THE **CALL** TO **CREATE**

Celebrating Acts of Imagination

LINDA SCHIERSE LEONARD, PH.D.

Harmony Books/New York

Anna Akhmatova: A Poetic Pilgrimage by Amanda Haight. (New York: Oxford University Press, 1976). By permission of Oxford University Press.

Published by Harmony Books, 201 East 50th Street, New York, New York 10022. Member of the Crown Publishing Group.
Random House, Inc. New York, Toronto, London, Sydney, Auckland
www.randomhouse.com

HARMONY BOOKS is a registered trademark and Harmony Books colophon is a trademark of Random House, Inc.

Printed in the United States of America

Book Design by Susan Maksuta

Library of Congress Cataloging-in-Publication Data
Leonard, Linda Schierse.
The call to create : celebrating acts of imagination / Linda Schierse Leonard.—1st ed.
I. Personality and creative ability. 2. Creation (Literary, artistic, etc.)—Psychological aspects. I. Title.
BF698.9.C74L46 2000
153.3'5—dc21   99-41778

ISBN 0-609-60093-1
10 9 8 7 6 5 4 3 2 1
First Edition

For Keith,
my soul-mate

CONTENTS

ACKNOWLEDGMENTS   ix

PREFACE: CREATING FROM THE WILDERNESS   xi

INTRODUCTION: ADVENTURE OF THE SOUL   1

Part 1   THE SEEDING

1 Inspiration: The Muse of Nature   23

2 Commitment: The Sower   37

3 Doubt: The Cynic   58

Part 11   THE CARING

4 Courage: The Witness Confronts the Tyrant
and the Victim   81

5 Consciousness: The Sentinel Awakens
the Escape Artist   112

6 Discovery: The Adventurer Challenges
the Conformist   139

7 Toil: The Artisan Teaches the Star Humility   168

Part 111   THE BLOSSOMING

8 Play: The Dummling Shows the Perfectionist
How to Play   191

9 Compassion: The Lover Opens the Critic's Heart   219

Part IV   THE HARVESTING

10 To Praise Is the Whole Thing: The Celebrant   249

NOTES   269

INDEX   275

ABOUT THE AUTHOR   285

ACKNOWLEDGMENTS

My thanks and gratitude go to all the people who helped me in so many different ways through the struggles of writing this book. In alphabetical order they are:

Ashley Anderson, Pat Bixby, Leslie Black, Harold Booth, Deborah Bowman, Jesse Boyce, Lisa Braunstein, Stu and Shelly Braunstein, Phyllis Bronson, Betty Cannon, Keith Chapman, Norma Churchill, Marilyn Corrigan, Lynne Foote, Marjorie Foster, Richard and Diane Bradford-Goldstein, Gloria Gregg, Noni Hubrecht, Sherri and Steve Hunter, Karen Kaho, Phyllis Kenevan, Sally Klemm, Lorraine Kreahling, Lynn Leight, Reed Lindbergh, Paula Lowitt, Phyllis and Saul Lowitt, Martha Meagher, Lara Newton, Cathleen Roundtree, Don Sandner, Mary Schlessinger, Myra Shapiro, Suzanne Short, Karen Signell, Elaine Stanton, Rennick Stevenson, Katherine Thalberg, Janine Vernon, Jane and Joe Wheelwright, and Don Williams.

Special thanks to Katherine Thalberg and the staff at Explore Booksellers and Bistro in Aspen—my writing "home"—for providing a beautiful and creative space where I always find nourishment and inspiration.

Many thanks to the Aspen Music Festival, which renews and inspires me every summer. In the Music Tent, set in a mountain meadow abundant with wildflowers, I listen to the melodies of the Muse while looking out toward the aspen trees and the movements of the heavens.

Every autumn I am grateful to the Aspen Film Fest and the Telluride Film Festival that excite and enliven me with their array of independent films.

Acknowledgments

Thanks also to my editors at Harmony Books—Leslie Meredith and Dina Siciliano—for their vision, encouragement, and editorial suggestions; and to my agents, Ling Lucas and Ed Vesnesky, who advised and supported me during my struggles to write the proposal, a linear part of the book process that is foreign to my natural intuitive way of writing.

So many thanks also to the people who so generously gave me permission to share their stories in this book. (The names and other identifying facts were changed to protect the identity of all contributors and some of the stories are composites of many people.)

And finally, my deep and loving gratitude and thanks to my muse, companion, and flesh and soul-mate, Keith Chapman, who inspires and challenges me to set out on our adventures in the outer and inner wilderness.

PREFACE:
CREATING FROM THE WILDERNESS

Before I began to write this book, I had the following dream: I was in the wilderness. Suddenly twenty-five wild beasts surrounded me in a circle. I saw that to survive, I had better learn to feed them and discover how to relate to each one.

When I woke up, I realized that the wild beasts symbolized an abundance of instinctual creative energy. If I did not feed these forces and learn to honor and respect them, they would devour me. I needed to learn how to live in the wilderness. The dream reminded me of the fairy tale "Beauty and the Beast," in which a simple maiden learns to love a fearsome beast. When she frees the beast from his enchantment by loving him, she discovers that his princely kingdom contains the secrets of creativity.

Every time I approach a new project, I feel just like I do when I trek in the wilderness. Creating is like being in the wilds, surrounded by beasts. The sense of wonder before the magnificence of the wild lands and the awe before exotic animals is beautiful and terrible. Imagine being in the jungle and seeing a Siberian tiger approach. This is the way I experience the creative process. I am thrilled with the spirit of adventure, yet alert and anxious before the danger.

In nature's wilderness death is always near—in the sudden strike of lightning, the unexpected freeze, the flash flood, the avalanche, or the chance encounter with a bear. The wild psyche, too, brings us face to face with death every time we transform our lives or create something new. Our inner wilderness is like the great white space of an endless snowscape. There, in solitude, we enter the infinite mystery and meet the ineffable. Even if we are with others, we still make a solitary journey.

In the beginning of transformation—whether in personal life or in creative work—people sometimes feel alone, lost, and disoriented. When we create, we enter into uncharted territory. We may fear that imagination will fail us or that we will not be able to find the trail markers that we need to write, paint, choreograph, or create the next phase in our daily lives. Do we have a compass? Have we lost the map? Do we know how to pitch a tent in a snowstorm? Have we brought the right equipment, and do we have the training to find our way in or out of unknown country? Can we even find the hint of a track?

The anxiety that can seize us in the wilderness when we fear to enter or when we are lost in dense forest as darkness descends is like the anxiety that can overwhelm us at the start of creative life. I may fear that I have nothing to contribute or that I will not be able to express my vision in an inspiring and beautiful way. But if I dare to put that first word down on paper or take the first step on a new phase of my life, I feel the flow of fantasy and imagination arising from unknown places within, a force far more powerful than my mistrusting mind and as potent as the mysterious moods of nature. As the Irish writer Sean O'Faolain once expressed it: "All good writing in the end is the writer's argument with God"—in other words, the struggle with creation.

Before a mountain trek I anticipate the dangers of the wilderness. Yet I thrill to discover unknown terrain. The anxiety that I experience before such a journey is like my apprehension prior to creating or to undertaking a new venture in my life. Setting out in the wilderness of creativity takes enormous effort; it can be excruciating to get to my writing table or to the trail. If I want to climb a mountain peak or cross through dense forest to a hidden glade, I must prepare to face lightning storms and be ready to slog through muddy bogs on my way.

If I risk setting forth, I feel both agony and ecstasy as I ascend the mountain. The exertion of the climb presents me with struggle and exhilaration. When I smell the evergreen's fragrance or see a wild columbine showing her violet bonnet in a grassy meadow, I feel grateful to be alive. As I reach the pass and feel the wind blow through my hair, I sense the greater forces that surround me. At the peak I see the far chain of mountain ridges ripple like waves in a great sea. The mysteries hiding in the rocky chasms below and the wonder of the changing faces of the clouds that move above are like the discoveries that astound me whenever I create or change my life. As I descend, crossing through rivers on my return, I hear the mountain's melodies just like John Muir, who exclaimed while exploring Yosemite, "The snow is melting into music."

The wilderness of the creative psyche is analogous to the wilds of nature. The wilderness is a place where humans are guests, not owners. If you hike into the wilderness at the start of a trail, you will see signs reminding you that you are a visitor and must respect the ways of the wild. When humans disregard nature, injury and sometimes death can result. Similarly, we are guests in the domain of the psyche; we must respect and care for the soul. The terrain of the creative psyche requires our consideration and our care as we traverse its peaks and valleys, ford its turbulent waters, and explore its caverns and its crevices.

Preface: Creating from the Wilderness

Mother Nature is greater than human attempts to dominate her. Likewise, the creative psyche is beyond our attempts to control. But we can learn their ways and what they ask of us. If we do not accept the greater wisdom of nature and psyche, we ignore, neglect, and violate their life-sustaining realms. As a result, we are likely to wreak their havoc; yet if we respect and care for them, we will receive their gifts.

The Polish composer Henryk Górecki expressed his reverence for the relationship between nature and creativity when he remarked: "In every piece of mine there is something of the Tatra Mountains. I need them like fish need water, like a man needs air." We, too, feel graced with awe and wonder and the bliss of inspiration when we see the luminous sunrise that comes over a mountain peak at dawn or the translucent changing colors of the sunset at dusk.

In the wilderness we struggle with the dilemmas of the psyche transposed into physical form. Behind the outer adversities of the wilderness and the inner obstacles to creativity lies the deep paradox of human existence. For this encounter we need courage. The word *courage* stems from the Latin word *cor,* for "heart."

Finding heart and passion within oneself is at the core of creative life and bids us to develop the courage to be compassionate with ourselves and others as we create. Responding to the call to create is not an isolated act. Creativity entails conversation with all beings in the wild and wondrous weaving of relationships that is the cosmos.

So now, on a windy day in March, as I sit before the empty page of the "book of life" hoping to create, I need only remember that I am not alone. I glance out the window toward the holy mountain, Sopris, and see the sun shining through the snow as the snowflakes dust the branches of the aspen trees. I take heart as I remember the words of Athol Fugard, the South African playwright, who emphasizes that sharing is implicit in the act of creation: "I make it because I want to share it with you. At the end of my process you are waiting for me . . . that is the act of faith. That is the hope that every artist has."[1] And that is the hope that I have too—to share the passion for creativity and nature with you.

INTRODUCTION:
ADVENTURE OF THE SOUL

I believe that creativity is an adventure of the soul in its quest for meaning in this earthly life and that all of us are called to create in different ways.

A mother giving birth, an infant saying its first word, a child expressing joy at the wonder of a flower, an adolescent discovering his or her own way in the world, an adult consciously choosing to confront a midlife crisis, the artist seeking to give original expression to a new reality, a person trying to transform his or her life—all are responding to the call to create.

Similarly, the lovers who honor the holy in each other, the healer caring for a wound, the scientist who searches for a new way to describe the universe, the entrepreneur or work team that develops and launches a new product, the philosopher probing the meaning of existence, the revolutionary trying to effect social change, the philanthropist hoping to contribute to humankind's well-being, the person embraced by the arms of death—all face the challenge of creativity as they consciously struggle to find purpose in life.

The Call to Create

The call to create bids us to bring something new into being. I love the way Maya Angelou expresses the creative challenge by saying that she seeks to live a "poetic existence." She takes this to mean assuming responsibility for the air she breathes and the space she occupies with others in the world. She intends to be immediate and present in whatever she is doing, whether it is writing, caressing a child's head, or cooking a pot of beans.

Like Maya Angelou, all of us can respond to the call. We answer the call whenever we appreciate the world around us by being thankful for the gift of life. A blade of grass struggling to push its way through a crack in a city sidewalk stirs us to admire its tenacity. A geranium blooming in a window box calls for us to see its beauty and to acknowledge the care of the person who tends it. An infant looks into our eyes and waits for us to smile. A pet dog nuzzles us to touch it with affection. If we taste and savor a meal prepared with love, we appreciate the creativity of the cook. A young girl plays the violin by her window; if we enjoy the melody of her music, we hear the call. The fragrant scent of a lover evokes a passionate caress. We respond whenever we look up with awe and gratitude toward the sparkling stars that show the way in the dark midnight sky.

NATURE'S WOMB: THE THEATER OF CREATIVITY

I perceive the call to create to be grounded in nature. Nature is a major source of creative inspiration, healing, and renewal. Since life is creative and a natural process, we need to understand nature and its cycles to flourish creatively. Knowing more about the seasons and their rhythms can help us comprehend the phases of creativity.

Ralph Waldo Emerson expressed the relationship between nature and creativity this way: "Behind nature, throughout nature, spirit is present, spirit, that is, the supreme being, does not build up nature around us but puts it forth through us." However we wish to understand the words *supreme being*, Emerson is talking about our ability to evoke the creative spirit residing in nature.

Our dwelling place in the cosmos is unique—a space in being in which we, as creatures with consciousness and choice, can respond to life by giving expression to it. We live at a crossroads of creation—where we can choose to participate and cocreate with the cyclical process of nature.

As members of the natural world, we have the eyes, ears, nose, mouth, and hands to see, hear, smell, taste, and touch. As human beings we have the extraordinary capacity to consciously wonder at, probe, analyze, and assimilate these sensations. We also have the capacity to choose to participate in the discovery of life's meaning and to give expression to what we experience. It is this capacity that calls us to create.

The definition of the word *create* is "to originate, to cause to exist, to bring about, to produce, and to form by artistic effort"; it stems from the Latin word *creâre*. Its many meanings include the following actions: to start, to establish, to organize, to constitute, to found, to originate, to generate, to procreate, to hatch, to write, and to compose. For example, whenever we grow spiritually or transform ourselves or something outside of us, we form a new way of being or understanding through our skillful efforts. When we create, we can generate new human and societal relationships, and we can originate increased ecological understanding of our relationship to the greater environment—nature. This requires liberating our "everyday genius."

Everyday genius refers to the innate natural gifts and capabilities that are part of being human. In Latin and in Roman mythology "genius" is the guardian spirit of a person or a place. The Greeks used the word *daimon* to describe this inner force, a higher spirit within us that calls us to create. The dictionary describes daimon as "an indwelling divine power that energizes humans with extraordinary enthusiasm." The original Greek meaning of the word connoted both divine and diabolical energies—hence, the conception that creativity is dangerous. Jung described the energy of the psyche—libido itself—as daimonic and as carrying the tension of good and evil. Thus, the call to create asks us to live consciously in the tension between the divine and the diabolical and challenges us to learn to direct our energies toward creative life.[1]

I see the call to create as key to being human. We are called to create by our ability to understand why we are here on earth as part of Creation. As creatures with the capacity of consciousness and choice, we can cooperate with and contribute to the greater process of creation, or we can deny or refuse our vocation and fail to reach our own potential. Creativity, as a response to the care of nature and psyche—to the wilderness within and without—is related to spiritual growth, to creative transformation, and to ecological wisdom.

As in any venture into the wilderness of nature and the soul, the elements act upon us, and we experience different climates and weather patterns. In nature we learn the feel of fire, air, earth, and water. The thunderstorms and lightning, the snow, hail, rain, sun, and warm spring breezes that we encounter in nature are like the moods that overtake us in creativity. Valleys and mountain peaks, icy glaciers and dense jungle heat, muddy bogs and marshes, arid deserts and dense jungle, meadows lush with flowers—each of these marvels of nature reflects various landscapes that we encounter when we create.

In urban areas especially, people turn to nature for inspiration and regeneration. New Yorkers love to be in Central Park. Chicago offers city dwellers the respite of the Great Lakes. In Los Angeles people can escape the smog by going to the ocean. Parisians stroll in the Luxembourg Gardens. In San Francisco, where the bay and ocean meet, the gleaming Golden Gate Bridge spans the cliffs, revealing the cooperation between nature and the human spirit. In Rome the fountains surge with the waters of life, reminding people of the mountain springs—the dwelling place of the legendary Muses, feminine nature spirits who bring imagination and inspiration to our lives.

When we are caught in situations in which we feel imprisoned, nature can nourish our faith. A tree gave hope to a young girl trapped in an unhappy home in the novel *A Tree Grows in Brooklyn*. A bird is a muse for a prisoner in the film *The Birdman of Alcatraz*.

In actuality, the political activist Rosa Luxemburg sustained herself by tending to plants when she was incarcerated for revolutionary activities. Similarly, a tree growing near his childhood home in the remote impoverished farming area in Ethiopia offered a vision of freedom, faith, persistence, and endurance to Haile Gebrselassie, the winner of the 1996 Olympic gold medal for distance running.

Artists, spiritual leaders, and scientists have given expression to this intimate relationship between nature and creativity throughout the ages. Ancient drawings by primitive people to revere animals, as in the Lascaux caves in southern France, are in the bowels of the earth. Greek and Roman temples, built to praise the divinities, are set high on cliffs above the sea. Egyptians built the pyramids in the desert, while Buddhist temples adorn mountainsides in Tibet and the jungles of Cambodia. Ancient astronomers charted movements of the sun and the stars at solstice sites in India and Persia.

In modern times artists like Georgia O'Keeffe and Vincent van Gogh reveal the beauty of the countryside and the brilliance of flowers in their paintings. Poets like Wendell Berry and Mary Oliver invite us into animal presence in their poems. Choreographers like Martha Graham and Vaslav Nijinsky show the dance between humans and nature in ballet. The novelist Albert Camus described the healing capacity of the sea in *The Plague*, and Pearl S. Buck depicted the sustenance of the soil in *The Good Earth*. Musical masterpieces like Vivaldi's *The Four Seasons*, Beethoven's *Pastoral Symphony*, and Mahler's *The Song of the Earth* resound with nature's creativity, inspiration, and meaning for our lives.

Gustav Mahler understood that his creative work, his life, and nature were inextricably interwoven. For inspiration he walked in the mountains, a practice essential to his creativity, and composed *The Song of the Earth* at his alpine home in Austria. The songs are based on Chinese poems that emphasize the earth as our spiritual home. Despite the finitude of human life, they proclaim that we experience the promise of eternity on earth through the cycle of blossoming flowers and green grass, through the birds as they welcome spring, through the murmuring melodies of brooks, in the clouds that float across the sky, and in the fire of autumn leaves. Mahler's symphonies resound with the growl of beasts and the songs of birds, echo the changes of the seasons and of weather, and reverberate to the movements of the moon and sun—all musical metaphors that express the emotions of creativity.

Introduction: Adventure of the Soul

A major obstacle to creativity is wanting to be in the peak season of growth and generation at all times. For example, if we want to be productive all of the time, we may push ourselves beyond our natural limits and not acknowledge our bodily and psychological needs for rest and regeneration. This is an unrealistic expectation because the creative process has necessary ebbs and flows like those of nature.

Both nature and psyche require the recurrence of soothing sleep and wakefulness. Honoring the changing phases of life from birth through midlife to old age is another organic need. By listening to their bodies, women passing through their monthly cycles appreciate this instinctive wisdom about the seasons of the body and the psyche. Men have their circadian cycles too. If they have not been estranged from nature's rhythms, both men and women understand that the ebb and flow of energy that they experience in their bodies is rooted in organic cycles like the phases of the moon and of the tides.

Those who resist the rhythmic energy of nature and of the psyche by attempting to deny dark periods are likely to fall into cynicism and become entrapped by their own tyrannical will to power and control—a motif I will explore in chapters 3 and 4.

But if we see the soul's journey as cyclical, like the seasons or like the menses, then we can accept the reality that periods of despair or fallowness are like winter—a resting time that offers us a period of creative hibernation, purification, and regeneration that prepares us for the births of spring.

Nature's creative process is organic. As the wind breathes over the mountains and grasslands, it blows seeds from the trees, plants, and bushes into the air and carries them until they fall into the ground. Animals sow seeds too. When they gather and eat fruits, berries, and grasses, their scat teems with fur, feathers, and seeds. As it decomposes, the scat becomes part of the the ground, thereby sowing the seeds and fertilizing the earth.

Preparing the ground is a natural process. Roots reach down into the earth and spread to support and strengthen the growing plants and trees. The matted weavings of fallen leaves fertilize the soil so the seedlings can grow. They are protected to survive and develop as they sleep deep in the ground during winter. When the time is right, the buds seek the sun and begin to blossom. Nature celebrates this process with gorgeous fruit, brilliant multicolored flowers, and golden fields of grain.

Humankind's creative process reflects that of nature. But we must consciously choose to accomplish her innate activities. First we must prepare the ground to receive both the gifted seeds of inspiration and the ones we have sown ourselves. This happens in the phase of seeding and surrender when we become ready to receive and accept the time of waiting and nourishment inherent to all growth and transformation.

Then we must work and struggle to till the soil, to weed out the saboteurs to growth and creativity, and to hone our skills so the seed can be embodied. This is the time of caring and tending, the phase of conscious work and effort. We must learn to cope with the hurricanes, floods, and droughts of creativity.

To prepare for the time of blossoming, we must learn to appreciate the phase of rest and regeneration. During this phase we comprehend how control and interfering can sabotage the creative process. This is the time when playfulness and compassion are essential.

Finally we come into the time of harvesting, when we gather the fruits of creativity and share it with others. With wonder for the mysteries of growth and transformation, we give thanks, celebrate creativity, and praise existence. And knowing that we must be ready for the process to resume, we save some seeds for the new sowing— for the cycle that will renew itself.

I experience the journey of creative transformation as moving in a continual cycle, somewhat like the seasons. And similar to the seasons, I have experienced four main phases. Inspiration—that mysterious surge of creativity—can spring forth at any time in any of these cyclical phases. Throughout our lives and at different points of the creative journey, we are in these seasons of the soul's creativity.

First, there is the time of *surrender.* In every creative act we have to take a leap into the unknown so that we can discover the new vision, idea, or feeling and bring it into being. This is a time of letting go and letting be, a time of being open to whatever spontaneously arises and reveals itself. It is a time of giving up control. Sometimes strange and dark images appear, and sometimes a blaze of light and beauty. To surrender means to give up habitual ways of looking at things so that we are free to see and experience whatever appears. The surrender stage of creative transformation requires facing death so that rebirth can occur. In times of surrender we test and refine our faith, trust, and hope in the creative process.

Second, there is the time of *work and struggle.* Toil and discipline are required to wrest the new image, perspective, insight, feeling, or behavior from the chaotic welter of old, clinging habits and forces.

The new thing struggling to be born requires conscious work and effort to release it.

Third, we need times of *rest and relaxation* from the periods of work and struggle. We need meditative time to revive, renew, and regenerate ourselves so that we can continue to create and transform. Animals like the bear instinctually know that hibernation and incubation are essential to growth.

Finally, *giving*—sharing the newborn being in its embodied state with others—completes the creative cycle and at the same time commences it again. Passing the creative gift along to others and contributing to the world inspires others and calls them to create, thus continuing the creative process.

Learning to follow nature's rhythms offers us a helpful model for the adventure of creative life as the soul passes through the seasons. With the gift of life comes the call and the choice to create—an invitation from the Muse of Nature who asks us to preserve our experiences and stories through memory. In our day this includes the ecological reality that respect, understanding, and care of nature will make a crucial difference for life on our planet.

The backdrop of this drama of creativity is that immense landscape of nature and psyche whose destiny is intimately interwoven. Nature is the grand stage upon which the psyche's characters of creativity—the Muse of Nature, the Sower, the Witness, the Sentinel, the Adventurer, the Artisan, the Dummling, the Lover, and the Celebrant—interact with their detractors—the Cynic, the Tyrant, the Escape Artist, the Conformist, the Star, the Perfectionist, and the

Critic. In the following pages I will explore how the psychodynamics of these inner characters can help and hinder us.

CHARACTERS IN THE DRAMA OF CREATIVITY: THE DRAMATIS PERSONAE

As Shakespeare said, "All the world's a stage; and all the men and women merely players." In the same vein we can imagine the human psyche as a vast stage where the great drama of creativity is enacted by various archetypal characters—the universal human figures in ourselves, in different cultures, and throughout time.

The call to create requires us to recognize and choose between the inner characters that help us to create and those that hinder us. At different times and in different contexts each character can help us. Just as dark times are part of our growth, so the darker figures in ourselves can show us truths we need to recognize and thus deepen our creative life, while the more beneficial figures can deter creativity if they lack conscious direction and are used to excess. These inner characters exist in both men and women and are not limited to gender.

I identify characters at play in the drama of our own creativity—our soul-work—so that you can get to know them, see how they operate in yourself, and learn to cultivate and direct their energies toward creative instead of destructive ends. To do this effectively, we must treat them with consciousness and compassion.

The first character we meet in the drama of creation is the *Muse of Nature.* The Muse is well known by creative people from ancient to modern times as a spirit of nature and imagination that brings us inspiration. Since the beginning of creation, poets and artists have cherished the Muse and prayed to her to inform their lives. We find the Muse of Nature revered in fairy tales and legends, novels, poetry, painting, film, dance, and music. The Muse is that mysterious, elusive spirit that inseminates our imagination, enlivens us, and invites us to cocreate with nature; thus we must learn how to invite the Muse into our lives.

Next we meet the *Sower,* the life-affirming character in us. The Sower listens and responds to the voice of the Muse by planting the seeds of hope, faith, and commitment to the creative process. The Sower, who says yes to life, calls us to respond to the challenge and potential of creativity in our daily lives.

At our best moments we all become the Sower by listening carefully and understanding that waiting and quiet patience are required to become one with the regenerative rhythms of nature. Similarly, this book explores how the art of patient waiting nourishes the creative process, and how fretfulness can prolong creative blocks.

In dark times the first saboteur we are likely to encounter is the *Cynic,* who says no to life. The Cynic lacks faith and, due to frustration with imperfection, doubts, neglects to care, and asks, "Why bother?" The Cynic's attitude usually stems from disillusionment because life has not met idealistic expectations. In despair, due to the lack of relationship with a greater force, the Cynic causes us to doubt ourselves and interferes with the natural process of development. When the Cynic predominates in us, we try to force life to conform to our own expectations rather than surrendering to life's natural process.

Learning to transform the Cynic entails understanding despair and the leap of faith that creativity requires. I will show ways to heal the Cynic so that this character in ourselves can hear the nurturing yet truthful voice of the Muse. In turn we can usefully acknowledge the dark truths the Cynic perceives.

The *Witness* and the *Tyrant* act as dramatic opponents. The Tyrant is a power-monger who wants to rule with absolute control. The Tyrant would like to be more powerful than nature herself and take the Muse of Nature hostage, as in the Russian legend of the Firebird, which Igor Stravinsky expressed in music and dance. The Tyrant has no patience for creation's need to go through a period of quiet growth. Thus the Cynic's doubt and despair become the Tyrant's rage. The Tyrant starts to bully the creator, who begins to feel like a passive victim, helpless and weak.

If we allow the inner Tyrant to stifle and strangle the muse within ourselves, we choose to be victimized. Instead, we can fight the Tyrant by standing our ground through *active* patient waiting, through listening, watching, and recording the truth as we see it.

The Witness helps us have the courage to stand ground and the wisdom to know how to do it. By observing and remembering—as the Muse encourages us to do—the Witness can record the words and behavior of the Tyrant. The Witness observes and notes the Tyrant's threats to censor creative acts in external life, to quell inspiration, to stifle our spirits, and to attempt to terminate our inner efforts. By developing the Witness we learn to deal with the fears and anxieties that keep us victim to the Tyrant.

A tempter that can divert us from the creative path is the *Escape Artist*, who avoids the difficult and exhausting struggle inherent to creativity. The Escape Artist wants to evade the pain, anguish, and tension that constantly confront the creative person. The *Sluggard*, the *Compulsive Doer*, and the *Dilettante* are all components of the Escape Artist. The Escape Artist tempts us to become discouraged and to slip back into unconsciousness by choosing complacency or a passive, inertial state like that of the Sluggard, who sidesteps useful activity by falling into idleness. In contrast, the Compulsive Doer's busyness and workaholic approach to life allow no time. The Dilettante seeks pleasure and immersion in worldly distractions to dodge the internal work of creating.

Creativity requires that we stay alert so that we do not succumb to destructive temptations and lose the consciousness and insights we have gained. We need to be alert so we can raise the new from the unknown to discover new seeds. But going into the unknown can be dangerous, because sometimes we get lost there. Thus we need to keep our balance. Creativity obliges us to become aware of the border between the unconscious and the conscious so we can pass back and forth between them.

The helper here is the *Sentinel*, who actively stands watch at the borders of consciousness to prevent retreat and regression. Like those who seek awareness through meditation, the Sentinel is aware that solitude allows the quiet communion with the self and nature that is necessary to develop centered consciousness.

If we listen to the Tyrant, we are likely to cling to the rigid route of the *Conformist* who discourages discovery and creativity, which threaten security, profit, and safety. The Conformist tries to maintain the status quo and, under the thumb of the Tyrant, warns and chastises those who venture out of preordained straight-and-narrow perimeters.

The *Adventurer* is the Conformist's dynamic opponent. Unlike the Escape Artist, who avoids conscious focus, the Adventurer purposefully breaks out of the given structure to go in new directions by taking a leap of faith and risking failure. But while the Adventurer accepts the challenge to create, this character must learn to be centered and to balance on life's tightrope, that is, to exist in the paradox of creation and destruction.

By accepting the challenge, the risks, and the responsibility to live life as consciously as possible, the Adventurer will learn to survive and then thrive in the tension of opposites. This requires respect for our human practical needs as well as for the greater mysteries; it requires the courage to live resolutely in the paradoxes of life and death, creation and destruction, all the while struggling to direct energy toward divine creation. Here we explore the fine art of balancing that creative discovery requires.

The *Star*, who becomes inflated with success, fame, and power, becomes arrogant and loses humility. Stars lord it over others, threatening the creative process because they want to take all the credit for creating. The egoist in us feeds the Star with inflated fantasies of fame in which to indulge, or lures us to rest on our laurels. This short-term gratification seems—for the moment—much better than the constant process of risk and work that go into creative life. The inflated ego of the Star can be a major, serious pitfall, for it leads to neglect of the craft inherent to creativity.

To transform the egoistic Star, we must turn to the humble *Artisan* in ourselves, who acknowledges that creativity is a gift rather than something that can be possessed or to which one is automatically entitled. The Artisan knows that the ways of nature are subtle, nonlinear, and powerful and will humble us all sooner or later. Just as the many medieval artisans worked anonymously together to build the cathedrals, exemplifying the humble toil of creating, so the Artisan in ourselves already knows that we must work continually and collaboratively to hone the skills of our craft.

Who, in our culture, has not abandoned creative efforts by succumbing to the absolute standards and constant criticism of the *Perfectionist*? The Perfectionist thrusts before us a goal that we have no chance to reach because we are finite beings. When the Perfectionist tells us, "You'll never measure up. You'll never do it right. Don't show it to others if it isn't perfect," we often hang our heads in shame. We may feel like failures, fear that we are frauds, give up, and abandon our projects.

To counter this obstacle, we must take refuge in our simple appreciation of the creative act itself. Paradoxically, the way to reclaim self-respect and self-esteem from domination of the Perfectionist is to accept a certain tolerance for naïveté and even foolishness in ourselves—like that of the classic *Dummling* figure in fairy tales.

In contrast to the Perfectionist, the Fool or Dummling proceeds without a plan, without knowing the way or the outcome—and stumbles upon wisdom. This is actually the way of creative people who view the creative process as a quest and search for the path of discovery.

The *Critic* is an inner figure who can either function as a fearsome opponent that discourages creativity, or help us make the crucial decisions required to lead a healthy and creative life. If the Critic malevolently judges everything we do, it objectifies the creative process and undermines our passion for learning and for life. At worst, the Critic can collude with the Tyrant and the Cynic and lead people to destroy what they have composed at any point in the creative process—a tragic occurrence that I have heard described many times in my psychotherapy practice and in my work in the field of creativity.

Since we need to discriminate in order to hone our creations, we must develop an honorable, compassionate inner judge who helps us decide whether to delete, add, or reorder things in our lives and artworks.

To counter the Cynic and Critic and guide them toward helping our creative efforts, we must look to the inner *Lover* who is compassionate and who participates passionately in life's flow. The Lover accepts imperfection, has tolerance for the necessary adjustments in the process of creating, and assumes an active role by joining and sharing with others in the struggles of creative life and in harvesting its fruits. Acting from the heart, the Lover calls others to creative communion.

The Lover leads us to the *Celebrant* who praises existence and gives thanks for the gift of life. The Celebrant affirms both life and death and understands that we are all part of the greater whole of nature.

The Celebrant understands that the appreciation of creativity is itself a creative act. In order to appreciate a work or life of art, we, too, must be creative. By appreciating the work of other artists, creative people are inspired to create their own work, and they in turn inspire and mentor others in a cyclical chain of creativity. The Celebrant's appreciative attitude counters the cynicism of the "demon-like" characters and transports us back to the Sower if we have fallen into the grip of the "demons."

The same process occurs in self-transformation. We are inspired by others who have transformed. And as we transform, we inspire others—thus honoring the Muse and singing with her. If we praise life, we will return to the process of seeding anew, which requires accepting death, rebirth, and the continuing transcendent cycle of creativity. Likewise, if we praise our creations, we nourish our psyche.

Consequently, if we respond to the rhythm of creativity, we will return to the Sower. As Rainer Maria Rilke, who traveled this great orbit many times in his life, expressed it in *The Sonnets to Orpheus*, "To praise is the whole thing."

Nourishing the Creative Spirit

Over the years many people have asked me how to nourish the creative spirit. How can we break through the obstacles that block the way? How, in our attempts to create, do we pass through the maze of difficulties entailed in the creative process?

A multitude of temptations lure us to quit our endeavors. At various times in our lives we are likely to experience a lack of inspiration and passion. We may fear success or failure or suffer from despair in fallow periods. Exhaustion from the constant work and struggle to give form to a new vision may overtake us. Often we feel hurt and tormented by criticism from others and from within ourselves, and we ache from the rejection of our work or the way we live.

In order to create, we must face the anxiety that accompanies its process. We need to tackle the guilt that haunts us if we become obsessed with perfection. And we must counter feelings of fraudulence and shame that ensue from wounds to self-esteem—injuries that interfere with the inner authority that empowers us to give birth to something new.

The act of creation requires us to commit to our projects. It demands consciousness to confront and transform the cynical doubts that discourage effort. We must be vigilant to identify distractions and other obstacles that divert us from our aims. Creating requires courage to face fears of failure and even of success. And throughout the process we must embrace compassion for ourselves and for all who dare to accept the call.

This book is about the call to create and about responding to that call. My aim is to help you, the reader, discover how to recognize that call, to identify the inner tendencies that sabotage your creative efforts, and to detect the inner helpers that can help release your creative energies so that you can reap the spiritual, emotional, and instinctual joys of creating, self-discovery, and transformation.

If you come to know the dynamics of the inner characters that I describe, you can understand how they function in yourself and how calling upon them will further your creativity. By seeing how they interact and work together to create or, conversely, collude to sabotage your efforts, you can learn to avoid the pitfalls that prevent and deprive you from living fully.

Each chapter in this book has many stories that illustrate the many different difficulties and feats we encounter along the creative path. I have described the inner characters by using examples from myth, fairy tales, literature, and the visual arts. There are accounts of well-known artists because their creative struggles often reveal themselves in bold, dramatic strokes so we can better see and understand them. And there are stories of our "neighbors"—ordinary people meeting the challenges of creativity in their daily lives. I also relate some of my own struggles along the creative path that we all travel together. It is my hope that my analysis of the internal forces or "characters" within us, and their ground in nature, can help those who seek to find, recover, devote, and apply their inherent creativity to their personal lives and to society.

Whenever I hear people say they are not creative, I surmise they are passing through a "dark night of the soul," the despair that accompanies a spiritual crisis that calls us to mature. If we are not able consciously to identify and to accept this period as one phase of growth, we can remain stranded in it.

Members of Western culture, especially now, want instant success, and they evaluate achievement in terms of money, power, fame, and possessions. We relegate creativity to a corner of our lives instead of seeing life *as* creative. Thus we reduce its meaning in our lives. This behavior reveals a society that has lost faith in the notion of creative growth—planting, waiting, digging into the divine soil when the time is right, harvesting, giving thanks, and then sowing again. But if we value and choose the path of creative growth, we will find ourselves on a journey of discovery that will lead us to treasures beyond our wildest expectations.

Part 1
THE SEEDING

Seeds are a handful of miracles.

Athol Fugard

1
INSPIRATION

Then, dearest Maiden, move along these shades
In gentleness of heart; with gentle hand
Touch—for there is a spirit in the woods.

William Wordsworth

Slowly, I discovered the secret of my art consists of a meditation on
nature.

Henri Matisse

THE MUSE OF NATURE

Since the dawn of consciousness, creative people have invited and prayed to the Muse to inspire their lives, understanding that the Muse brings transcendent energy that cannot be forced or controlled.

For many creative people, the Muse resides in nature. Artists like Vincent van Gogh and Georgia O'Keeffe, sculptors like Constantin Brancusi and Auguste Rodin, poets like William Butler Yeats and Anna Akhmatova, composers like Beethoven and Stravinsky, all honor the Muse as an intrinsic part of nature as well as an interior source of creativity—an energy that they cherish.

When the Muse graces them with her presence, they give thanks; when she withdraws, they mourn her disappearance. In legend it is said that mortals who take sole credit for their creativity, and brag about their excellence and achievements, or forget to thank the Muses for their gifts, will lose the Muses' encouragement and inspiration.

THE MUSE IN MYTH

In legend the Muse was a source of inspiration related intimately to nature. In Greek mythology the Muses were honored as nature goddesses of creative inspiration for song, poetry, and the other arts and sciences. These nine daughters of Zeus and Mnemosyne, the goddess of memory, were originally nymphs—female spirits dwelling in waters and woodlands. The Muses were also said to be daughters of

Mother Earth and Air. They were "mountain goddesses" who presided over natural mountain springs, waters that held the extraordinary power to give inspiration.

One of their dwelling places was the sacred spring Hippocrene, on Mount Helicon, where the goddess Athena, patroness of the arts, is said to have visited them to listen to their songs and stories. The name of this sacred spring was derived from two Greek words meaning "horse" and "fountain," since the spring water flowed from a rock after it had been struck by the hoof of Pegasus, the winged horse.

In paintings the Muses are depicted as playing their instruments or leafing through books by streams on a wooded mountainside, where Pegasus can be seen leaping from a high rock from which the water flows. Later, the Castalian spring on Mount Parnassus became their special dwelling place.

As the daughters of the goddess of memory, who recalled all that had happened since the beginning of creation, the Muses retold their mother's great stories in verse and song so that humans would remember the ordeals of their heroes and heroines and how they dealt with them. Even before there was writing, the Muses helped people preserve their stories through memory. Thus the Muses, with their knowledge and their tales of creative effort, knew how to inspire royalty, enthrall the common people, and relieve both when in despair.

Among the ancients, the Roman poet Virgil invoked the Muses in the *Aeneid;* Ovid described them in *Metamorphoses.* The Greek poets Pindar and Aristophanes appealed to them as well. Homer wrote about them in the *Iliad* and the *Odyssey.* But it is Hesiod's religious poem, *Theogony,* written in the eighth century B.C., to which most seekers turn for the story of the Muses.

Hesiod celebrated the Muses, relating how they inspired him to sing the praises of the deities. He described the Muses as nine daughters "whose hearts are set upon song and their spirit free from care." They were born of the union of Zeus and Mnemosyne, near the topmost snowy peak of Mount Olympus. The Muses dance on "soft feet about the deep-blue spring and the altar" of Zeus, and veiled by the mist at night, they arise and sing hymns to honor the gods and goddesses. One day while Hesiod was shepherding his lambs under the holy mountain of Helicon, the Muses plucked and gave him a marvelous shoot of sturdy laurel. Then they breathed into him a divine voice so that he could celebrate what was to come and what had passed.

In Roman times each Muse was said to direct a different aspect of the arts and sciences. Calliope presided over epic poetry, Melpomene over tragedy, Thalia over comedy and pastoral poetry, Erato over love poetry, Polyhymnia over sacred poetry and religious mime and dance, and Euterpe over lyric poetry, music, joy, and pleasure. Clio held sway over history, while Urania governed astronomy. Terpsichore led dance and dramatic chorus.

Although various writers have ascribed different attributes to each of the sisters, in essence the Muses were bonded by their heavenly singing. Indeed, the Muses were said to sing together with such rhapsody and harmony that even the birds would listen to them in wonder.[1]

We still call upon Muses today. Anna Akhmatova, one of Russia's greatest twentieth-century poets, revered the Muse in her verse. She understood that her inspiration was a gift from a source higher than herself. Akhmatova saw the Muse as a feminine spirit—a pagan sister who could restore her creative relationship to nature when her poetic voice was silent from grief, parched and barren from exhaustion, or forced to be fearful and mute by the tyrannical ban of her work during Stalin's reign of terror. Akhmatova's Muse is also akin to the Russian mother of Jesus, Mary, who inspires her suffering daughters to be courageous heroines in times of tyranny. We will see how Akhmatova battled with the Tyrant and became a Witness in chapter 5, which deals with courage.

When Akhmatova was a young girl, the Muse came to her in dreams in the form of a mysterious maiden who bathed with her in the sea, taught her to swim, and sang with the voice of the wind whispering through a silver pipe. Once when Akhmatova's tongue was muffled, the Muse told her:

> Your hair has grown gray. Your eyes
> Have grown dull and misty through tears.
>
> You no longer understand the birds' song,
> Understand the lightning or the stars.
>
> For long now the tambourine's not been heard
> Yet I know you are frightened of silence.
>
> I have come to replace your sister,
> By the high fire in the woods.[2]

MODERN-DAY MUSES

Since the Muse speaks through the lives and works of creative people, we sometimes first experience her as embodied in external figures who inspire us—public figures, lovers, spouses, friends, parents, children, pets. When I was a little girl, Dolly, the horse that brought the milk wagon every Saturday, gave me hope, inspiration, and relief from a traumatic childhood. Dolly was my muse. Later, fictional dogs and horses like Lassie and the Black Stallion became muses for me. My artistic muses include Rainer Maria Rilke, Fyodor Dostoyevsky, Krzysztof Kieślowski, and Toni Morrison. My soulmate, Keith, whom I first met in Bali running up mountains, is a muse who inspires and challenges me to trek in the wilderness and to venture writing another book.

Popular singers who express a people's deepest feelings act as muses in our culture. Elvis Presley, the Beatles, and the Grateful Dead inspired their generation. Billie Holiday, Judy Garland, and Edith Piaf vocalized our fears and longings, our desperation and our hopes, in their plaintive songs. Movie stars like Ingrid Bergman, Juliette Binoche, and Marilyn Monroe—along with their male counterparts like Paul Newman, Marcello Mastroianni, and Sidney Poitier—serve as cultural muses.

Various aspects of the Muse are portrayed in films. The loving Muse, who inspires a man to change his life, was embodied by Ingrid Bergman in the classic *Casablanca* and by Irène Jacob in Kieślowski's contemporary masterpiece, *Red*. Susan Sarandon and Geena Davis, in *Thelma and Louise*, personified revolutionary muses who inspired many women to make changes in their lives. Susan Sarandon also led viewers to reflect on moral issues such as capital punishment in her role as a nun in *Dead Man Walking*, and as a mother fighting the medical establishment to save her son's life in *Lorenzo's Oil*.

The Muse of Nature

Oprah Winfrey is a muse for many; she inspires people to look at the suffering in their lives and in society so they can heal. Her book club has introduced her viewers to the art of reading. Revolutionary figures like Martin Luther King, Jr., John F. Kennedy, and Hillary Rodham Clinton inspire people to aim for social reform and take political action.

Artists like Picasso paint portraits of their models who serve as muses to them. The dancer Suzanne Farrell was a muse for choreographer George Balanchine. The pianist Clara Schumann was a muse for her composer husband, Robert Schumann, and also for Johannes Brahms. The sculptress Camille Claudel was a muse who revivified Rodin when he was in a dry period in his forties.

Film directors often work with the same actors with whom they have intimate and intuitive relationships. Ingmar Bergman worked with a cast of muses including Liv Ullmann, Harriet Andersson, and Max von Sydow. For Federico Fellini the Muse was embodied through his wife, Giulietta Masina, in classic films such as *La Strada, The Nights of Cabiria,* and *Juliet of the Spirits.* Catherine Deneuve served as Luis Buñuel's muse for many years. Robert De Niro, Harvey Keitel, and Joe Pesci are among the many "tough fellows" who act as muses for Martin Scorsese. Françoise Truffaut has filmed Jean-Pierre Léaud many times, starting with *The Wild Child.* Woody Allen has left a trail of muse-lovers, including Diane Keaton and Mia Farrow. Hanna Schygulla and Barbara Sukowa were muses for the German director Rainer Werner Fassbinder.

Maud Gonne, a political activist for Ireland's freedom, served as a muse for Yeats. Lou-Andreas Salomé, the writer and lay psycho-analyst, inspired Friedrich Nietzsche and Rilke. Anaïs Nin inspired Henry Miller. Alma Mahler, well known for her creative salons, was a muse for geniuses all over Europe including the painters Gustav

Klimt and Oskar Kokoschka, the composers Alexander von Zemlinsky and Gustav Mahler, the Bauhaus architect Walter Gropius, and the poet-novelist Franz Werfel. Marilyn Monroe, a muse for Joe DiMaggio and Arthur Miller, is still a tragic muse today.

Although these modern "muses" are creative in their own right, most had to learn the hard way that it is dangerous to identify as the Muse. By equating oneself with *the* Muse, it is easy to fall into the pitfall of inflation, a topic discussed in detail in chapter 7. An attendant danger is to become a mere reflection of others' wishes and desires, thus losing or failing to develop the relationship with one's own creative center.

Although we may first experience the Muse through an external figure, we must remember that the Muse's energy is transpersonal and cannot be possessed. The Muse is mysterious—an inspirational, interior source of creativity.

The word *inspire* stems from the Latin word *inspirare.* It means "to breathe, to inhale, to fill with noble and reverent emotion, to exalt." Inspiration is like a breath of fresh air. Inspiration enlivens us, excites us, stimulates us to creative action and to incite creativity in others. The breath of the Muse ignites creative fire. When the Muse is present, she breathes enthusiasm—the breath of the divine spirit—into us. By inseminating imagination, the Muse is a link between nature and psyche.

Down through history, artists and writers have served as muses for each other and their audiences through their creative works. For example, Stéphane Mallarmé's poem *L'après-midi d'un faune (The Afternoon of a Faun)* inspired Claude Debussy to compose one of the greatest musical masterpieces of impressionism; the prelude by the same name in turn inspired ballets by Stravinsky, Nijinsky, and Jerome

Robbins. Debussy first heard the poem at one of Mallarmé's Tuesday evening gatherings, which he regularly attended.

The Afternoon of a Faun expresses the faun's fleeting longings and desires as they rise and fall with the heat of an afternoon fading into night. This piece fuses the outer world with an inner vision of nature. The nymphs and naiads are dreamlike yet also seem to have an earthly presence. Both the dance and music call us to sense the unity of psyche and nature.

The Muse reveals herself in the form of animals, birds, trees, rocks, flowers, stars, and other beings of nature. Rachel Carson, the naturalist and marine biologist, wrote with her pet cat lying by the side of her typewriter. The novelist and poet May Sarton wrote odes to her feline friends. Flowers and rocks inspired Georgia O'Keeffe to paint. Birds inspired Olivier Messiaen, the French composer.

Messiaen nourished his muse by taking frequent field trips in nature to see and hear the birds he loved. On these trips he recorded their songs and reproduced them in his music. Inspired by the canyon lands of Utah, Messiaen composed *From the Canyons to the Stars*, which begins in the desert—a metaphor for the spiritual desert, the emptiness from which we can begin to contemplate the divine mysteries. In silence we can hear the song of birds, the winged earthly angels that sing God's music and, like the heavenly angels, bring spiritual messages to us.

Messiaen wrote that the birds that inspired *the Oiseaux exotiques*, one of his compositions, have feathers that encompass all the colors of the rainbow and that circulate in the music. Messiaen believed that specific musical sounds represented certain colors, so that the plumage of the birds can be heard. In this piece one can hear birds from all over the world, including the Baltimore oriole with its orange and black feathers, the green color of the lesser green leaf-bird, and the black Hindu mynah with its yellow neck.

In the novel *Green Mansions,* the naturalist W. H. Hudson described his experience of the Muse of Nature. *Green Mansions* depicts a writer who is disillusioned by his failure to find fame and fortune and has become cynical and alienated by the pettiness of town life. Searching for solace, he travels to the rain forest of Venezuela, where he encounters the ethereal Rima, as elusive and graceful as a rare butterfly or a hummingbird.

Rima is a wild solitary bird-girl whose home is the forest and who warbles with the melody of birdsong that penetrates the soul. A child of nature, Rima divines supernatural truths and can guide a man through jungle and desert in the darkest night.

Like those of us on the creative path, the protagonist of *Green Mansions* must enter the dark wood, push through the dense foliage of the tropical forest, and follow the birdcall he hears for many days before he finally encounters Rima, who brings him hope for beauty and the simple joys of nature. Reflecting on Rima's power to bring meaning to his life, he describes the Muse and her inspiration:

> My every action, word, thought, had my feeling for Rima
> as a motive. Why, I began to ask myself, was Rima so
> much to me? It was easy to answer that question: Because

nothing so exquisite had ever been created. All the separate and fragmentary beauty and melody and graceful motion found scattered throughout nature were concentrated and harmoniously combined in her. How various, how luminous, how divine she was![3]

He realizes that his former desire for fame, wealth, and acceptance by the social elite is an illusion when compared with the innocence and spirituality that he feels with Rima, a pure muse of nature who inspires him and restores his sense of grace. Although in the end he loses Rima to those who fear her strange purity and kill her, her memory lives inside his soul as a lasting source of inspiration and hope.

The pilgrimage to find Rima is like the journey that people on the creative path must take to find the Muse. Like Hudson's protagonist, we often become disillusioned and cynical when our fantasies of success do not come true, when we lose hope for meaning in our lives, or when we cannot find inspiration. The venture to enter the unknown and unfamiliar terrain of the creative psyche is necessary if we want to recover or find new meaning.

Pushing through dense jungle is like the effort needed to cut through the thickets in our psyche—the chaos that clutters, confuses, and impedes our thoughts, feelings, and visions. If we are given the gift to hear the elusive birdcall, we must make the effort to trace it and follow it to its source. Only then will we be strong and ready to receive and honor the inspiration of the Muse by remembering, incorporating, and integrating her divine disclosures, revelations, and sacred truths into our lives, works, actions, and relationships.

MEETING THE MUSE

We cannot control the Muse; nor can we command her presence. But we can prepare ourselves to be ready for the Muse when she visits us. We must acknowledge and understand that the Muse is a seminal energy of existence at play in the great unity of nature and psyche—the mystery of being in which we ourselves participate. In doing so, we can invite her into our lives by valuing her and allowing her to dwell in the sacred spaces within ourselves.

Rilke learned this lesson when he traveled through the terrain of the vast Russian steppes with his external muse, Lou-Andreas Salomé. At the end of their trip she told him that it was time for them to separate as lovers so that he could discover his inner muse. Rilke said that Lou's advice, together with the experience of passing through the grand steppes for days on end, freed him to discover the great expanses within himself. By learning to dwell in solitude, spaciousness, and silence, Rilke was able to listen to the interior muse's call to create.

Learning how to dance with nature's time instead of being a slave to clock time is essential if we want to invite the Muse to be with us. If we flow with time, we can welcome the Muse with the freedom and openness to the timing and movement that is her realm.

Once during a dark and dry period, I went to see a Matisse retrospective at the Museum of Modern Art in New York. The vibrancy of colors and Matisse's dancing women danced with me; I had to stop to catch my breath. That day the Muse inspired me and breathed new life into my soul. If I had not pulled myself out of my malaise by initiating the act of going to the museum, and if I had not been open to receive the beauty shining through Matisse's paintings, I might not have met the Muse that day. Meeting the Muse and dancing with her was a call to me to believe in and return to my own creative work.

Although I cannot arrange it, I sometimes meet the Muse during a concert, a film, or a ballet. At other times I may find her in the poetry section of a bookstore or in conversation with my friends. Often she comes after I commit myself to sit down to write, or during meditation. But most frequently my meetings with the Muse occur in nature.

I walk in nature daily to find joy, renewal, and inspiration. This is especially important when I feel troubled, lonely, depressed, or in despair. In spring I see wild iris or yellow buttercups; a lark's song may lift my spirits. In summer wild berries refresh my taste for life. If I dare, I lie down and roll and revel among the flowers in the meadows and feel the ecstasy of life. In autumn, when the magic maple foliage turns red and the aspen's golden leaves tremble in the wind, color comes into my imagination. In winter the snowflakes lace the fir trees, giving sparkle to my life. Animals, fish, birds, wind, stars, rain, snow, flowers, grass, the changing seasons—each living thing reveals its own mystery, inspires me, and renews my life with wonder. I know I have received the gift and the grace of nature's Muse.

Welcoming the Muse into our lives requires us to be tender and gentle, to be vulnerable and open to the love of I-Thou relationships.

The Call to Create

The Muse beckons us to listen to the sounds of nature and to breathe in her fragrant air so that her transcendent energy can flow through our bodies and enliven our imagination. By allowing our imagination to wander and wonder, we honor her and circumvent the trap of betraying the Muse by literalizing and reducing her to a concrete thing. The Muse nourishes us through her gifts of beauty and playfulness, encouraging us to care for the soul and let the child in us be free.

Ultimately, the Muse is the voice inside us that encourages us to understand the seasons of nature and creativity as an organic, cyclic process of creation and destruction, life and death. She invites us to participate and cocreate within this cyclical process instead of trying to fight or control it.

Our active role in meeting the Muse is to prepare ourselves, to be ready and open to listen to her, and to respond with thanks and appreciation for her gifts. This requires surrendering our hidden, calculated agendas that attempt to control her, along with the illusion that creativity is at our command. Then we must accept her offering of inspiration by forming and embodying it. To this end we must also learn how to recognize and contend with the voices of other characters in ourselves that want to hinder, possess, abuse, and silence the Muse. We will look at the ways these saboteurs stifle our creativity in the following chapters.

2
COMMITMENT

Though I do not believe that a plant will spring up where no seed has been, I have great faith in a seed. Convince me that you have a seed there, and I am prepared to expect wonders.

Henry David Thoreau

THE SOWER

I was in that fragile period between creative works when I needed to help my gestating book enter the world safely. My next project had not yet begun to take shape in my soul. I had fallen into a distressing abyss of apprehension and doubt about the book—ironically, a work on creativity. This is a place known to every creator—the artist, the scientist, the entrepreneur—and in fact to all of us who are searching for the next meaningful project. It is a common situation we all share, whether we have already "successfully" created, want to begin creating, or are readers seeking deeper understanding of the creative process.

This time is tense and vulnerable, but it is an essential part of being human, of the soul's quest for a creative life. In this respect the already-accomplished artist and the novice stand together naked at the starting point. The French writer Paul Claudel expressed this similarity when he remarked that each new book involves new problems that make the experienced artist as insecure as a beginner.

At such a time it helps me to remember that the creative process is akin to nature and has cycles that are similar to the seasons. When we embark upon a new project, we return over and over to nature as a basic ground of creativity. Just as winter—the time when growing things lie silently underground and can't be seen—is part of the cycle of development and is prerequisite as a ground of growth, so in our creative lives we must endure again and again the winters of doubt and anxiety that require an act of faith and commitment to waiting. Winter reappears regularly in nature, and similarly, most creative projects and lives encompass many winters. When the poet

Yeats wrote, "I sought a theme and sought for it in vain," he was expressing the anxiety, loneliness, and vulnerability that we all feel when we encounter the winter phase of creative life.

It was during a cold, rainy, dreary week in November when I was in New York City on a book tour that I noticed that one of my favorite playwrights, Athol Fugard, was there to direct and act in the premiere of his new play, *Valley Song*. Fugard's work has always been a source of inspiration for me, and I felt sorely in need of encouragement. Although I didn't know the theme of the play, intuitively I felt it would give me heart, since Fugard has always written about how we find meaning in our lives.

Valley Song is a meditation about seeds—the seeds we need to sow in the ground for growth, and that require the work of planting— the sacrifice and act of faith of letting go and waiting, and the continuing labor of tending. "Seeds are a handful of miracles," one of the play's characters declares.[1] Seeds insure continuing life. Seeds contain the embryos of a new generation, the kernels of creative life—and for the individual who hopes to create and transform, the kernels of *life as creativity.*

In the play three characters—an old coloured tenant farmer, his seventeen-year-old granddaughter, and an aging white Afrikaaner playwright—are confronted with the challenge of change.[2] The seeds are a metaphor for the growing pains of the new South Africa and for the creative struggles of every human being trying to find meaning and value in life.

The old farmer struggles to keep his granddaughter with him, but he learns to accept that she must forge her own way in the changing world, while he remains on home ground to plant his last seeds in the earth. Veronica, the young girl literally singing with life, dares to part from her grandfather and the valley she loves, to go to the city to sound her new song of hope. With them at home is the aging play-wright, who tests Veronica's commitment to be sure she is strong enough to venture forth on her journey—and who must also admit his own jealousy of youth and his fear of losing its melodies. In the end Veronica does leave for the wider world, and the playwright—remaining behind with the farmer, who is about to plant his last seeds in the ground—affirms the pumpkin seeds he holds in his hands, knowing they represent the words he cultivates on paper.

I could identify with Veronica's struggle to leave home, because when I was her age, I had to fight to leave my family so I could find my own path in life. Her grandfather's painful efforts to keep her with him reminded me of my mother's aching attempts to keep me with her. The playwright's concern about losing youth's exuberant songs reflected my new worry that I might lose my verve for writing as I age. But the pumpkin seeds he held in his hand offered me hope.

That night I left the theater in tears. The seeds Fugard planted in his play were sown in my soul as a source of hope for my own new writing. I could feel them, also, sprouting as buds of inspiration to help my transition into the next phase of my life—to come into the wisdom of becoming sixty. By going to see *Valley Song,* I had encountered the Sower.

THE GROUND

Just as actual seeds may be so small that we do not see their beauty, or so common that we overlook their elegance and do not really notice them—so in creative life we often overlook their importance or ignore that they are developing silently in the ground. Seeds have a marvelous tenacity. When they lie hidden in the ground, they are protected by a heavy coating. When the time is right to bud, they seem to know, and then the heavy coating softens and the seeds begin to grow and push above the ground. Sometimes as they encounter rocks in the soil, they change their path and go around the obstacle in order to bloom.

In nature seeding requires a time of death and rebirth in the dark, divine soil. So it is with life creativity: the seeds of our own creation must die and be reborn in the hidden depths of the soul. Dostoyevsky, who planted the creative seed in his books and in his life, acknowledged this fact in the biblical epigraph for *The Brothers Karamazov*, his novel of spiritual transformation: "Verily, verily, I say unto you, except a corn of wheat fall into the ground and die, it abideth alone, but if it die, it bringeth forth much fruit" (John 12:24).

We must dirty our hands in the earth and dig deep into the divine, darkened ground of the soul if we want to harvest its potential fruits. Perhaps this is why many artists and other creative people find that actually digging into the earth with their fingers is a physical embodiment of the creative act. The writers May Sarton, Alice Walker, and Wendell Berry are among the many artists who love gardening and planting—they understand that it is part of their creative process. The actress Catherine Deneuve has said that she uses her bare hands while pruning flowers—she accepts the dirt and bloody scratches to her hands as companions to the roses. Wendell Berry, who also earns his living as a farmer, wrote that the sower "has seen the light lie down in the dung heap, and rise again in the corn."

It is the same in our creative life, in which the ground is the unconscious, or the realm we sometimes refer to as imagination. There the seeds may be planted in many ways: through images in dreams, through events in our lives such as a mysterious meeting with a stranger who opens up a new part of ourselves, through our loves and relationships, through a robin's song that we chance to hear while walking. A fairy tale told to us in childhood, an artwork that we experience in adulthood, a character in a film—anything may show us new dimensions of ourselves, of our creative possibilities, and of the human condition. But whatever the seed may be, it needs time and receptive ground in which to develop and ripen.

During a long period of blocked creativity, the poet Rainer Maria Rilke was walking one day along some cliffs that towered over the Adriatic Sea. Suddenly a storm came up, and a great wild wind started to blow. Then the following lines of a poem came into his mind: "Who, if I cried, would hear me among the angelic orders? And even if one of them suddenly pressed me against his heart, I should fade in the strength of his stronger existence. For Beauty's nothing but beginning of Terror we're still just able to bear."[3]

These words expressed the awe, anxiety, and reverence Rilke felt before the creative process of life itself. He knew that they were the opening lines of a poetic cycle for which he had been waiting for over twenty years. In the meantime, however, he had worked to prepare the ground to receive these seeds, through years of writing hundreds of poems, letters, a novel, and other literary works.

The seed that was planted inside Rilke's soul on that stormy day ultimately became the *Duino Elegies,* one of the world's greatest poetic sequences. But Rilke still had to wait ten years—a cycle of many winters, through which he continued to work the soil of his imagination through his practice of writing—before he was able to finish the *Elegies.* Then, unexpectedly, in the days following his completion of the *Elegies,* a series of sonnets also came to him: *The Sonnets to Orpheus.*

A major obstacle to creative growth is to forget or to neglect this time of concealment, protection, and mystery. If the sensitive seed is exposed too soon, it may not survive other forces that work to stop its growth. Most of us have had the experience of sharing a precious insight or feeling to someone before they are ready to receive it, and have known the resulting pain when it is not understood or is rejected. On the other hand, if we allow our secret seeds of inspiration to lie untended, they may never be noticed and thus remain unborn.

Just as the physical seed must be planted in ground that is good for growth, so the seeds of our creative and spiritual life can grow only if they are planted in the soil of a soul that is receptive. In another biblical seed parable (Matt. 13), Jesus of Nazareth tells us that the "good ground" is the receptivity of the listener who can understand that the seed is the spiritual teaching. Seeds that fall by the wayside and are untended are like germs of wisdom and potentialities to create that are lost, denied, or remain unchosen. We need to know where and when and how the seeds can grow best.

THE SEEDS

Fugard takes care to demonstrate that the seeds in his play are not to be understood as only metaphorical. Acting the part of the "aging playwright" in his own play, Fugard connects with the substance of the pumpkin seeds, which he carries around with him. At the start of the play he walks around the theater and shows the audience the seeds that he holds in his open hand. Thus, he invites all those present to become the "good ground" in which the images found in his play may be implanted. He invites them to begin, with him, the process of germination, which bears fruit according to the receptivity and nature of each individual spectator. In the same way, every creative person sows seeds in the soul of the work's recipient—who in turn can become the creator of a new work and life, and thus continue the cycle of creativity.

In his comments about the play, Fugard said that he personally took the pumpkin from the ground in South Africa and cut it open to gather its seeds. The seeds are so precious to him that every night before he leaves the theater, he makes sure he hasn't dropped one. He honors the divine imminence in the actual seeds of nature, as well as the seeds of imagination that he sows in his play.

PSYCHE'S TASKS

Recently I reread one of my favorite stories, the tale of Eros and Psyche.[4] I return to this tale over the years because I admire the brave, gentle, natural way that the heroine, Psyche, works through creative challenges. By understanding how Psyche's struggles correspond to my own, I have gleaned many insights about the creative process.

Psyche is ordered by Aphrodite to sort through a jumbled pile of seeds and to separate each kind of grain from the others. This is the first of four tasks she must perform if she wants to recover her lost lover, Eros, who symbolizes love or the creative heart, and give birth to a child bred from their union.

Psyche was assigned this task by the goddess Aphrodite. Aphrodite, jealous because Psyche's earthly beauty was said to rival that of the goddess herself, had ordered Psyche's father to take her to the top of a mountain and leave her there, where a monster would come to devour her. But the kind West Wind carried Psyche gently from the mountaintop down to the kingdom of Aphrodite's son, Eros. There she fell in love with Eros, even though she did not know who he was and could not see him, for he visited her only in the night.

Psyche had been separated from Eros because she disobeyed his order not to look at him; he had told her she could be with him only in darkness. Fearing that he might be a monster—a suspicion implanted by her sisters, jealous of her relationship with the mysterious lover—Psyche lit an oil lamp so she could see him. Her attempt to see him in the light is like the action of the soul by which we bring something unknown into consciousness; it is an essential act of creativity that requires attentive love by those who create.

Aphrodite, who wants to possess her son, represents the pull to keep Eros in the unconscious. Yet paradoxically, the tasks that she sets for Psyche are tasks that require becoming conscious. In this sense, Aphrodite is the Sower who implants the seeds of creative work to be performed by Psyche in her struggle to create a new way of being. Similarly, in our personal lives, it is often the very figures who give us trouble that launch our attempts to change, transform, and mature.

Psyche's tasks, in my view, are the tasks of transformation of every human being engaged in the creative process, and so I will return to her again and again throughout this book. At the beginning of her first task, Psyche is overwhelmed by its enormity, and sits stupefied before the disordered mass of seeds. The job of sorting them seems so immense and impossible that Psyche falls into despair and considers suicide.

Just as Psyche must learn to sift and distinguish the different kinds of seeds, so must we discern and sort the seeds for creative birth. We, too, must learn to differentiate the diverse seeds, whether they are words, feelings, thoughts, musical notes, images, movements, or bodily sensations, in order to find the unique form that best facilitates their expression. Like Psyche, I often feel overwhelmed by the confusion and chaos of all these "seeds," and by the colossal difficulty of the ordering process.

This is the point where many of us are tempted to abandon our creative projects. We may expect rapid results and turn to easy "how to do it" solutions—the "quick fix"—which has become an addiction in our technological times. Baffled and perplexed, feeling too weak or uncertain to make the choice to begin, some of us quit the job of differentiation altogether, thus deserting our creative potential. Before starting each new book, I have had to struggle with this temptation. Each time I must face the anxiety that comes with the chaotic jumble of ideas, feelings, and experiences, into which I must dive in order to find meaning.

Psyche's name stems from the Greek word *psukhe,* which means soul. In my view, her tasks are part of the difficult soul-work that is required by and for creative life. In other words, creating *is* soul-work. And so much is at stake—our *soul* is at stake—whenever we try to develop, improve, and refine ourselves, that we often are afraid to start, or get discouraged and give up midway in the process.

The Sower

So we have left Psyche in despair faced with her first creative task. But as she contemplates suicide, some little ants come to her aid and sort the vast heap, separating the seeds grain by grain and distributing them according to their kind. When I heed Psyche's story and consider how the ants came to her aid, I recall that I, too, have inner helpers like the ants. These beneficial creatures call to mind our instinctual ability to discriminate, to sift and sort, to correlate, to value and to choose—all activities necessary in order to create from the jumble of fertile potentialities we have within ourselves. By sorting the seeds we can direct these natural predispositions *and* possibilities, and, literally, bring order out of chaos—the ordering that we all need to induce the as-yet unknown and uncreated to emerge into consciousness.

I generate thousands and thousands of scribbled pages for every book that I write. Every time an insight comes to me, I jot it down on whatever is near: the corner of an envelope, pieces of napkins, scraps of paper. I know that I need to listen carefully to the inner voice to allow these intuitions to come forth. However, my intuitions often disappear if I don't write them down. By now I know that I must record them in some way. Only then can I begin to work with them.

I regard this jotting action as a long-term seeding process. Some of these seeds come to fruition and others lay fallow in the ground and take root much later. But whether or not they burst out of the soil or stay there silently, I know they form the background for creation. Their silence and invisibility remain an essential part of the completed work and of the creative life.

Elie Wiesel, the Nobel prize–winning author, once said that his finished book, *Night,* included only ten percent of what he had written. Behind any completed work or act lies another ninety percent of ideas, feelings, experiences, and words that are the environmental foundation, the ground that embodies, comprises, and contains it. The same is true for the dancer who spends hours stretching and practicing, for the scientist who researches, for the businessman who develops and promotes a new product, and for all of us as we grow and develop by understanding and integrating our life experiences.

Like Psyche, we all have inner helpers that work by instinct and we can call upon helpful images that encourage us not to give up. Images like the ants can remind us that creative work requires many little steps and invokes many different aspects of ourselves. It is very important to honor this set of "small" processes that sometimes seem ordinary and minor, but are actually extraordinary and essential to creative growth.

Honoring the necessary, subtle process of simply noting random thoughts or images, by writing or in any other medium, is actually tantamount to a *commitment to the creative process.* In our lives, this is the beginning of all transformational work.

THE SOWER

The act of commitment that is essential to the creative process is embodied by the archetypal figure of the Sower—the initiating force in us that plants the seed and has hope and faith that it will bear fruit. The Sower works even when the obstacles seem to be insurmountable and understands that it takes many seasonal cycles to carry through the work of creation. The wisdom of the Sower is exemplified through Antonia, the heroine of *Antonia's Line*, the 1995 Oscar-winning film by the Dutch director, Marleen Gorris.

After her mother's death, Antonia returns with her daughter to the country village that she left twenty years earlier to escape an abusive, alcoholic father, a mad mother, and a village wracked with patriarchal mistreatment and defilement of the feminine. Antonia begins life anew and plants seeds in the earth on their farm while her daughter, Danielle, paints and sculpts.

Antonia sows seeds of love, humor, and feminine wisdom as she and her daughter confront the bullies in the village. She finds allies in a benevolent farmer and an old friend who has become cynical in word, but is good-hearted and compassionate toward Antonia and the rest of her line: her daughter, granddaughter, and great-granddaughter.

Among the bullies whom Antonia successfully confronts with the help of her daughters is a priest who denigrates women in his sermons and sexually harasses a young woman in the confessional, and a bully who rapes his retarded sister and later, in revenge, Antonia's own granddaughter. But the fruitful seeds of self-respect, independence, and self-esteem that Antonia has sown in her generational line of women are stronger than the rotten, corrupt seeds of the abusers.

With the faith, endurance, and commitment of the Sower, Antonia initiates a life of love and compassion in her line of new women (and men) in the village—a way of life that also acknowledges and follows the rhythms of nature and the cycles of life and death and of creation. I mention the fictional character of Antonia (who can be seen as symbolic of the "Great Mother") because she has been a source of inspiration, courage, and hope for many viewers—both women and men—who identified with her while watching the film.

Ultimately, the Sower is a character who works in the sacred soil of cosmic creation. The artist Vincent Van Gogh cultivated for us, in us, a sustaining image of the earth, by painting its divine radiance. In "The Sower," he illuminated humble toilers in the field, patient delvers and tenders of—partners of—the earth. In "The Peasant Shoes," the bits of earth which cling to the rough, well-used boots become as radiant as the sun's purifying light—the same light which bathes the humble sowers, the golden, responsive sunflowers, the entire radiant, divine world as Van Gogh reveals it to us in his moments of great illumination.

For Van Gogh, all of life was a whole—the earth, plants, animals, humans, and the heavens. He dreamt of cosmic union. He once wrote:

> I have a terrible lucidity at moments, these days when nature is so beautiful. I am not conscious of myself any more, and the picture comes to me as in a dream . . . I look upon the real human feelings, life in harmony with, not against nature, as the true civilization, which I respect as such. I ask, what will make me more completely human?[5]

The commitment to being human requires an affirmative act of faith in creation and challenges us to meet troublesome obstacles as we enter into the drama of creative work. The magic theater of creative life presents us with many characters that we can understand as archetypal figures in ourselves—inner actors in the psyche of the creative person. Their energies can either help us or hinder us throughout the various modes and moments of the eternal act of sowing, which is a lifelong process.

The Art of Listening

Once the seeds of creativity have been sown, we need to wait for them to develop. Waiting requires the ability to listen to the silence and accept the state of grace inherent to conception. Abiding in solitude and silence, dwelling in the empty times, awaiting while the ground seems fallow, is one of the most difficult tasks in creative life. Yet, patience is required of all of us if we want to survive. Here I think of Psyche's second task—one that we all encounter at various stages of our growth.

The jumble of seeds presented to Psyche by her jealous mother-in-law, Aphrodite, had been sorted by the ants. But this enraged the goddess, who assigned to Psyche an even more difficult task: to gather a wisp from the wool of the golden rams. By day the rams raged with maddened frenzy, inflamed by the burning sun, and their horns could gore to death anyone who dared approach them.

Psyche's first reaction is to think again of suicide. She goes to the edge of a cliff over a river, intending to jump in. But before she hurls herself down, she hears the whispering of a reed from the river's bed.

The reed tells her not to pollute the river's sacred waters with the misery of her self-murder. Taken aback, Psyche listens while the reed tells her how to accomplish her task.

The reed advises Psyche to hide beneath a leafy tree which drinks from the same waters. She must wait until nightfall since, during the day, the rams are frenzied by the fierce heat from the burning sun. At nightfall, though, the rams' anger and madness will be allayed, and the tired beasts will fall asleep. Then she can safely search the branches of the bushes through which the fearsome sheep rush to graze, and take the remnants of the golden wool left clinging to the twigs.

Psyche listens to the reed with attention and follows its counsel. She also listens to the rustic shepherd guide, Pan, who sits by the river and counsels her that the tasks are a way to win the love of Eros. By waiting until dark, she is easily able to take the soft, golden fleece and bring it back to Aphrodite. By waiting and listening to nature, Psyche is able to fulfill her task.

Waiting is one of the most perplexing tasks of creative life. Waiting is different from passivity. Rather, it is an act of receptivity that requires its own brand of courage. Waiting does not mean that we should not act, or that we are not creative. Psyche's waiting *is* creative; she returns with the beautiful golden strand of energy, the golden hair that is the weaving of creativity.

Rilke's *Letters to a Young Poet* can guide all of us in our efforts to hold steady and find strength during difficult times. Rilke suggests that the poet go deep within himself and listen to his heart. He writes, "find patience enough in yourself to endure, and simplicity enough to believe; . . . acquire more and more confidence in that which is difficult, and in your solitude among others. And for the rest, let life happen to you. Believe me: life is right, in any case."[6]

When barren times occur, many of us get depressed, feel hopeless, fall into despair, and even abandon creative life altogether. After all the labor of sowing and sorting the seeds, suddenly it seems that nothing is happening. This is a time when the Cynic in us is likely to question all of our efforts. Some of us become paralyzed, fearful of the emptiness of the vast abyss ahead. Others are so angry at the silence that they hurl themselves into the waters to drown in fury, or run right in front of the raging rams.

I often feel frustration before starting a new work. For example, I wrote the following words in my journal in January, just before I began this book.

> Today I sit before the void. I try to create. But emptiness is all I see. Emptiness confronts me every time I begin a new book or dare to enter a new phase of growth in my life. I am challenged with the question: How do I take the first step toward transformation? I exist in that terrifying space between books. As the novelist, Daphne du Maurier, once said: "Writing every book is like a purge; at the end of it one is empty . . . like a dry shell on the beach, waiting for the tide to come in again."

I share my personal experience at the beginning of my own creative process because I know that many other people feel frozen at this point. It is as though they are on the edge of a great glacial precipice that they must traverse. But they are paralyzed with fear. So they remain numb, afraid to take the next step, which may hurl them into the abyss. At this point many people give up and turn back.

Convinced they are not creative, they sink into depression and feel too helpless, weak, or devastated to try again. Others react with anger, refusing bitterly to attempt the quest anew. They turn their backs on creativity and sit and brood in resentment, like the "underground man" in Dostoyevsky's novel, withholding what they have to give. Whether they feel weak and helpless or are infuriated by their failure, they may decide to live below their potential. Some choose to reside in a gloomy cellar of their creative capability; others opt for a dusty attic covered with cobwebs. Like the mad Mrs. Rochester in the novel *Jane Eyre*, sometimes people even burn down their house of creativity until nothing is left but raging flames and ashes.

In times like these it helps to remember that creativity has cycles, just like the seasons. The barren time is reminiscent of winter. If we can learn to wait, to honor the time of silence, to accept that life flows according to natural cycles, if we can learn to listen to the whisperings of the reed, like Psyche, then we will understand that desolate times, too, are times of growth.

For example, if you look closely in winter, when the trees are bare and seem dead, you can see the already-formed buds of next spring's flowers and leaves at the end of each twig. They are covered with a hard coating that protects them from the cold snow and wind. This covering doesn't soften, even on the occasional warm day, until the time is truly right—and the tree knows when that is. Although we cannot see them, the tree's roots are growing, too, preparing to support the coming spring growth. It is the same during the winter season of creativity.

During transitional times such as the passage from winter to spring, it helps to be alert to the signs of new growth. Once on an early June hike to Arapaho Pass, high in the Rocky Mountains, a friend and I were trudging through the snow. Suddenly she pointed to a beautiful flower just emerging from the translucent crystals of ice. I hadn't been looking carefully, because at the time I didn't know I could see flowers in the snow. The snow buttercup, she told me, grows under the snow at high altitudes and waits for the right time to show itself. Then the yellow color of the blossom attracts the sun and melts itself a path around and through the snow. Glowing with light, the golden flower is a sign of springtime and hope for those who can see her.

Similarly, seeds of creativity lie silently in the psyche's ground. They need to be protected until the time is right for them to come forth to be developed. We must be alert to what lies deep within ourselves to notice the transitional time when our visions are ready to emerge and flower.

PATIENCE

Rilke emphasizes how important it is to accept the natural growth of inner life with love and patience, as we accept the way a tree grows naturally and slowly. He says:

> All progress must come from deep within and cannot be pressed or hurried by anything. *Everything* is gestation and then bringing forth. To let each impression and each germ of a feeling come to completion wholly in itself, in the dark, in the inexpressible, the unconscious, beyond the reach of one's own intelligence, and await with deep

humility and patience the birth-hour of a new clarity: that alone is living the artist's life: in understanding as in creating.

There is here no measuring with time, no year matters and ten years are nothing. Being an artist means, not reckoning and counting, but ripening like the tree which does not force its sap and stands confident in the storms of spring without the fear that after them may come no summer. It does come. But it comes only to the patient, who are there as though eternity lay before them, so unconcernedly still and wide. I learn it daily, learn it with pain to which I am grateful: *patience* is everything![7]

Patience is a virtue that I tend to forget when I am in that troublesome space between books, or in the transition from one stage to another in my life. When I fear I am in the abyss of a writer's block—or in a dark time preceding rebirth and transformation—I sometimes forget my own long and hard-won knowledge about the creative process—life itself is cyclical.

Toni Morrison, like Rilke, points out that writing is a way of life; it is a process that goes on all the time even when she's not at her desk. As I reflect upon her words, I am reminded of Psyche listening to the wisdom of the reed. In an interview, Morrison remarked that a "writer's block" should be respected. A "block" may be telling the writer she needs to wait until she is ready. The frustration and the fear of fear often come from artifical deadlines.[8]

Along with Rilke and Morrison I have learned to affirm the waiting process, the natural cycle of winter, and the fact that growth is happening all the time, even in what looks like silence and darkness.

The Sower

The novelist Marguerite Yourcenar, the first woman elected to the Académie Française, talks about how necessary it is for a writer to be able to listen. She creates her characters by trying to listen to their voices and to understand the melody of their being. To hear another's voice, Yourcenar remarks, we have to create silence within ourselves. It takes work to listen with an open ear instead of interrupting with our own talk. This is the work of receptivity. It is the art of the listener.

The art of listening, so central to the healing process as all therapists know, is a subtle skill. We must listen to both the spoken and to the unspoken, to the silent ground behind the word. Attending to our intuitions, believing in them, and living by them requires the keen tending care of the inner ear. The listener pays heed not only to the obvious and the literal sound, but to the mysterious musical tones resonating in the background.

The Sower must be able to hear the call of the Muse and to listen to her wisdom about the natural way of creation—a process that, like pregnancy, requires trust, faith, patience, and conscious waiting. Like the pregnant woman, we will not be successful in creating if we don't heed birth's natural process. Just as Psyche listens to the moods of nature through the reed, we must listen to our inner nature, to what moves us from within.

After listening to the Muse of Nature and attending to the seeds she inseminates in imagination, the Sower sorts, plants, and tends the seeds of transformation and creativity, knowing that they will bear fruit if they are cultivated with care.

3
DOUBT

In a dark time, the eye begins to see.

Theodore Roethke

THE CYNIC

Whenever I commit to a creative project, I know that sooner or later I will encounter a character inside myself whom I have come to call the Cynic. Sometimes I become cynical toward myself, sometimes toward others, and sometimes toward the world at large.

After years of soul-searching, I have learned that my inner Cynic stems from disillusionment due to excessive idealism and intense romantic naïveté, and can be a defense against full exposure to the whole of life. If I start to look and listen with cynical eyes and ears and become hostage to my own mocking thoughts, it is usually because my idealistic fantasies have been disturbed. Underneath the disillusionment a hidden wound often festers. At bottom the secret longings, feelings, and aspirations of my inner Cynic have been injured; its heart is suffering from hurt, neglect, and rejection.

Let's take this book, for example. My original vision was to write from the lighter side of creative life—an inspirational book in which I could share my love of nature. I felt I had spent time enough delving down into the dark side, digging into human wounds, as I had in my earlier books. I hoped to continue with my fifth book's "reindeer spirit": that gentle strength of the heart's transcendence, so free and open that it crosses over into other realms.

When I first thought of writing this book from its original title, *Creating from the Wilderness,* I imagined strolling on mountain ridges to find the spiritual wisdom that Emerson, Thoreau, and Muir had gathered from roaming the wilds. I hoped to convey the sense of awe that Rachel Carson felt as she walked along the Maine coast, exploring the wonders of the sea and the beauty of the tide pools. I wanted to tell inspiring stories about Mahler composing music on alpine hikes, and how Ingmar Bergman wrestled with the demons that haunted him in the middle of the night, by taking them outside for a brisk walk in the fresh ocean air on Fårö, the isolated island where he lives. I yearned to share my love for Kieślowski's films—the way he sets a mood through music, color, cinematography, and the mysterious meetings of the characters he portrays. I wanted to introduce readers to the wisdom, compassion, and hope I found in Fugard's plays and to Dostoyevsky's characters, who struggle to find meaning in his novels that changed my life. I wished to write as lyrically as Rumi and Rilke.

In nature I love to feel the ecstasy as I ascend to the top of a mountain peak. There I can see the sweep of mountain ridges rising in the distance, their reflections shimmering like opals in the lakes below. I luxuriate in the luminous colors and the sweetness of the blooming wildflowers, and I breathe deeply to inhale the pure and fragrant air. I long for such idyllic moments when I take up my pen to write—in fact, whenever I begin a creative project of any kind.

My vision was to write about the relationship between nature and creativity and its parallel to the passage of the seasons. But right there, embedded in the seasons, was the genesis of the Cynic, whose despair about hard times gains ground in winter when we can't see things growing. Even in the first bloom of spring, the Cynic is likely to complain that a late frost will most likely freeze the budding plants.

The proclivity for cynicism is buried underneath idealistic longings. The Cynic is a disillusioned romantic whose idealism has been disturbed by limitations in life. I fell into the Cynic's clutch, began to doubt my vision, and fell into despair. I experienced a writer's block. But this experience brought me to realize that I could not ignore the Cynic.

The dictionary describes a *cynic* as "one who believes all people are motivated by selfishness." If I confine my view of life to the perception of this single character, I limit the sweep of my vision. For example, if I am motivated to create in order to make money or to be a success, I limit myself and become victim to prevailing dictums of the marketplace. Yet the Cynic's outlook also has an important function. Since humans are confronted with egotistical motives, we must learn to deal with the inner Cynic as well as the trenchant cynicism pervading society.

If I wanted to write a book linking creativity and nature, I could not neglect writing about the Cynic, because its energy is part of human nature. Dealing with the Cynic *is* part of the creative process. To write about creativity requires writing about its dark sides as well as its joys.

And so with this book, too, I had to dive into the darkness—meet with the Cynic inside myself who sneered: "You fool. You thought you could escape me in your valley of wildflowers. Wilderness has its dark side too. Remember that on mountain climbs you encounter mud and rocks, sweat and toil. Danger lurks on high peaks and ridges when the thunder and lightning gods show their dominion. My seed is also there in the creative compost of the soil, and you must see its worth."

Immersed in idealistic fantasies, it is easy to neglect the painful times of growth. Similarly, in relationships we naïvely forget the struggles and conflicts that must be faced to enable these relationships to endure. When another point of view disturbs our fantasies, we are confronted with an obstacle. We need to look at it and ask ourselves whether we have something to learn from this experience. Minimizing difficult times makes it harder to get through them and breeds the Cynic's discontent.

The same is true in the act of creating—whether it is an artwork, a relationship, an innovative project at work or at home, or a way of life. First comes the flash of inspiration, a new vision, along with the longing to express it as artfully as possible. Then comes the struggle with reality. As human beings, we are faced with limitations. Our incomplete finite nature always causes us to fall short of the ideal.

My experience with the Cynic is like that of many people. The Cynic disarms us by preying on our fears and worries. By smirking about lost faith and laziness, the Cynic induces negative feelings and thoughts that try to stop us at the beginning of a creative journey. Sometimes it may seem to "save" us from failure by discouraging commitment to a creative project at the start. The Cynic challenges us with that troublesome question: "Why bother?"

To the potential writer or artist, the Cynic might ask, "Why does the world need another book, poem, or painting? So many already are on the market; there's no time or space on the shelves for another. Yours won't make a difference." To disconcert the potential parent, the Cynic is likely to pronounce: "There are so many children in this world that the earth can't supply food enough to nourish them. Why bring a child into a degenerate world wracked with injustice, pain, suffering, and evil—a world that is headed toward annihilation?"

One of Dostoyevsky's cynical characters, Ivan Karamazov, tries to torment his younger brother, the faithful Alyosha, with his rationale damning a Creator who allows suffering to happen. But Alyosha, knowing that Ivan longs for life and love, reminds him of the signs of hope—the little sticky green leaves in spring, the blue sky, and the woman whom he loves.

In his novels Dostoyevsky named and described the archetypal characters that he knew held himself and others prisoners. Through fictional characters such as the "underground man" and Ivan Karamazov, Dostoyevsky described the Cynic by portraying his own doubts and resentments. These troublesome attitudes of the Cynic manifested themselves in Dostoyevsky's compulsive gambling and in the debts that he accrued—destructive behaviors that began to rule his life, endanger his marriage, and threaten him with lifelong bondage in debtor's prison. By writing about inner saboteurs like the Cynic, Dostoyevsky brought them to consciousness and learned how to transform his life.

Dostoyevsky described his remedy in his last novel, *The Brothers Karamazov*, when he offered us the Lover, Alyosha—a character with heart and faith—in counterpoint to Ivan, the Cynic. In the meeting between the brothers Alyosha and Ivan, Dostoyevsky offers resolution by affirming and celebrating life. Alyosha's love for his brother leads Ivan to admit that, despite all the cruelty and injustice that he attributes to the Creator, even Ivan—the Cynic—loves the sticky green leaves in springtime.

Like Ivan, the Cynic represents that tendency of the human personality to question our motives, doubt the value of what we do in life, and hint that life is spoiled. The Cynic insinuates that whatever can go wrong will go wrong. Disillusioned by life's disappointments and unable or unwilling to go beyond the obstacles it encounters, the Cynic drowns in sour feelings about the world.

Cynicism develops in people's lives for a variety of psychological reasons. Developmentally, children may mirror cynical parents or teachers who discourage them from exploring new or better possibilities. Cynicism can stem from a materialistic society, like ours, that is greedy for profit, jaded, and weary from too many distractions and possessions. Or it can pervade a country, group, or family whose resources are diminished. At a fundamental level cynicism is an inherent component of the human condition, since the Cynic sees and confronts the dark side of life that most of us prefer to ignore.

In my work as a therapist and teacher, I find that the Cynic arises as a defense against the exposure to human reality—the beauty and terror of being who we are. As humans, our creative challenge is to learn to live with the ambiguity of not-knowing and to balance on the tightrope stretched between our longing for the infinite and the limitations of our finite modes of perception and expression.

Afraid to live in this paradox and under the influence of the Cynic, many people give up from fear of failure before they get started. Others abandon their projects midway because they expect finished results too early in the creative process. Still others destroy or hide their works. The Cynic's way of "giving up" is self-defeating and contrasts with the "surrender" required in creativity. By closing us to help, wisdom, and appreciation from sources other than ourselves, cynicism sabotages creativity because it devalues receptivity.

How can we recognize the Cynic in ourselves? By paying attention to our unspoken "self-talk"—habitual tapes that play repetitively in our minds—we can identify and purge self-destructive thoughts such as "I'm not creative. Why try?" Observing dreams that portray the Cynic can help us identify this figure and bring unexpected insights. Actual stories of women and men who have struggled with the Cynic, along with those of fictional characters in novels, films, and fairy tales, help us to detect cynical attitudes so we can transform them.

Cynthia's story is like those of many men and women trying to respond to the call to create. One day she walked into my consulting room and, in tears, described her doubts and despair over her creative abilities. As a girl Cynthia had wanted to write a novel. Reading books had helped her throughout a difficult childhood. After she began to earn her livelihood, she saved enough money to take off six months from work to realize her dream. But she became distracted and could not write. When the six months passed, she fell into despair because she thought she didn't have what it takes to write a book. She abandoned her book project and resumed her former job.

Nightmares began to haunt her. She dreamed that adolescent boys were trying to murder her. These killers, she came to see, represented the inner Cynic that sabotaged her creativity by taunting her with her failure to write the novel in six months. The nightmares caught Cynthia's attention, and she saw the necessity to confront her inner Cynic by reexamining the romantic and idealistic notion that she could write a novel in such a brief time.

Cynthia tried to understand how her cynicism and her romantic notions about writing might have developed. She remembered that her mother had complained about abandoning her own desire to create. Her mother was taught that women shouldn't try to juggle marriage and a career; nor could they succeed in a man's world. When Cynthia told her mother that she wanted to write a book, her mother criticized her for being too idealistic. Cynthia rebelled by holding to her ideals, but sabotaged them by her unrealistic expectations about the length of time that creativity requires. She had been influenced unconsciously by her mother's cynical attitude.

The Call to Create

When Cynthia understood how her mistaken ideas about creativity had been formed, she could separate herself from them and develop a more realistic approach to writing. She read interviews with writers and learned that creating is a complex, many-faceted activity. After the work of inner and outer exploration, Cynthia was able to surrender her ego's tight time plan and return to work on her novel. She had learned that it takes time and a concerted decision to work through inner obstacles that block our creative efforts.

If, like Cynthia, you identify the snide inner voice that says you will fail, that your project is worthless, or that others will not understand it or reject it, you can detect the sneering chatter of the Cynic. The Cynic lives in a passive bitter state that breeds resentment and rejects the call to create. The emotional energy that could be directed actively toward creative life is diverted and convoluted into hostility and spite, cynical attitudes that hurt.

Instead of feeling the joy of inspiration and enthusiasm, the Cynic actually becomes tormented by its own creative imagination since it is not being utilized. As Nietzsche expressed it, the Cynic's "soul squints," for it is an expert in self-deprecation and self-humiliation—ugly judgments that it eventually twists and turns to degrade others. Rather than responding to the creative challenge of being human, the Cynic stagnates in impotence and impoverishment. In reaction, it starts to project its own hostility upon others, expects the worst from people, and is likely to become a misanthrope. Like Oscar the Grouch in *Sesame Street* who lives in a garbage can and emerges only to growl, the Cynic can discourage us by saying that our creative work is trash.

The tragedy of the Cynic is that it does not follow its heart, for its heart has been hurt. Instead of accepting the risk to live in the warmth of love and passion, it slogs around in a bog of spite. Like Dostoyevsky's "underground man," the Cynic confines himself to a cold corner in the cellar of his inner mansion and lives in despair. He turns into a devilish doubter who pretends to know all the answers or claims there are no answers. The Cynic scoffs at trust, discourages risk, and takes perverse pride in humiliation. As the archetypal Cynic, Dostoyevsky's despairing underground man exclaims in frustration, "I know myself that it is not underground that is better, but something different, quite different, for which I am thirsting, but which I cannot find! Damn underground!"[1]

THE CYNIC'S DESPAIR AND THE LEAP OF FAITH

In order to confront the Cynic, we must face our human propensity for despair and understand it. In despair we lose hope and faith—two essential components needed to create. Reading Kierkegaard helped me to understand that despair comes from being split in two within ourselves. Despair stems from a divided self that resists the tension and movement between interior conflicting opposites, such as matter and spirit, actuality and potentiality, the finite and infinite. We encounter these conflicting poles within ourselves whenever we struggle to embody and to realize our visions.

The call to create confronts us with paradox because creating entails forming matter, actualizing potential, and making the "invisible" visible. Transformation challenges us spiritually, emotionally, and psychologically to learn how to live in the tension of these opposites. The call to create summons us to become conscious of the human condition and to choose to take responsibility for this mystery of conflicting desires and tensions that we are.

If we do not accept the soul's creative challenge, we live in despair, split apart within our center, alienated from our authentic self. This is the state of the Cynic, who perceives inner division as absolute and refuses to surrender to life's changes or to nature's cycles. The Cynic in ourselves lives in a state of passive resentment, which is a hidden, tyrannical form of control and which rejects the receptive state of mind necessary to create.

If we remain unaware of our capacity to change, we become hostage to a state of unconscious despair and live like robots, clones formed by mass society. Then we become like the prisoners in Plato's parable of the cave. They believe that reality consists only of the dim projected shadows they see on the cave walls. People in this state of mind tend to limit their lives to hedonism or conformity without commitment to anything higher than ego-impulses. In effect, they become trapped by acting out these tendencies, unwittingly reducing their existence to the Escape Artist or the Conformist—two inner saboteurs described in chapters 5 and 6. The film *Pleasantville* portrays the dilemma of unconscious despair that afflicts the Conformist, while Fellini's classic *La Dolce Vita* shows the spiritual malaise of hedonism.

If we become conscious of our ability to change, yet feel too weak to do so, we remain victims who suffer from the despair of weakness. Conversely, if we consciously deny or refuse our potentiality to change, we suffer from the despair of defiance. In either case, we try to force life to conform to our limited perspectives rather than accept life's natural, organic process. The despair of weakness that culminates in suicide is depicted in *Anna Karenina;* and in *Scent of a Woman* Al Pacino portrays a blind and bitter ex-Vietnam military officer caught in the despair of defiance.

The Cynic's despair results from an idealized expectation of perfection. Since perfection is impossible due to human finitude, the Cynic can veer to the extreme of weakness, stagnating there as a failure. Or the Cynic can shift to a state of defiance, refusing the possibility of change and growth. When trapped in the despair of weakness or the despair of defiance, the Cynic rejects help, whether it comes as compassion from other people or inwardly as inspiration from the Muse.

The way out of despair is to risk a creative leap of faith that acknowledges both weakness and strength and dares to balance on the tightrope between our finite and infinite sides and to believe that help can come from a source greater than the ego. To live authentically and creatively, we must commit to living in this paradox. In the Brazilian film *Central Station,* Fernanda Montenegro portrays a cynical old woman who transforms her despair as she, at first begrudgingly, helps an orphan boy.

If we want to escape from the clutch of the Cynic in order to transform ourselves, we need to learn to be open to the Muse, who can redirect this energy with the inspiration she can bring to us. If the Cynic and the Muse can learn to play together, we can transform our approach to creativity.

Sometimes we can initiate the meeting with the Muse. For example, before writing *Valley Song,* Fugard said that he felt tired and had been thinking he might stop writing. Yet he also knew he had an appointment to keep with some inner characters.

In order to keep that appointment and to write the play that eventually became *Valley Song*, Fugard decided to meet with five teenage girls, each of whom represented the different ethnic groups in South Africa. He asked the girls, who volunteered to meet and work with him, to keep journals of their thoughts and feelings. Then Fugard and the girls worked together on a play that they produced onstage in South Africa. Because he chose to learn from these young women, Fugard was finally able to write with the jubilant voice of Veronica in *Valley Song*.

HEALING THE CYNIC

Whenever we dare to create we risk becoming hostage to the Cynic. In the Cynic's clutch we lose flexibility, openness, and human warmth and frequently congeal into rigid, hard, stony versions of ourselves.

Sometimes the Cynic's ridicule leads to addictions in which we try to drown the mocking voice that insults us by saying we have failed. The film *Leaving Las Vegas* shows this by the extreme example of a man who chooses to drink himself to death. Like Dostoyevsky's "underground man," who rejects a young girl's love, Nicolas Cage plays the protagonist who refuses help even after he has found a woman who accepts him and offers him genuine love.

The Cynic can assail us at any phase of the creative process and tends to appear periodically. In order to transform this character, we must be able to identify the Cynic in its various guises and in the different ways that it discourages us from our creative and spiritual lives. It is important to name this inner saboteur so we can begin to confront it successfully and help it meet with the transformative energy of the Muse. This is one of the major tasks of soul-work.

By identifying and personifying the Cynic in ourselves, we can learn how it obstructs our creative efforts. Then it is possible to separate from this character in order to stop reducing our whole self to just one facet. By confronting this character, we can see how it developed, where it came from, and how we use the Cynic as a defense against creating. Perhaps a cruel rejection from a teacher or from siblings or peers in our school years, or a critical parent who doused enthusiasm early in our lives, is behind our lack of faith and confidence. Or, we may feel the Cynic rising up inside ourselves if we are slighted at work.

For example, Michelle, a woman in her late twenties, had wanted to rise to an executive position in a large corporation. When someone else was promoted to the higher position, Michelle became jealous and bitter. Michelle was more innovative and had worked harder. However, the other woman flattered the boss while Michelle remained quiet and independent. After her lack of promotion, Michelle lost interest in her work and became cynical; she stopped doing her best. Her boredom at work spread to a general listlessness in her life which in turn affected her relationships.

Finally Michelle became so depressed that, at the advice of a friend, she consulted with a therapist. After some work in therapy, Michelle realized that she had regressed to becoming a victim, a role that she had experienced in childhood. In fact, the woman who had been promoted reminded her of her youngest sister, the darling of the family, while her supervisor reminded her of her mother who liked to be dominant and to be flattered.

Michelle, like many middle children, felt like an invisible child. For the most part her parents had ignored her and let her go her own way. The only time she received attention was when she made a witty remark. Her father encouraged her older brother's career but gave no attention to Michelle's. Her mother affirmed her younger sister but neglected Michelle. Michelle chose to enter a corporate career only because her friends headed in that direction. At the time, she had no other focus.

Michelle's creative challenge was to identify her cynicism, its source, and its victimizing effect upon her life. She recognized that she had to surrender the resentment that she held about the lack of recognition of her potentiality and merits—a resentment that fed her tendency to be pessimistic. She also learned to wait patiently since she did not know where, when, and how her creative seed would sprout.

During this period Michelle realized that she did not want a nine-to-five corporate job. She had a dream that pointed to a new direction. In the dream Michelle was doodling while her supervisor was giving instructions. The supervisor reprimanded Michelle and pointed to the sketch. When Michelle looked down at the drawing, she saw that she had created a satiric cartoon. Michelle's quick wit and dry sense of humor amused others and had become a defense. The dream helped Michelle to see that she could develop skills to draw cartoons—a creative vehicle through which she could use her humor in effective ways, such as social satire. By turning her wit toward a creative direction, Michelle transformed the habit of using her wit in a cynical way against herself and others.

The Cynic

When cynicism arises in us and darkens our spirits, as it did to Michelle, we need to ask: "What act of consciousness and courage am I defending against?" Instead of hiding behind the Cynic's complaints and remaining passive, we must dare to be creative. In this way we can improve the quality of human life.

While writing this chapter I had to confront my own cynicism by writing about my feelings of doubt, skepticism, and discouragement so that I could get beyond the Cynic's comments to find my voice. Indeed, I realized that every time I write a book I encounter the Cynic and must learn to deal with it anew. When I feel apathy, a sense of pessimistic futility that what I write is not important or already has been said, or when I feel that I'm not up to the task, I know I must understand how the Cynic is functioning in my life.

My dreams alert me to the Cynic when it lurks in a corner of my psyche. For example, while I was writing *The Wounded Woman,* my manuscript was rejected forty-two times. My enthusiasm began to dwindle, and I fell into a deep depression. Even though my heart told me otherwise, I began to think that all my work was of no use.

In the midst of this despair, I dreamt one night that a mean old man was following me around. As I turned around to confront him, he lunged at me and I kicked him away. Suddenly he grabbed a bucket of dirty water that had been used to wash some strawberries and tried to douse me with it. Just then I heard a voice telling me to grab the bucket and throw the dirty water back on him. After I did this, the voice congratulated me for carrying out a task that was prescribed in the fairy tales of four different languages.

When I awakened I realized that this mean old man represented an old cynical side of myself that had been following me around for years. This time the Cynic tried to drown enthusiasm for my book by relying on the despairing way that I reacted to rejections. The dream showed me that I should not allow trust and confidence in myself and my creative work to be drenched with dirty water. Rather, I needed to act by throwing the water back at the old cynic so I could free myself to enjoy the fruits (the strawberries) of my accomplishments.

By now I know that if I stay vigilant and confront my inner Cynic, eventually he skulks away. More important, if I continue to face him and work with his energy, he may be transformed like the frog in the fairy tale, *The Frog Prince*, which can be seen as a story about transforming the Cynic.

In the Grimm Brothers' version of *The Frog Prince*, a princess has lost her golden ball which has fallen into a well. The frog agrees to retrieve the ball if she will feed him and allow him in her bed. After she gets her ball back, the princess forgets about her promise, but the frog croaks so loudly at the door that her father orders her to take care of the creature. Repulsed by the frog, the princess feeds him but refuses to take him to her bed. When the frog persists in his demands, the princess gets so angry that she throws him against the wall, whereupon he is released from his bewitchment and is transformed into his original form: a handsome prince. In Charles Perrault's version of the tale, the princess must kiss the frog to turn it into a prince.

In my view, the golden ball that the princess loses is like creative intuition, which can so easily roll back into the well of unconsciousness. The frog is a creature that, like the Cynic, knows the depths and can descend into the unconscious but can also move above ground, as we can with our consciousness. Like the frog the Cynic can descend into the deep well—a repository for creativity—to retrieve images that are new or have been lost.

The Cynic's familiarity with the dark, hidden corners of the soul is an aid for creativity, which requires descending into unlit realms. Like the frog that was remade, so the Cynic can be transformed from bewitchment into royalty. In both versions, whether it is through anger or a kiss, the frog needs attention from the princess in order to be transformed. Just as the frog asks for consideration, so the Cynic needs our care if we are to transform him.

In creating we need to use both anger and the kiss. The attention that we offer the Cynic often needs to be "tough love"—the care and consciousness to sort out the fruitful qualities from those that breed malcontent. We need to sort out the dark truths that the Cynic perceives from the despairing pessimism that makes him impotent.

In Dostoyevsky's novel *Crime and Punishment,* the cynical Raskolnikov murders an old abusive woman and, accidentally, her sister, because he believes he is above human limitations. He is transformed when he listens to the helpful wisdom of Sonia, a kind, humble young woman who loves him. Sonia listens to Raskolnikov and nourishes him through her charity, devotion, and patience. But she also confronts him sincerely and honestly with his crime. Sonia looks into his eyes, shakes him, and tells him to acknowledge his crime and ask for forgiveness by bowing down to Mother Earth, kissing the ground, and watering it with his tears.

Telling the Cynic to stop complaining and to act constructively to change things is a task of creativity. Just as Sonia shook Raskolnikov, we need to shake our inner Cynic so we can open our hearts in humility if we want to transform our lives.

Remember that Psyche fell into despair when she was given the task of sorting out the seeds. But listening to her natural instincts, she accepted help from the worker ants. If, like Psyche, we can separate the seeds that will bear fruit on the earth from those that fester underground, we will be able to benefit from the Cynic's view of the darker side of life. For to move creatively, we need to be aware of all the elements in a situation. By addressing the realities that the Cynic sees, we can make the necessary changes.

LISTENING TO THE MUSE OF NATURE IN THE "WORLD'S DARK NIGHT"

The new millennium is here. If we want to transform the cynicism that sabotages hope for a humane world, we need to understand how the Cynic functions at a cultural level. The travesties of poverty and war, addictions to drugs, power, control, greed, and violence, our inhumanities to each other, and denial about our abuses all threaten to destroy the earth and humankind. Technological advances have brought progress but, with it, the potential to destroy our planet. Grim realities such as these foster cynicism, *and* they also call us to work together with creative cooperation if we want to survive. Western civilization has fallen into an abyss—into the "world's dark night"—a descent into the "dark night of the soul" as described by Saint John of the Cross.

He asks us to imagine the soul as a burning log. At first the log becomes black, sooty, and smelly as it burns. If you have ever been around a campfire, you will know what I mean. The burning log is beautiful to see and warms us. But when the smoke drifts toward us, the soot irritates our eyes to tears and drives some of us away. If we remain present while the log continues to burn, we will see it transform into radiant flames—a fire that is so beautiful and dazzling that it inspires awe.

The soul is like a burning log, according to Saint John. Just as the black and sooty log can make us feel dirty, smelly, and obnoxious, so our soul sometimes looks dark, ugly, and disagreeable as it smolders in the fire. Cynicism and despair are the black burning logs of creative fire, and dealing with them is a stage on the soul's journey for purification.

The soul may look black and ugly to us, just like the smoking log. But if we are willing to accept the discomfort and suffering—the rage and tears that accompany this process—we will see the soul become beautiful as it merges with the fire's divine radiance like the log that bursts into brilliant flames.

Passing through the dark night is a cyclical process that recurs throughout our lives to increasingly refine and purify the soul. It is like nature's passage through the seasons—a continuing journey of renewal that has moments of descent and ascent, death and rebirth.

Confronting the Cynic and the other shadowy saboteurs of creativity *is* part of the soul's passage through the "dark night." Choosing consciously to face the Cynic and other saboteurs is necessary to transform ourselves and our world. To create and to do our soulwork, we must learn to pass through our personal dark nights and the world's dark night too.

Throughout the creative process it is necessary to recognize and listen to the interior and exterior adverse voices in order to know how to cope with them and how to act in a given situation. Detecting the prejudiced, condemning voices in ourselves and in our global culture is central to the soul-work required to redirect our energies toward creativity.

In this dark time we need to struggle consciously to invite the Muse of Nature to help us out of our dilemma. Global warming, smog, and decreasing rain forests are just a few of the increasing signs that show our need to respect nature's rhythms and learn how to follow them. Otherwise we may destroy our planet due to greed for power, profit, and personal aggrandizement.

If we can be humble, admit failures, bow down, kiss the earth, water it with our tears, and *listen* to the wisdom of the Muse of Nature, perhaps we can transform the ashes of personal and cultural cynicism into creative fire.

Part II
THE CARING

"Care" first gave humans their being. Once, when she was crossing a river, Care saw some clay and began to give it shape, meditating upon what she had just created. She had taken the clay from the body of Earth and had asked Jupiter to give it spirit. Care wanted to give this new being her name. But Jupiter and Earth each claimed their right to the name. Saturn (Time) settled the dispute by saying the name would be "homo" since it is made from "humus" or earth. At death, Earth would receive the body, and Jupiter the spirit. However, the new being would belong to Care during its lifetime, for it was she who had first shaped it.

Ancient Latin Fable

4
COURAGE

The rottenness of others is in us too. . . . I really see no other solution than to turn inwards and to root out all the rottenness there. I no longer believe we can change anything in the world until we have first changed ourselves.

Etty Hillesum

THE WITNESS CONFRONTS
THE TYRANT AND THE VICTIM

Everyone who creates faces the threat of the archetypal Tyrant—a character that dominates through fear tactics to hold on to the illusion of complete control and power. The Tyrant speaks within us and throughout the course of history in outer society. The internal and external tyrants play off each other. When either one seeks power, the other tends to collude. As with all of the other characters, the voice of the Tyrant is not restricted to gender.

Whenever we hear explosive words within ourselves that thunder, "Do as I say, or else . . . !" we can recognize the internal tyrant speaking. We encounter the interior tyrant whenever we attempt to change our lives.

We face the exterior tyrant in family conflicts, discord in relationships, dissension at work and at school, and during social, communal, and political strife. In daily life we experience the tyrant at work when a boss yells at us, at home when a spouse, sibling, or parent blames us, and at school when teachers and peers ridicule our efforts.

In order to be the most powerful, the Tyrant rules with oppression and even wants to eclipse nature by forcing its own will upon it. Because the Tyrant uses people's creativity for its own ends, it tries to bully the creator into submission. If the creator submits, he or she becomes the Victim.

Creative action and soul-work inevitably bring us face to face with this power-monger that tries to usurp and suppress individual creativity for its ends. If we do not stand up to the Tyrant—whether internal or external—it will subvert our purpose to its own.

The Tyrant interferes with passion and our natural call to create. When we lose passion, we lose the fire we need to create. This happens if we follow dictums that betray our integrity and disregard our emotional truths. When we permit ourselves to be forced to do something disloyal to the care of the soul, we suffer in the form of guilt and shame.

While we may or may not be called to confront the Tyrant in outer life, we face the Tyrant inside ourselves whenever we work to create or transform our lives. Transformation asks us to surrender outworn rigid regimes to cultivate flexibility and growth—an act that threatens the Tyrant's reign.

RECOGNIZING THE INNER TYRANT

How can we recognize the Tyrant so that we know how to cope with this power? And how is the Tyrant related to the Cynic, whose skepticism discredits creative integrity and effort in its early stages?

If we are not alert to the Cynic, this inner saboteur turns into the Tyrant, who then tries to abuse the Muse, our inner source of inspiration, by using her energy for its own ends. While the Cynic sabotages creative effort by doubting its worth, the Tyrant aims to possess and control creativity for its oppressive ends. If the Cynic betrays moral conscience and integrity by succumbing to power, it loses heart and becomes tyrannical.

In contrast to the Cynic, whose mean-spiritedness tends to be passive-aggressive, the Tyrant operates overtly through intimidation, lies, and terrorism. The Tyrant is likely to assume an angry, threatening demeanor, the body language of rage, to manipulate us through fear.

The Tyrant maneuvers to be the central figure in both outer and inner life. Wanting everything its way, the Tyrant imposes its will upon others. It speaks with a punitive voice to have the last word and refuses to listen to whoever disagrees with it. Eventually the Tyrant suppresses all traces of criticism and makes greater demands on its workers, its people, and even its allies.

When all else fails, the Tyrant uses censorship to stamp out human dignity and creative freedom that threatens its dominion. If the Muse protests, the tyrant tries to deaden imagination. On the outer level we saw this happen during the reigns of Stalin and Hitler, who suppressed, censored, and threatened artists with imprisonment, exile, or death.

Inwardly the same thing happens when our personal censors threaten: "If you dare to utter your ideas out loud, you will be punished." How many of us shrink and quell before such inner intimidation and thus become victims who construct our own prisons?

In the end the Tyrant's actions become predictable. In order to uphold power, pride, and prejudice, the Tyrant refuses to face reality, chooses to believe what it wants, and ignores the facts. The Tyrant begins to label and stereotype people, to denigrate them, and to blame others as a scapegoat for its own mistakes. In history this occurred at the end of Hitler's reign, when he extended his notion of "anti-Semitism" to encompass all of his prejudices against whoever disagreed or offended him—for example, to gypsies, to homosexuals, to the maimed and impaired, and to German expressionist artists who offended his aesthetic taste and criticized him through their artworks.

Arrogance leads to the downfall of the Tyrant, who becomes hostage to inflation, identifying with godlike rights and powers. The voice of inflation bellows, "I am entitled to do and have whatever I want," thereby feeding a voracious narcissism that ignores and violates earthly limits and human boundaries. Wanting to be "the best," the most successful, the wealthiest, or the most famous is an inflated temptation of which a person must be wary, and it will be explored further in chapter 7.

The inflated Tyrant plots to possess everything, especially creative imagination, which exceeds finite grasp and comes from an indescribable source. In a state of possession, the Tyrant wants to control the Muse. The Tyrant schemes to control creative life by conniving with egotistical desires that feed an artist's inflation. When they identify and equate personal creativity with the transcendent energy of the Muse, artists and others lose touch with humility, forgetting that creative inspiration comes from a greater source.

Sooner or later inflation leads to a fall, in which the Tyrant hits bottom, loses power, and is seen as a mere mortal with human possibilities and limitations. To be found out humiliates the Tyrant even though the possibility for genuine transformational power requires acknowledging errors, becoming humble, and valuing humility.

Thus, the call to create inevitably introduces us to the Tyrant, whose rule is threatened by ventures that are foreign to its own. The Tyrant's desire to be center stage and to reign with absolute control and power is antithetical to creativity—a process that requires open receptivity in balance with the skill to bring form out of chaos. When we create, we need the freedom to plunge into the unknown and to allow imagination to roam freely in foreign territory to discover what is there.

Creative life requires surrendering ego-control to transcendent energies that are greater than any single system, person, or part of ourselves. The freedom so central to creativity threatens despots, whether they seek power in the outer world or inside the psyche.

THE VICTIM

The interior voice of the Tyrant threatens us with accusations, questions our legitimacy to create, and criticizes what we have composed. This inner voice may indict us as mad, as a fraud, or as a victim too weak to fight for creative integrity.

When the Tyrant dominates our inner life, we lose the feeling of inner freedom. Intuition ceases to flow. We become afraid to model or express what is new or unconventional. If the Tyrant prevails, we shrink down, slump our shoulders, and speak weakly or not at all. These physical signs show that the Tyrant has stepped forward in the psyche to prevent us from taking new directions that threaten its web of power.

Despite the Tyrant's show of force, underneath the show of power, the Tyrant feels insecure. Like a frightened and helpless child, the Tyrant's threats are desperate manipulations to maintain control. Some who become hostage to the inner Tyrant try to hide their feelings of victimization by acting like a tyrant; others act out the Victim role.

If we allow the Tyrant to possess our inner life, we might hear its voice tell us to destroy our work, as the French sculptress Camille Claudel destroyed nearly half of her sculptures when she felt victimized by Rodin's rejection of marriage. Unconsciously she acted out the wish of her tyrannical mother, who did not want her to be an artist. Opera's diva, Maria Callas, succumbed to her inner Tyrant by abandoning her singing—an unconscious act of rebellion against her overly ambitious mother. In this way Callas killed her inner creative child, just as Medea—the legendary character she portrayed in opera and in Pier Paolo Pasolini's film—murdered her children to avenge her betrayal by their father, Jason.

Artists can become hostage to the creative process itself if they neglect the healthy needs of body and soul as they answer the call to create. In such cases the artist becomes a pawn to the Demon Lover, an archetypal Tyrant that lures us away from creation and toward destruction. In the film *The Red Shoes*, a tyrannical impresario discovers a young dancer and makes her a slave to her art. Once she ties on the red ballet shoes, she must dance to her death, a symbolic fate for many artists. The Tyrant's abuse of the artist is also portrayed in Fellini's film *La Strada*, the story of a simple waif who is ordered to play a clown in a traveling circus. She becomes a slave of a cruel circus strongman who brutally mistreats her. In the film *Mephisto*, a talented actor becomes a marionette to a fascist puppeteer. He rationalizes his betrayals and performances, which are dictated by the Tyrant to whom he has sold his soul. The Russian legend "The Firebird," which I will discuss in detail later in this chapter, shows the conscious struggle that is required to resist a demonic tyrant.

The Call to Create

In contrast to the tyrannical Demon Lover, the Daimon is an inner force, a higher spirit within us that calls us to create. The dictionary describes *daimon* as "an indwelling divine power that energizes humans with extraordinary enthusiasm." The original Greek meaning of the word connoted both divine and diabolical energies—hence the conception that creativity is dangerous. Plato referred to it as the "divine madness." Jung said that the energy of the psyche—libido itself—is daimonic and carries the tension of good and evil. The daimon carries the intensity of creative fire—which can enliven us or destroy us.

Creative people down through the ages have recognized the creative daimon's presence in human existence. The daimon, Socrates said, was an inner voice that guided him. In the *Symposium* Plato remarks: "Eros is a daimon." Homer, Aeschylus, Aristotle, and Goethe all referred to it. Yeats called it that "Other Will." In his diaries the artist Paul Klee wrote about the daimon's presence in his paintings. For Michelangelo the sculptures were already housed within the block of marble. Michelangelo responded to the daimon's call through the work and struggle required to release them.

Prokofiev, the Russian composer, wrote about his hymn to the free, noble, and happy spirit of human beings—the theme that infuses his Fifth Symphony: "I cannot say that I deliberately chose this theme. It was born within me and clamored for expression." Prokofiev considered his response to this call as the culminating point in his creative life, for it enabled him to return to composing symphonies after a fourteen-year period of interruption.

Down through the ages artists have talked about the difficulty of living in this tension. Rilke described a time when he was at a creative crossroads. He felt defeated by despair in both his life and his writing, and he fell into a debilitating depression. For a time he was diverted by the Demon Lover's temptation to consider suicide. But Rilke knew that the call to create summoned him to endure the tension by withstanding "the demons" so he could be alive to hear "the angels" singing.

As in the case of Rilke, the call to create asks us to struggle consciously in the paradox that creative choices require; it bids us to learn to live in the inherent tension between the divine and diabolical. The human challenge is to direct our energy toward creative life rather than toward destructive ends that culminate in suicide, murder, and annihilation of earthly life. Hence the call to create asks us to resist both the Tyrant and the Victim and to survive by developing our potentiality to be a Witness.

THE WITNESS: COPING WITH THE TYRANT

We all have different ways of coping with the Tyrant. Yet defenses tend to further tyrannical ends. In order to protect ourselves from the tyrant, some of us react through rebellion or by passive-aggressive behavior. Hypervigilance and escape through sleep are additional modes of defense.

People who have grown up with parental tyrants are likely to internalize the Tyrant, thereby enabling this interior despot to direct their lives. A person whose inner Tyrant rules them is likely to succumb to an outer Tyrant's control. Or a person might enact the Tyrant in a misguided attempt to escape from chaotic or despotic situations. Frightened underneath, some people put on the Tyrant's mask of power to try to survive.

A helpful witness to a child's abuse can influence whether the child develops into a creative person who can help others by describing his suffering. If there is no witness, the child may become a despot who repeats repressed feelings of helplessness by turning them brutally on others. The psychoanalyst and artist Alice Miller contrasts the case of Stalin, who became a Tyrant, with that of Dostoyevsky, who became a Witness.

Stalin was beaten by his father while his self-involved mother looked away, a story typical of many abused children who become abusers themselves. Dostoyevsky's father was tyrannical, but his mother actively loved him, as did the peasant nurses who held him on their laps and told him the legend of the Firebird, his favorite story and a tale that helped foster his faith in the possibility of creative freedom.

Dostoyevsky experienced the Tyrant on a political level when the tsar condemned him to be executed for subversive writing. As Dostoyevsky stood blindfolded at the scaffold, the tsar reprieved his life at the last moment, sentencing him instead to ten years in a Siberian prison. Facing death, then miraculously receiving the gift of life, was the turning point that helped Dostoyevsky to reexamine his life and to develop spiritually and creatively. He used his time in prison to look within and observe other prisoners. Then he wrote about the suffering of prison life in his novel *House of the Dead*.

As we saw in chapter 3, Dostoyevsky wrote about inner saboteurs as well as the supporters of creativity and spiritual life. He described them in his novel as characters who grapple with the complex dilemmas of injustice, good and evil, and despair and faith. Like Dostoyevsky, we can learn to look at our own times in "prison" as opportunities to reflect on our lives and to transform.

THE LEGEND OF THE FIREBIRD

Since fairy tales and legends speak to us directly on the universal level by taking us to the heart of human conflicts, I would like to tell a story that helped me understand how the Tyrant obstructs creativity. The story also shows how a young girl's courage leads her to witness the demonic Tyrant so she can be free to share her gifts with others. As we have seen, "The Firebird" is an ancient legend that nourished Dostoyevsky as a child and helped him face his own demons. This legend still influences creative people today.

Long ago, in a small village far away in Russia, there lived an orphan girl whose gift for embroidery and weaving was so extraordinary that reports of her brilliance spread throughout the land and across the sea. Maryushka made such beautiful weavings that merchants came from afar to beg her to work for them. Maryushka always thanked the merchants, but she refused their offers because she wanted to live and work in the village where she was born and where her parents were buried. She felt her inspiration came from the countryside.

Praise for Maryushka's work spread so far that Koschei the Immortal, a sorcerer who believed he possessed all the beauty in the world, heard of her artistry. Furious that her creativity had escaped his possession, Koschei decided that he must capture Maryushka so he would have her creations for himself. So he flew far away to Maryushka's village and, arriving at her doorstep, changed his appearance into that of a handsome young man. When Maryushka answered his knock upon her door, he bowed to her and asked to see her artwork.

As soon as he saw Maryushka's dazzling embroidery, Koschei became enraged that he did not possess her creativity and her works of beauty. So he asked Maryushka to become his bride. She could live in his palace, enjoy the golden apples from his garden, wear all the beautiful jewels in his possession, and see and hear the songs of the birds of paradise that he kept on the castle grounds. Maryushka thanked him, but she told him that she could not embroider for him alone and declined his marriage proposal. She wanted to stay in the village where she was born, live in the countryside that inspired her, and continue to give joy through her creations to the simple peasants who lived in the village.

Upon hearing her reply, Koschei went into a frenzy. In an instant the evil sorcerer changed Maryushka into a beautiful firebird and himself into a gigantic black falcon. He flew down upon the exquisite Firebird, clutched her in his claws, and soared away with her toward his palace. But Maryushka, who witnessed this demonic sorcery, chose to sacrifice herself rather than to become his hostage. One by one, she shed her radiant rainbow-colored feathers, which fell upon the earth, so that she could bequeath her creative gift to others. Thereby she released herself from the Tyrant's clutches. And until this day it is said that the Firebird's brilliant feathers are divine gifts of grace hidden in the ground and aglow with splendor. The Firebird's luminous feathers are in the earth to inspire all who see and cherish beauty to create loveliness for others.

"The Firebird" shows how a creative woman confronts and

thwarts a tyrant who attempts to possess her. The legend shows that an act of love and spiritual sacrifice has more power than a despot who tries to capture creativity by taking the Muse of Nature hostage.

The Firebird legend is compelling because we all have within us a character like the tyrant sorcerer Koschei, who wants to control and to possess creativity, to grasp its transcendent energy with clutching claws that will destroy it. But we also have within us the generous spirit of the transcendent Firebird—the Muse of Nature that inspires us to receive gifts of imagination and commit ourselves to the sacrifices necessary to create works and lives of beauty. Like Maryushka, we must be able to recognize the tyrant who wants to dominate, direct, and subdue our imagination and hold us in his power. As in the Firebird legend, it takes conscious sacrifice, choice, and courage to detect, grapple with, and outwit the Tyrant who would violate our lives.

Creativity requires freedom and space to allow the mind to wander into unexpected places. By planning to marry and possess Maryushka to keep her creative energy caged in his palace, Koschei exemplifies the Tyrant who plays on our fears and keep us from exploring. But in her earthly form as Maryushka, and in her transcendent form as the Firebird, she is not afraid of the tyrant.

In the legend, as soon as the Firebird sheds her feathers, she is free of the Tyrant's grasp. Then she offers her beautiful feathers, symbols of her courage and creativity, to others. Creativity itself actually frees us from the power of the Tyrant because being creative requires commitment, courage, consciousness, choice, and compassion for oneself and others. Creative life requires us to be authentic and fully present. Despite past personal and cultural conditioning, we are still the authors of our being.

The Call to Create

Creative energy is not an object that can be owned. Nor is it a force that can be maintained and directed by sheer will alone. The weaving of original insights and dazzling images that culminate in an artwork or a beautifully embroidered life require us to be ready and open to receive the ebb and flow of inspiration. Meanwhile we must work to develop the necessary craft and skill to work with whatever the muse offers us.

Maryushka's simple wisdom, humility, and devotion all acknowledge that she is aware that her ability to create works of beauty is a gift from something greater and does not belong to her alone. Intuitively she knows that if she works only for a merchant or accepts the temptations of Koschei, she will have sold her soul. Maryushka, in her earthly form, represents the spirit of groundedness and demonstrates the patience, integrity, and courage that creative life requires.

A tyrant like Koschei does not have the patience to listen and to wait in order to appreciate and cooperate with the creative process. He is the greedy one in us who wants to have a finished product in hand—the one who wants what he wants when he wants it. The Tyrant is possessed by self-will run riot. Instead of enjoying the rhythm of giving and receiving that creativity entails, the Tyrant wants to catch and dominate the elusive free spirit. But like the transcendent Firebird, creative fire is too potent and mysterious to be captured and possessed.

Whenever artists believe they are the sole originators of a work of art and presume to master the creative spirit, their penchant for personal power interferes with the creative process. In ordinary life this happens whenever we value the results of creativity more than the inherent joy that comes from the activity of creating. For example, if we value money, fame, and adulation, we appraise the product as worth more than the process. By forgetting that we are cocreators who cooperate with a force greater than ourselves, and by neglecting to give thanks for its wondrous gift, we become like Koschei, who claims that he alone is entitled to possess creative beauty.

THE WITNESS: FACING FEAR AND TRICKING THE TYRANT

Since the Tyrant plays on our fears, acknowledging and facing fear is essential to freeing ourselves. Dealing with fear is frequently the first and most difficult step to take in creativity. Developing the inner Witness is essential for this task. While the Tyrant thrives on hiding truths and concealing abuses, the Witness exposes denial and hidden acts that contribute to the habit of fear.

The Tyrant's presence actually forces us to focus on facing our fears and to tackle them so we can survive. Whether we encounter the Tyrant on the inner or outer level, confronting this figure calls for courage and for focused consciousness to see, understand, and testify to violations of human dignity. People who bear witness to fear by telling their stories through words, painting, music, dance, film, or any other way have a chance to confront and redirect the Tyrant.

Throughout history we find models of courage to help us. For example, Nelson Mandela, Vaclav Havel, Rosa Luxemburg, Etty Hillesum, and Viktor Frankl were held hostage by tyrants in their respective countries. All of these heroes and heroines opposed outer tyranny. They were able to bear witness to it because they consciously developed the inner strength that enabled them to survive in times of terror.

Viktor Frankl, who was interned in a concentration camp, maintained his inner strength and dignity by composing in his mind a work that later became the inspiring book, *Man's Search for Meaning.* The imprisoned Havel wrote letters to his wife to maintain his moral fiber. Hillesum chose to become a "living conscience" for people by recording her experiences in her journal. Before she died in Auschwitz, she smuggled the journal to friends outside the camp; it was later published as the book *An Interrupted Life.* Dmitri Shostakovich, who composed under Stalin's reign, tricked the censors and exposed the Tyrant's thumping step in his music—a reminder to all those who knew how to listen.

The children interned in the Terezin concentration camp were encouraged to draw pictures and write poems about their lives by teachers who witnessed their creativity while they were imprisoned by Nazi tyrants. Through artistic expression the children created an imaginal realm that helped them endure the fear and torments of the camps. Through creativity they were able to reach across the abyss of horror to testify to others.

THE MUSE AS WITNESS—ANNA AKHMATOVA

In order to confront the tyrants that try to sabotage creativity, it helps to find examples of creative people, like Dostoyevsky, who survived and matured by successfully dealing with tyranny. When I discovered the true story of a Russian woman, Anna Akhmatova, who became one the greatest poets of the twentieth century by witnessing the Tyrant, I was inspired. Her life story gave me a model to help me fight the inner Tyrant that haunts me during times of rejection. From her story we can learn how the Cynic and the Tyrant can be countered by the Muse and how it is possible to stand firm, to listen, and to wait in order to bear witness.[1]

Although Akhmatova served as a muse for the Russian people, she had to struggle with her inner Cynic and the outer Tyrant during times of personal despair and wartime horrors. By becoming a Witness to what she saw, she transformed her cynicism, even though her poems were dismissed as trivial and sentimental expressions of personal feelings and were later banned as a threat to the goals of Communism.

In her youth Akhmatova's lyrical poems, personal charisma, and striking beauty drew people toward her. She became a romantic muse for men, for other artists, and for the Russian people. Her first husband, the poet Nikolay Gumilyov, called her a "mermaid," a "moon girl," and a "water nymph" in the love poems that he wrote for her. She wandered dreamily in the Luxembourg Gardens and in the bohemian quarters of Paris with Amedeo Modigliani, who immortalized her in a portrait. The Russian poet Marina Tsvetayeva called her a "heavenly fire"; Osip Mandelstam called her a "black angel" who was burnished with God's strange stamp; and Alexander Blok said her beauty was so great that it inspired terror.

Akhmatova, who at first was a romantic muse for her lovers, suffered the realities of two unhappy marriages. Gumilyov betrayed her through numerous affairs. Her second husband, a scholar much older than herself, was a jealous tyrant who tried to burn her poems.

During such times of personal despair, Akhmatova lamented that the Muse had withdrawn her divine gift, since her own poetic voice remained silent.

When her inner Cynic imprisoned her in despair, Akhmatova pleaded with the pagan nature Muse to visit her. At such times she wrote that her hair seemed gray, her eyes dull, her voice silent, and that she could no longer understand the bird's song, notice the stars, or hear the music of the tambourine. The muse who came to restore her was, like Rima in *Green Mansions,* a young girl at one with nature. Akhmatova's muse bathed with her in the sea, taught her to swim, called the fish and the sea gull to her, and spoke with "the voice of the silver pipe."

When Akhmatov began to realize that being a muse for others did not compensate for the loss of her personal life and love, she understood that fame is a joyless trap. She learned that she misused the Muse's interior, inspirational energy whenever she projected it outward on concrete people, such as the men she loved, or when she personally identified with the Muse's transcendent energy. Akhmatova recognized that she would betray her vocation as poet if she believed she was the romantic embodiment of the Muse, as she had done in her youth. During times of the Muse's silence, when she discovered she must invite the inner Muse to return, Akhmatova learned to surrender her concrete role as romantic muse with its accompanying cynicism about her joyless fate as a poet who continually lost the love of men.

Akhmatova's leap of faith in the gifts from the transcendent Muse helped her to withstand the Cynic's despair and the Tyrant's abuse. She found inspiration in the embracing earthly arms of Mother Nature and in the heavenly grace of the holy mother, Mary.

Their inspiration helped her to be free to accept the call to be a poet who bears witness by accepting the responsibility to record the tragedy of war in her Motherland. She developed her gift to formulate in poetic images and words the brutal chaos she saw happening in Russia.

After the Russian revolution, Akhmatova's poems were disparaged for their personal expression of emotions, their lyricism, and their spiritual mysticism. In 1921 politicians—and the poets aligned with them—denigrated her poetry as a relic of the past that did not conform to the purposes of the revolution. Critics maligned her poems as anachronistic lyrics representative of the old religious Russia. They denounced them as inferior and lacking literary merit. Then in 1925 they banned all publication of her work.

Stalin threatened poets during his reign of terror. Osip Mandelstam was tortured and executed. Alexander Solzhenitsyn and Joseph Brodsky were interned in prison camps. Boris Pasternak was held hostage in his house. Marina Tsvetayeva escaped to France but hung herself after she learned that her husband had been murdered and her daughter imprisoned. Akhmatova chose to remain in her Motherland but was banished to a remote area in South Central Russia where she lived under constant observation. Akhmatova described the condition of the artist confronting the inner and outer Tyrant in a poem she wrote after visiting Mandelstam shortly before he was executed.

> And in the room of the disgraced poet
> Fear and the Muse take turns on watch.
> And the night goes on
> Which does not know of dawn.[2]

The Call to Create

In this poem Akhmatova shows that the Muse who helps us witness and the Victim who fears the Tyrant alternate in ourselves during the dark night of the soul. By remembering, we can illuminate the darkness and face our fears.

In the early 1940s the ban upon her writing was lifted briefly, but it was reinstated in 1946 when Akhmatova was expelled from the Union of Soviet Writers. Tyrants destroyed her poems in print and publicly announced in Russia and abroad that her poems had been censored. Akhmatova's health declined due to the harsh conditions in Russia, and she was put under house arrest. To assuage the Russian people who loved her, her oppressors ordered her to appear at her window twice a day so that guards could prove that she had not committed suicide or escaped. The dictators feared an uprising from the Russian people if they learned that their Muse and Witness had been murdered.

As early as the beginning of the revolution, Akhmatova had intuited the bitter bloodshed that would ensue in Russia. She foresaw that the politicians' blind patriotic fervor would end in a war that would lay waste to the earth and wound the soul of Mother Russia and her people.

Akhmatova recognized that she had two tasks. First, she must assume the personal obligation to overcome and transform the cynical Tyrant inside herself that was stifling her Muse. Second, she must accept that her call to be a poet required that she assume social responsibility to bear witness to the horrors of war and to the abuses of Tyranny.

Although many artists chose to escape from Russia during Stalin's reign of terror, Akhmatova's unconditional love for her Motherland required her to remain. She knew she must bear witness in her poems so people would not forget. She also wanted to share the beauty, love, and inspiration through the poetic word that opens up the heart and gives courage.

Akhmatova was told she would be executed if her poems were found written on paper. She wrote her poems on tiny scraps of paper that she quickly destroyed after she had memorized them with the help of women friends. During the four decades during which her writing was censored, she expressed the war's terrors in poems such as "Requiem," and "Poem Without a Hero," which took her twenty-two years (1940–62) to complete.

After Stalin's death in 1953, Akhmatova was allowed to do translations and to stay at a small dacha in a writers' colony near Leningrad. In 1956 her poems were published again, and she was allowed to see foreign visitors. She received many literary honors and prizes from abroad. It was expected that Akhmatova would be nominated for the Nobel Prize, but she died before that could happen. But Akhmatova did survive to become the "living conscience" of literature, a poet who wrote courageously through catastrophe to be a witness in a time of war.

The story of Akhmatova's battle with the Tyrant is one that serves as a model, from which we can learn how to resist our inner Tyrants. We all have an "inner Akhmatova" who knows the value of patience and waiting for the right time to confront the Tyrant. Learning from her, we can listen to our intuitions and feelings about the Tyrants who oppress us and remember to record events in order to stay alert to despotic abuses in ourselves. Remembering—an inherent act of the Witness—is essential to prevent future violations of the Tyrant. By surviving the tension of the opposites, the Witness can prevail over the Tyrant and the Victim to become the champion of creativity.

The Witness knows that observing and confronting abuses, acknowledging suffering, and showing conscious compassion can break the vicious cycle.

DEVELOPING THE INNER WITNESS

If we are to respond to the call to create, it is essential to confront the inner Tyrants that block our way and to bear witness to our process.

Developing the inner Witness enables us to see the whole layout of the Tyrant's trap. Then we can identify the Tyrant and describe the way it works inside ourselves. By stepping back, taking a breath, and looking at the reality of a Tyrant's power, we can reduce the catastrophic proportions that we may have added to the picture—extra torments that have come from our own particular fears and humiliations.

Writing down experiences is a way of witnessing in our own lives. We saw how Akhmatova and Dostoyevsky did this. By writing each of my own books, I have been able to witness different inner characters that I needed to transform.

The easiest way to get started is by recording feelings, dreams, and images every day in a personal journal. To develop the inner Witness through journal work, describe the instances in your life where you have become hostage to an inner Tyrant. Then try rewriting the event by imagining other ways to relate to the dominating force within that obstructs creative life. By describing these events, it is possible to see the patterns used to escape the Tyrant's domination—patterns that I describe in this book.

The Witness Confronts the Tyrant and the Victim

Once defensive patterns have been identified as obstacles, it is easier to see how the Tyrant actually uses our defenses to hold us hostage. We will be able to see our inner despots more clearly if we envision ways to face and talk to the Tyrant. Writing, dance, and movement, painting the Tyrant's portrait, or sculpting it in clay are other ways to do this work.

Sometimes it helps to find outer Witnesses in order to develop the inner Witness. One way to do this is to seek out people whom you can trust and that can serve as outer Witnesses. By joining a group of women or men, it is possible to develop an inner Witness who can help disengage from the Tyrant.[3] The Witnesses in the group can help a person observe his or her obstacles to creative work and how the inner Tyrant may have developed. They can also support people in their creative efforts by helping them to recognize and disengage from an inner Tyrant and to sustain faith and trust in the battle with the inner saboteur. We saw this work effectively in Anna Akhmatova's case, when her women friends supported her by helping her memorize and hold her poems until the Tyrant's ban was lifted.

A powerful way to get to know the Tyrant's fears, methods, and manipulations is to enact the Tyrant's character in the safety of a group by making a mask and costume of the Tyrant, wearing it, and playing the part. The Witness can be enacted in the same manner. This is a method that actors use to get to know more deeply the characters that they portray.

Once we identify the Tyrant in ourselves, it helps to face it directly and to ask why it is afraid. This may need to be done in a safe, protected place with the help of others—for example, a therapist, a spiritual adviser, or a group focused on creative issues. Once the fear is identified, the Tyrant should be asked how it might redirect its energy in a more constructive way. If we discover that the inner

Tyrant stems from insecurity and alienation, we can transform it by developing our strength and compassion.

FEAR: AN INNER TYRANT

For many people fear itself becomes the Tyrant that keeps them from taking the risks that creative life requires. Fear has a specific object that can be dealt with; if this object is identified and faced, it can be removed, as in the case of Claudia, a successful executive who shared the following story.

In childhood Claudia had unconsciously absorbed the fears that permeated her family. Her mother acted like a victim who was fearful of everything, a tendency that women in her family had repeated throughout the generations. In contrast, like many men of his time, her father would not acknowledge his fears.

As she grew up between these opposite reactions to fear, Claudia became confused. She had no models to show her a healthy way to deal with fear. Claudia was committed to intensive inner work that helped her see that she herself tended to repeat these two extremes. Outwardly she acted like her father. Inwardly, however, she felt fearful like her mother, a quality that she hated.

To others, Claudia seemed sure of herself, successful, and in control of her life. She had a warm, expansive way of relating to people that was genuine. Her warmth also helped ward off a secret fear of being abandoned, humiliated, and shamed. To counter her apprehension of being ostracized, she gathered groups of people around her for security, so she wouldn't feel left out. She put so much energy into relationships that she left little time for herself.

Claudia defended herself against her fears by taking on an overload of work. At one time she even burdened herself with two full-time jobs plus part-time work. Between her overextension to people and to work, Claudia had little time or energy to find the creative relationship with a soul-mate for whom she longed, nor for the screenplay she wanted to write. Shame and guilt about not actualizing this creative potential gnawed away at her.

The overcommitments she made to people and to work, her longing for relationship, and the secret shame that she was not fulfilling her lifelong dream to write the film script put her under so much stress that she began to suffer from intense and painful migraine headaches. Like many people, Claudia developed a life pattern that perpetuated the tyranny of fear she had absorbed as a child, one that fueled an inner Tyrant who told her she could not find happiness in relationship or creative work.

The energy she used to counter her fears culminated in worry that began to hold this brilliant woman in the torturous vice of the migraine headaches. Her body had become a prison like the concentration camps.

If Claudia had not looked within to face her fears, she would still be hostage to the Tyrant. But while in therapy she remembered a dream that gave her a powerful image to help her cope with her fear. In the dream Claudia saw a misshapen gigantic leper. She felt threatened and afraid and worried about what to do. Then she saw Mother Teresa go over to the leper, touch his head, and caress him. Responding to the caress, the leper was no longer frightening.

When she awoke, Claudia was surprised that Mother Teresa had been in her dreams, because she was not religious. If anything, she was agnostic. When she thought about the dream, however, she understood that if, like Mother Teresa, she could develop compassion for the fearsome inner leper—an image for the frightened fearful Victim in herself—she could deal with the fear in her life.

To work with the dream in order to understand the leper, she talked with him imaginally and allowed herself to experience his feelings. Sitting in a chair, which she consciously designated as the leper's, she heard the leper acknowledge certain masochistic attitudes that she recognized in herself and in her mother—including feelings of rejection, the fear that she had done something wrong, and gigantic guilt. If spurned by a friend, she worried obsessively about what she might have done and about the motives of the other person. Then she overextended herself through work and social engagements to escape from her worries. Worry consumed much of the time and energy she could have used to create.

By talking with the leper, Claudia realized that, in her obsession to please everyone so as to avoid rejection, she had been dissipating her creative energy. Claudia also dialogued with Mother Teresa as an imaginal figure and asked her how she could touch the leper without fear. Mother Teresa's answer was simple. "Through loving every living thing," she said. This reply struck Claudia to the heart. She realized that she had neglected loving herself. This incredibly successful woman had to accept both the crippled leper and the Mother Teresa in herself. Claudia acknowledged that although she had given Mother Teresa's love to others, she had not given it to herself.

Claudia became more open to herself and less fearful that others would reject her. This freed her to meet the "soul-mate" whom she later married. She creatively redesigned both her outer house and her "inner home" and began to work on her screenplay. Because she chose to commit to look within, Claudia was able to let go of her inner Tyrant—the one who had power over her through her denial of fear. Calling upon Mother Teresa, as the Witness, helped release the Victim—the crippled leper that had been an image for how she felt.

Claudia's story is similar to that of many people who remain hostage to the Tyrant. Successful and accomplished in their outer lives, inwardly they suffer from low self-esteem because they are afraid to follow their creative passions. Even people who have already successfully created still feel that no matter what they do, it is not enough. Their fear keeps them from enjoying their creativity and from loving themselves.

FACING ANXIETY

Anxiety is an inherent part of the creative process. Sometimes we confuse anxiety with fear and tend to flee from it. But anxiety is different from fear, which has a specific object that can be identified, confronted, and removed.

Although many think that anxiety is something negative from which to escape, I see anxiety as a mood that overwhelms us, disrupts our habitual routines, and calls us to face the unknown. The Witness has developed the courage to accept the anxiety inherent to creativity.

Imagine anxiety as similar to electricity; it can shock, energize, and open us to the beauty of the unknown if we learn to be with it and witness it. Anxiety forces us out of accustomed habits and paths, revealing mystery and illuminating unknown aspects of being that are strange and unfamiliar. In all creative ventures we transcend the limits of the familiar to explore new territory. Creative people consciously confront anxiety, because they realize that it opens them to encounter the mysterious gap between what is known and unknown and to receive the revelations that emerge.

Artists attest that anxiety accompanies the creative process. Poets like Emily Dickinson and W. H. Auden, artists like Frida Kahlo and sculptors like Alberto Giacometti, composers like Beethoven and Shostakovich, scientists like Albert Einstein and Marie Curie, film directors like Andrey Tarkovsky and Ingmar Bergman, actors like Anthony Hopkins and Sally Field—all acknowledge that the encounter with anxiety can initiate the breakthrough into a vision struggling to be born. This requires an attitude of active listening and alertness in order to receive the new truth and a leap of faith into the psychic abyss that the mystics describe—the source of divine illumination and of that which is still unborn.

THE LISTENER AS WITNESS

We must listen to develop the Witness. This is shown vividly in the film *Dead Man Walking.* Based on the true story of Sister Helen Prejean, the film is an example of developing the art of listening that can open the way to redemption.

In the film Sister Helen, played by Susan Sarandon, receives a letter from a prisoner condemned to death who asks her to listen to him. When she goes to the prison to meet the man accused of rape and murder, she is thrown into doubt. In her gut she doesn't like this man. Although he claims he is innocent, he spouts prejudices and seems to respect no one, including Sister Helen and himself. Still she listens, hoping to find his redeeming side. She becomes the Witness for two figures within the prisoner—one a Tyrant, the other a Victim.

Like Psyche separating the seeds, Sister Helen has to sort out her own confusing and contradictory reactions—not only to the accused but also to his accusers. And like Psyche, she must be patient and wait to gather the golden strands from the raging rams. She must confront her own outrage and the anger of others toward her.

Because she listens to the condemned man, Sister Helen herself is faced with censure and reproach. The prison priest, a bigot whose parochial biases are not unlike the unsophisticated prejudices of the prisoner, reprimands her for her naïveté. The priest orders her to quit her foolish role, but she refuses. She knows she must stay with her task.

The children who attend the school at which Sister Helen teaches begin to avoid her. They feel she has betrayed them by her absence and have become suspicious of her because they have heard rumors about her unorthodox relationship with the prisoner.

The parents of the murdered teenagers criticize Sister Helen. They question her spiritual intentions and blame her for taking sides because she has not listened to them. Acknowledging her oversight, Sister Helen goes to them to hear their side of the story. They assume she will agree with them, but she affirms her integrity by insisting that she must try to be impartial. To truly listen, Sister Helen knows, she must try to free herself of the prejudice that interferes with the capacity to be open and receptive.

Her task, as she sees it, is to listen to both sides without judgment. She prays and hopes to try to find the saving grace that can help liberate both the accusers and the accused so they can face and forgive the revengeful killer within themselves and find mercy, compassion, and grace.

Day after day, as she listens to the prisoner, Sister Helen instinctively waits for the appropriate moment—the opening to ask him probing questions that will help him confront himself about his values, his actions, and his faith. When that time comes, she does not flinch.

The prisoner confesses that he was too weak to resist participating in the rape and murder that his partner had initiated. By following the Tyrant, he became a Tyrant himself. Before his death he accepts responsibility for the crime and asks for forgiveness.

Just like Sister Helen and the mythological Psyche, when faced with a creative task, we must develop our capacity to listen and to wait for the proper moment to take action. To be creative, we need to recognize and rid ourselves of biases that compete with listening and clear perceptions.

Sister Helen knows that listening is essential, but that spiritual transformation requires a further step—to bear witness. So she commits to the creative task of writing down what she has heard and seen in her book, *Dead Man Walking*. She chooses to enact the love and sacrifice that creativity requires—to courageously bear witness to the Cynics and the Tyrants who attempt to deaden spirit and soul. Because she understands that she must confront the paradox of good and evil that lies within each human being, rather than simply condemning an accused man, Sister Helen accepts the challenge of consciousness and courage.

The Witness Confronts the Tyrant and the Victim

The power of listening is essential to find healing in the paradox of creation and destruction. Nature herself holds this dark enigma in her womb since death is inherent in every birth. As humans, we can choose between good and evil; we can direct our energies to create or destroy. Accepting this challenge in our creative and spiritual lives means confronting the dark and shadowy sides of ourselves, the inner saboteurs who undermine us personally and who, collectively, lead toward planetary destruction. Creative life requires the courage to confront inner and outer cynics and tyrants who can take us hostage into the "world's dark night." Our task is also to learn whatever they can teach us.

At the deepest level, combating the Tyrant is an inner task. Resisting the outer Tyrant entails transforming the inner Tyrant—a moral imperative that *is* an act of creation itself. After every creative act, we need to sustain our strength of character by developing moral courage, so that we do not fall prey to self-destructive tendencies that dissipate dignity during dull or empty times.

Whether we create by making something in the external world or by shaping our own inner life, we need to develop deep inner peace and serenity as the ground of survival and transformation in order to withstand and bear witness to any form of tyranny. Ultimately, our creative task is to prepare a dwelling place within ourselves for dignity, love, beauty, and hope—a realm of radiance where the beauty of the Firebird flourishes.

5
CONSCIOUSNESS

Daily, hourly we must keep the crystal clear that the colours may assume their order. I pray to fulfil my task, don't elude me now for my soul's sake. I must live so that clarity produces the order of diversity. Nothing less than bearing it all will do, for it is the creation of a change of consciousness.

Florida Scott Maxwell

THE SENTINEL AWAKENS
THE ESCAPE ARTIST

Because the struggle and toil to create can be so difficult and exhausting, the temptation to flee from the task of consciousness can induce the Escape Artist, an inner figure who uses many different masks and costumes to disguise its habits of avoidance.

One of the Escape Artist's ploys—to remain asleep by slipping back into unconsciousness—is an enticement that constantly confronts the creative person. Choosing complacency or a passive, inertial state in order to avoid pain, anguish, and tension is a lure of the Sluggard who avoids work and useful activity.

Another way to escape from the conscious labor of creativity is by keeping busy all the time. The Compulsive Doer, who occupies himself with busy work or by worrying and working so hard that he has no time for the reflection and the immersion into empty space that creativity requires, avoids consciousness just like his shadow sibling, the Sluggard.

Still another maneuver of the Escape Artist is to be a Dilettante, who is tempted by a constant series of exciting possibilities but abandons each one for the next, thereby avoiding the constant effort to actualize his projects.

The Compulsive Doer's frequent state of exhaustion, the Sluggard's inertial laziness, and the Dilettante's frenetic attempt to find exciting distractions that actually tire him in the end—all detract from the conscious effort required for creativity. Each of these

Escape Artist characters is a shadow figure for the others, and they tend to succumb to addictions such as overworking for power and control, pleasure-seeking, and sedation by substances. Addictions are a typical attraction for the Escape Artist, whose focus is easily diverted by the many distractions of modern life.

Creativity requires being alert, so one is not taken hostage by such unconscious, destructive drives. Some artists, exhausted by the struggle to remain conscious, are lured toward suicide. Sylvia Plath, Mark Rothko, Anne Sexton, and Jerzy Kosinski are only a few of such examples.

We need to be alert so we can raise the new from the unknown without becoming prisoners of chaos. Creativity requires that we become aware of the border between the unconscious and the conscious so we can pass back and forth between them. The helper here is the Sentinel, who actively stays alert and vigilant in order to watch at the borders of consciousness. The Sentinel prods us into wakefulness and prevents retreat into unconsciousness and regression. The Sentinel is the attentive character in us who keeps us on target, reminds us of our quest, and alerts us to the risk and effort it takes to make a creative journey.

THE SLUGGARD

The Sluggard draws us back into regressive patterns in order to avoid the work of consciousness and to remain asleep. This passive figure, paradoxically, can collude with other more active characters that are also prone to dodge the creative challenge via distractions. The Dilettante turns to pleasure, and the Compulsive Doer keeps occupied by taking on too many tasks. These characters can distract us from becoming conscious of our inner depths since they are afraid to be in the silent space that we must enter to create.

The Sluggard in us tends to function on automatic and resists risking the leap of faith to venture into the unknown—an endeavor that creativity and transformation require of us. If the Sluggard dominates in people's lives, they tend to procrastinate doing even the most necessary of life's practical duties. As a result, tasks pile up, and usually there is so much to do that the work becomes overwhelming.

Sitting in the chaotic heap of things to do and not knowing where to start confuses the Sluggard, who begins to feel hopeless. This paralyzing way of being is reminiscent of the mythological Psyche who sits before a mass of seeds that she must sort out into the categories to which they belong if she hopes to live. The tasks of discrimination and decision-making confront every human being in creative life. If we do not respond to them, the indolence and ennui that characterize the Sluggard tend to lead to a state of perpetual indecisiveness that paralyzes choice and leads to shame and guilt.

Sluggards often feel they have wasted their lives and are likely to say, "I don't know," in order to avoid commitment and action. Because Sluggards don't initiate and commit to life, they avoid conflict. As a consequence, they lose élan vital. The passivity and lack of focus that lead the Sluggard to forget causes us to lose track of the threads of meaning in life.

The Sluggard has been portrayed in Russian literature in the novel *Oblomov*, by Ivan Goncharov, and in film by Nikita Mikhalkov. Oblomov is a privileged recluse whose life becomes reduced to eating and sleeping and is an example of the extremes to which the habits of the Sluggard can lead us.

Anton Chekhov's protagonist in the play *Ivanov* is another extreme example of the nadir to which a person possessed by the Sluggard pattern can sink. In midlife Ivanov has lost his passion for life as well as his sense of meaning. He has fallen out of love with his wife, the tubercular Anna, who has sacrificed her relationship to both her religion and her family for Ivanov. Faced with Ivanov's unresponsiveness, Anna's illness gradually worsens, and eventually she dies.

Ivanov has mismanaged his money and landholdings and considers marrying Sasha, whose dowry might rescue him from financial decay. But he has fallen into an abyss of apathy, indifference, and guilt, which causes him to suffer from exhaustion, insomnia, debilitating shame, and unfocused anger. He feels hollow and futile and has lost hope. Unable to face the consequences of his attitude and actions, Ivanov commits suicide before the wedding.

Before taking his life, Ivanov exposes his internal predicament:

> I am forty, and already I am spending my days in a dressing gown. With a heavy head and a sluggish soul. Exhausted, broken, cracked. Without belief, without love, without hope. . . . In love I find no tenderness. In work I find no relief. In song I hear no music. In speeches I hear nothing new. Everywhere I go I feel revulsion for life.[1]

Ivanov is like many modern-day men and women who find themselves at a crossroads where they feel exhausted in their lives, overwhelmed by work, crushed by rejection, or bored by fleeting ardor. Depressed and anxious, such people are unable to find meaningful direction for their lives. Inertia is a decoy that traps those who crave an easy way out of dilemmas. The Sluggard's passivity afflicts artists who are publicly revered as well as ordinary people. We can see this in the story of Maria Callas. The Compulsive Doer dominated the first part of her life. Then in midlife the Sluggard took over.

DECLINE OF THE DIVA

The great operatic diva Maria Callas, whose electric singing inspired her public to call her "La Divina," fell victim to the Sluggard. In midlife she encountered a point in her career where she required extensive practice in order to make the changes necessary to further develop her voice. Callas was no longer able to consistently sing the high notes that her soprano roles demanded. She needed to work to adjust her voice to the mezzo-soprano range and to new roles more suited to her.

Up to this point Callas's life had been devoted to work—a syndrome partly due to her ambitious mother's influence. The only way Callas could find recognition from her mother, who rejected her love, was to please her by achieving success and fame. This trapped Callas into a vicious pattern of overwork. Callas had sacrificed her personal life—especially her love life—to this end. Once while suffering intensely over this loss, Callas paraphrased Descartes's famous dictum, "I think, therefore I am," by sarcastically remarking: "I work, therefore I am."

Around this time Callas met Aristotle Onassis and fell passionately in love with him. She became devoted to Onassis and began to neglect her singing practice. She now felt relief from the anxiety and nervous tension that had plagued her. Her panic attacks had partly been due to overwork, which had begun to possess and deaden her emotional life. Callas let Onassis, a Dilettante well known for his Don Juan behavior, become the center of her life. She hoped to marry him and have his child.

Onassis betrayed her love when he resumed his habitual pattern of courting other women. Then he demanded that Callas abort the child they had conceived if she wanted to keep their relationship. Callas acquiesced. She betrayed her desire to have a child, just as she had betrayed her inner creative child by abandoning singing. In the end Onassis rejected Callas when he married Jacqueline Kennedy, whom he had been courting.

Callas was consumed with jealous rage. She turned the rage against herself by falling into bitterness, anguish, and despair. But she tried to transform her rage by enacting the lead role in Pier Paolo Pasolini's exquisite film *Medea.* Earlier Callas had brought the mythological character Medea, depicted in Greek tragedy by Euripides, to public attention by singing this role in Cherubini's opera.

Through sorcery Medea helps her lover, Jason, acquire the Golden Fleece. She betrays her father and her brother to help Jason. The couple flees to Corinth, where Jason betrays her by arranging to marry the king's daughter. Medea is enraged and, in revenge, sets fire to their house, thereby murdering their children. Callas realized that she had reenacted this tragedy in real life when she aborted her pregnancy at Onassis's request.

Callas's work with Medea helped her for a while. Eventually, however, she began to seek escape through sleep. In her flight from the agony of consciousness, she became addicted to tranquilizers that dulled her emotional pain. She rarely left her apartment. Previously, as the Compulsive Doer, her obsession with overwork had consumed her life. Now the Sluggard took over in her psyche. Callas passively wasted most of her time by sleeping and watching television. She isolated herself from friends and regained the weight that had burdened her in her youth. At the age of fifty-three she suffered an early death from a heart attack.

In her prime Callas was called "the Tigress" by her fans who loved the raw primitive power of her singing. In contrast to the power of "the Tigress," toward the end of her life the great diva weakly lamented: "I have nothing. What am I going to do?"

Callas's tragic end shows the bottom to which the Sluggard in us can descend if we allow it to possess us. Instead of persisting in her struggle to face her despair and to try to transform it through inner work, Callas slid into unconsciousness. Succumbing to the Sluggard in herself, she neglected the difficult work to raise consciousness. Thus she fell into exhaustion and lost the balance, health, and wholeness that she might have found in her life. Although she could electrify, inspire, and awaken others through her art, the great diva neglected to use these creative gifts to inspirit and enliven her personal life.

ROSEMARY'S DREAM

Many modern men and women suffer from the conflicts that plagued the life of Callas—overwork, deprivation in emotional life, and rejection in love. Consider the story of Rosemary, who worked in New York as a waitress while trying to break into the acting profession.

One morning Rosemary awoke and could not force herself to get out of bed. She was exhausted from working at two different restaurant jobs to make enough money to live in the city. Rosemary felt discouraged by numerous false leads for acting jobs and by audition rejections. She also suffered from rejections by several lovers.

As she approached her thirty-fifth birthday, Rosemary left her career, and her love life was still at an impasse. She began to question her life decisions. She began to sleep late, then call into work that she was sick. Gradually she fell into a pattern of lying around her apartment, doing little except watching television, eating, and sleeping. Then she had difficulty getting dressed and leaving her bedroom.

As a result of her inertia, Rosemary lost one of her jobs; she could barely manage the second. By overeating she gained so much weight that it was harder to move around as quickly and easily as waitressing required. Because she stopped exercising at her health club, she felt sluggish. Secretly Rosemary was disgusted with herself, but she could not muster the motivation to reverse the encroaching habit of inertia.

Although she tended to sleep until noon, one morning Rosemary awoke early with a disturbing dream image that haunted her. In her dream a giant slug lay beside her in bed. Rosemary was afraid the slug might crush her. The heavy slimy body of the huge slug was repulsive to her, and this dream image shocked her from her idleness like a "slug" to the head.

Rosemary had been going to a therapist to deal with her depression. As with most of her other activities, however, she had taken a break from this inner work. The dream of the slug alarmed her so much that she called her therapist for an appointment. At the suggestion of her therapist, Rosemary researched the image of the slug.

The slug, she discovered, was a creature known for its idling, its slowness, and its meandering ways; it leaves a trail of slime behind it. This reminded Rosemary of the apathetic and procrastinating state into which she had fallen and that caused her to feel repulsed by herself. The dream of the slug awakened her to the way overwork exhausted her and resulted in her inclination to be sluggish.

Her research on the slug also revealed that the hieroglyphic sign for the slug had another and more ancient meaning.[2] In the Egyptian *Book of the Dead,* the slug is depicted as a small horned snake that symbolizes the male seed, the origin of life, and the silent tendency of darkness to move toward light. Moreover, from an ecological viewpoint, the slug, like other grazers that eat green leaves, helps regenerate the soil and thus is an important and essential contributor to the earth's ecosystem.

Rosemary realized that her recent sluggish way of life, along with her descent into despair, had some similarities with the dark night of the soul described by the mystics. Until then Rosemary had felt debilitated by darkness with no glimmering of light. She now began to wonder whether the symbolism of the slug suggested that her inner emptiness might be the darkness in which one could turn toward light and toward the possibility for transformation and rebirth.

As Rosemary worked with the dream image of the slug, it began to seem like a Sentinel awakening her. She started to reassess her life—her deep desires, her unexplored potentialities, and the activities that fulfilled her. Acting was still a genuine passion, but she found another way to actualize it. She reconsidered her decision to live in New York City and decided to move to a less expensive city that also had good acting possibilities.

During this time Rosemary happened to meet an old friend from acting school. They met for lunch, and her friend told her about a graduate program in which she was enrolled to become certified as a drama therapist. This chance meeting seemed like a miracle to Rosemary. Drama therapy was a profession that intrigued her and could supplement and support her acting.

Rosemary applied to the graduate school located in another city. She was accepted into the program, and she obtained a college loan to cover tuition. Although she still had to work to support herself, Rosemary needed only one job since her new place of residence was less expensive. Stimulated by her college courses and delighted at the prospect of this new profession, Rosemary smiled and said, "It's amazing that during my 'dark night' my dream slug turned into a seed."

Confusion about whether a sluggish period is a sign of sloth and laziness or an essential time for incubation is common to many of us. Even though the Sluggard can hinder our growth, it can also signal a genuine need for rest and regeneration—a necessary phase in creative life.

Hibernation, which is natural for the slug, is also a fundamental latency period. The psyche needs quiet intervals that allow the time and space to receive new images and intuitions, to see additional correlations, and to gain fresh perspectives and novel focal points for creative projects. In this sense the Sluggard can be a corrective for its conflicting cousins in the psyche—the Dilettante and the Compulsive Doer, who are so absorbed by distractions that they can avoid the task of looking within.

THE COMPULSIVE DOER AND THE DILETTANTE

These two characters disperse creative energy. The Dilettante seeks pleasure and immersion in worldly distractions so that there is no space to create, while the Doer works compulsively, eliminating spare time. Either way, these Escape Artists plunge into the external world in order to avoid the internal work of creating. Whether through an excess of pleasure or of work, we can become slaves to worldly diversions. The Dilettante and the Doer frequently take turns deflecting creative energy in the psyche of one person.

Marshall, a businessman in his fifties, came into my office for a consultation because he was bothered by his inability to return to work on a novel that he had started nine years earlier. He had stopped writing after he was diverted by other projects. Marshall said that one of his major problems was that his mind tended to go in a million directions at once.

Like many creative people Marshall had so many interests that he found it hard to commit to a particular project for any length of time. His fantasy life was so rich that he had difficulty devoting himself to one theme long enough to really work with it. The very sense of imagination and curiosity that stimulated his creativity, he said, was also what obstructed it.

For Marshall, the distracting directions could be either those of work or of pleasure. In fact, he tended to waver between periods when he kept busy by overworking and others when he pursued his pleasures. In his workaholic mode he could always find tasks that needed to be tackled—building shelves for his books, fixing the screen door, or sitting at his computer consulting the stock reports as they changed from minute to minute. He liked to go from one work project to another. In his working phase he could never find enough time or space to give consistent attention to writing a novel. Similarly, when his hedonistic lifestyle took over, everywhere he looked seemed to him like an enticing playground.

Despite his desire to write his book, Marshall defended his tendency toward distraction. By changing course continually, he felt free and unlimited. As a child Marshall had learned to escape from conflicts in his family. He distanced himself from his parents' expectations by enjoying his rich fantasy life. To an outside observer, Marshall appeared to be attentive to his father's compulsive lectures on the virtues of practicality. In imagination, however, he flew away into exciting adventures. He used the same technique in his marriage.

Then a nightmare awoke Marshall in the middle of one night and caught his attention. Marshall dreamed that he had rented a sporty and seaworthy speedboat to take his young son scuba diving. They had found a beautiful spot far offshore of a Mediterranean island. While his son was in the water, Marshall became bored. He decided to go exploring in the speedboat but planned to return soon. Time seemed to dissolve in his fascination with the beautiful panorama, when suddenly he remembered his son. Marshall panicked when he realized that he didn't know how to return to the place where he had left his son. The sea was so vast that it seemed hopeless. He had forgotten to pay attention to distinct features on shore and to note markers so that he could retrace his route. Marshall woke up from the dream in terror that his son might be trapped underwater. He feared his son would die unless he could find his way back to him.

In reality Marshall was a devoted father who was very attentive to his children, who were now adults. Moreover, in actuality, his son tended to be much more cautious than himself. The dream did not make sense to Marshall if he interpreted it as an actual event. So he began to look at the dream as a reflection of his own life.

As he pondered the dream, Marshall realized that the nightmare might be trying to reveal something about his creative life. In fact, just before he went to sleep that night, he had been worrying about his writing block. From this perspective, Marshall said, his son might symbolize the part of himself that needed consistency and persistence, the part that was endangered by his tendency to be distracted.

The dream suggested to Marshall that he was in danger of losing something valuable in himself—his creative child, which needed care and watchfulness. If he succumbed to impatience, boredom, and his desire for exciting distractions, as he had in the dream, he might not be able to retrieve this priceless part of himself.

Marshall noted that in the dream he hadn't taken into account the vastness of the sea. Nor had he considered that he might need to set markers to find his way. In many ways the creative unconscious is like a vast ocean in which we can drown if we don't keep a line to consciousness. Caring enough to value and record the little moments in the process of creating is as important as the more dramatic times of inspiration and peak experiences.

Writing a novel requires taking time to be solitary, going into the workplace, paying attention, and being focused. For Marshall this meant learning to set the limits and boundaries that provide a container for creative work. He had learned to do this as a father in order to guide his children when they were growing up. Now he had to learn to do this for himself.

A few months after the dream, Marshall was occupied with the stock market. He decided to gamble on a certain stock that was rising rapidly, and he took out a large loan, hoping to make a big profit. After he purchased the stock, it dropped sharply. This event shocked Marshall out of the fast track onto which his impulsiveness tended to take him.

When Marshall returned to his computer, he turned to writing his novel instead of perusing stocks. Because he felt guilty that he had lost the money, he decided to work creatively with his guilt by writing. Substantial loss through hitting bottom can lead a person to change. This was true for Marshall, who took a bad situation and made it good. He prepared himself to be open to the Muse. He wrote at night because he felt that he could better hear the Muse's voice in the dark. By day he edited what he had written. He was excited to meet the characters that emerged and to relate to them. In the first week he wrote a hundred pages, writing as fast as he could type. Although gaps appear in his writing process, Marshall has written more than two hundred pages—over half of his book—in the last year.

LEARNING THE VALUE OF SOLITUDE

The healer for the person trapped by distractions is the Solitary, of whom Henry David Thoreau, John Muir, Emily Dickinson, May Sarton, and Rainer Maria Rilke provide one kind of example.

The Sentinel Awakens the Escape Artist

Learning to dwell in the great wilderness—the vast spaces of both nature and the psyche—regenerates us and inspires us with the wonder of creation. The Solitary knows that quiet communion with the self and nature *is* active and is necessary to develop centered consciousness. For example, Haiku poets, Chinese landscape painters, and Japanese potters are among those who seek inner solitude through the art of meditation, which is part of the process of creating.

As in Marshall's case, some of us become overwhelmed by a desire to experience everything. When this appetite is insatiable, it pushes people into a frenzy of desire or busyness that obscures the creative need for solitary space. The novelist Thomas Wolfe confessed to "an almost insane hunger to devour the entire body of human experience." Wolfe said he felt driven to "unreasonable excesses to read all the books, to know all the people, to see all the countries in the world—in short, to eat the world and have it too."[3]

Although Wolfe valued the knowledge he had acquired through his travels in Europe to Paris, Madrid, and Rome, he came to realize that its importance lay in the intensity and depth with which he approached these experiences. He also saw that his frenzied, excessive craving to experience all of life's possibilities was actually an attempt to escape—"to fly from the stern necessity of conflict and of labor, somehow to get away from the indolence, the lack of substance, power, courage, or talent in our own spirits."[4] The power to work, he realized, was in himself.

Writing, Wolfe learned, requires commitment to a time of solitude in order to be alone with one's own work. While reflecting on the needs for creative life, Wolfe said, "During this time I reached that state of utter, naked need, utter, lonely isolation which every artist has got to reach, meet, live through somehow, and conquer if he is to survive at all."[5] It is necessary to learn to bear the existential state of aloneness. This requirement is not limited to the artist. It is a challenge for every living human being who meets the call to life, along with its twin companion, the call to death.

While writing, Wolfe was deluged with a storm cloud of images that broke as fast and furious as a hurricane that could sweep him away. He said that he struggled in a "floodtide of creation." This image symbolizes the struggle of creative consciousness to find order in the wealth of chaotic images that well up from the unconscious, as from a vast sea in which it is possible to drown.

Recording each image, sifting, sorting, and trying to find the skeleton of order in the chaos gave Wolfe some protection from the overflow of material. This effort provided an inner place to which he could return—a region in which not only writers but all human beings must learn to dwell. This dwelling place is like that place "in between river and rock"—the necessary space in which to live an authentic life, described by Rilke in his poetic cycle the *Duino Elegies*.[6]

In the five years that it took Wolfe to write his novel *Look Homeward, Angel*, he learned to face his creative task alone. Wolfe also learned that aloneness did not necessarily mean the torment of utter isolation that he feared. Wolfe had the help of his editor, Maxwell Perkins, who worked through the enormous manuscript, trying to persuade Wolfe to cut the voluminous material that overloaded and obscured the book. While Wolfe was away in Europe, Perkins sent the manuscript to press.

When Wolfe returned, he was bewildered and desperate. He protested his editor's decision and insisted that he needed to work at least six months before he could perfect the book. When Perkins advised him to stop worrying and to start his next book, Wolfe accepted his editor's wisdom. Perkins told Wolfe that he needed to learn to work without useless torment, waste, and confusion. To do this, he needed to curb his tendency to excess and the perfectionism that burdened him. By searching, struggling, and groping with this first book, Perkins added, Wolfe had discovered how to find his own way.

Wolfe believed that writing is a craft and that the artist must be a worker, not an aesthete. The artist, like every living person, is engaged in the work of creation. Wolfe saw the creative person as a prototype for all human beings. The story of the artist is that of a man and a worker, "a creature full of toil and sweat and labor and imperfection." The artist is not a fine fellow who is different from other people. Rather, the artist is a person who is derived from "the common family of earth, who is compacted of his father's common clay, of sweat and blood and dust and agony and who knows all the anguish, error, and frustration that his father or any man alive can know."[7]

CHARLOTTE'S WAKE-UP CALL

Because it is easier to follow the habitual routines to which we are accustomed, it often takes a disaster to awaken us. Even the most conscious people among us are not immune to the need for an extreme wake-up call. This was true for Charlotte, a psychiatrist who worked for many years helping others to find their own paths to health and creativity.

To the outer world, Charlotte did not appear to be a Sluggard, because she worked so hard. But she was hostage to a pattern of compulsive doing in order to deal with the demanding practical side of her life. Unwittingly she allowed her habit of overworking and worrying to dull her consciousness. As a result she became sluggish and inattentive to her own creativity.

Charlotte's story is an example of the way seemingly opposite characters in the psyche collude and work in tandem to seduce us from consciously attending to the call to create. Despite the time and energy that Charlotte spent working to raise the consciousness of herself and others, she was prone to an old pattern of duty and service that caused her to neglect her own needs.

Her position as the oldest daughter in her family cast her into the role of helping her mother, who was used to being served and acting helpless. When Charlotte's father died, she realized that her mother was dependent and confused. The household duties and the obligation to take charge of the family business fell to Charlotte, who automatically took over as the "doer" of the family.

Charlotte's natural love was painting, but it was her younger brother who went to art school. Unlike many women of her time, Charlotte had been focused on a career for herself since the early age of ten. She had always been drawn to the healing profession. She accompanied her paternal grandfather, a family doctor with whom she had a close relationship, on his round of house calls. In college she chose the pre-med curriculum and majored in psychology. Later she went to medical school and became a psychiatrist. This career choice, which continued her pattern of serving others in the healing professions, assured her independence and security for the future—a path opposite to the one taken by her mother.

Over the years, in the course of her own therapy, Charlotte became intrigued with learning to pay attention to the messages in her dreams. It was in a dream that she experienced the wake-up call of the Sentinel.

In the dream Charlotte experienced a visceral prick at the base of the back of her neck. It was her therapist trying to rouse her from sleep with a scepter. When she awoke, Charlotte knew the dream was important. Since she had worked with art therapy, she decided to paint the dream. She also made an appointment with her therapist, whom she had been seeing sporadically at the time of the dream.

Working with the dream spurred Charlotte's realization that she was not paying *enough* attention to her creative and spiritual life. But the demanding nature of her work and the normal routines of running her household consumed most of her attention. Even so, she was able to do many of the activities that she enjoyed—visits to art galleries and museums, dinners with friends, and occasional evenings at the cinema, ballet, and the opera. The major emptiness in her life at that time, she said, was the lack of a committed lover in a soul-relationship.

Although the dream intrigued her and popped into her memory from time to time, Charlotte resumed her normal life. Then she met an interesting man with whom she had much in common and who wanted to be part of her life. At last she had the prospect of the relationship she had wanted. But just a few months after meeting this man, she had another dream—a nightmare that alarmed her.

In the dream she was walking home when, near her house, she saw the bloody severed head of a cat that was screaming in agony. Charlotte woke up in terror. Again she consulted her therapist and worked with the dream by doing a sand play of it, a therapeutic technique that she often used with her own clients.[8] When she examined the sand play box, its contents revealed to her that much of her feminine energy had not been released and expressed in her life. From the sand play work she could see that her feminine instincts were in so much pain that they cried out through the dream image of the screaming severed cat's head.

A week later Charlotte woke up in the emergency room of a hospital. She vaguely remembered hemorrhaging so badly that she had felt faint. Worried, she had called a close friend who lived nearby and who rushed her to the hospital. Charlotte was diagnosed with cancer of the uterus. She was told she must first undergo radiation due to her condition and then have surgery.

While she was in convalescence after the surgery, Charlotte had time to reflect on her life. She followed the suggestions of her nurse to stop working for the extended time that was necessary so she could heal and recover. The process of healing from this serious illness, and of trying to prevent a recurrence, required her to reduce the stresses in her life. Charlotte was encouraged to recreate her way of life by resting and learning how to nourish herself by doing what she enjoyed.

As Charlotte looked back at the course of her life, she saw that both dreams were calls for consciousness from the Sentinel within her psyche—wake-up calls announcing that she was off center in her life. Learning that she had cancer was a summons so extreme that she could not ignore it. Nor could she evade this disease's exacting message to recover the lost and wounded parts of herself.

Charlotte realized that her lifelong pattern of neglecting herself by not taking time and care to protect her own needs and desires kept her off balance. She comprehended that her tendency to overwork and serve others colluded with the perfectionist in herself. Her perfectionism manifested itself through a scrupulous need to have everything just right. As a result, she worried compulsively. Her fretting depleted her energy and plagued her through alternating bouts of anxiety and depression. This stressful pattern in her life distracted her from being in touch with her feminine center and knowing her deeper self.

As a psychiatrist, she understood that this pattern resulted from the caretaking relationship she had with her mother. She knew that she must find and care for the inner nourishing mother in her own psyche and redirect that nurturing energy toward herself. The alternating pattern of anxiety and depression, which became concretized in practical worries, had its source in her upbringing to be the overly responsible child. After the shock of her illness, Charlotte understood that her anxiety and depression were actually Sentinels trying to reveal a deeper level of being and possibility for her life.

The treadmill of work and worry had diverted her attention from the inner call to creativity. Moreover, she had spent so much energy worrying about the relationship with her new lover that she had forgotten to enjoy it. Her social longing to be part of a "couple" exaggerated the place of relationship in her life—so much that she had neglected her femininity.

The dream of the screaming cat, Charlotte recognized, was a desperate attempt to wake her up to the fact that her feminine side was psychologically and physically in pain. The shrieking cat in her dream was an image of her own feminine instinct and spirit screaming for attention. Moreover, the dream in which her therapist had poked her with a wand in the back of the neck—the place where head and body join—pointed to the lack of integration of psyche and soma. Both dreams were dramatic calls to Charlotte to recreate her life. She knew that it was time to acknowledge the life-or-death summons to pay attention to the inner self and to respond to its call.

The project of creating her life anew drew Charlotte to focus on another path. She loved her career, but it had grown so large that it had gotten out of balance with the rest of her life. Actually, at this time of recovery, Charlotte didn't feel like listening to anyone—including her patients. She knew that she needed to listen to herself. So she decided to take the recommended sabbatical from work and enroll in art school.

Although Charlotte had always loved art and had taken some drawing workshops, until this time her relationship to art had been primarily passive—more the role of the viewer than the actual painter. She experienced the creative spirit in others' art but not in her own. While Charlotte valued her appreciation of art, she now felt the depth and urgency of her inner desire to be an active artist. As her health improved and her energy returned, she started painting full time and has continued with renewed commitment to create for nearly a decade.

Painting, Charlotte said, takes her beyond herself to a transcendent realm and a higher sense of consciousness. Painting at the easel also releases the dormant energy used up in depression into a creative art form. The redirection of her focus to art as a center of her spiritual life has moved beyond the personal sphere to another realm. Charlotte consciously answers the spiritual call by expressing and embodying it through her artwork.

Recently, since entering her sixties, Charlotte is aware of a new call to create. As she ages, she has less energy—a signal that she is entering a new phase of life. Charlotte wants to be as alert as possible to prepare for this new life phase instead of succumbing to temptations to avoid the aging process. Instead of falling into compulsive activity or inertia, she is learning to flow with her energy in order to make her daily life more enjoyable, creative, and meaningful. Charlotte is now cocreating as an active participant in the mystery of life's changes.

The Sentinel: Consciousness and Creativity

Creative life requires a descent into the unknown realm or, as Jung calls it, the collective unconscious—a chaotic but fertile maze of possibilities—to discover something new. But without the return to consciousness, original discoveries cannot be actualized.

The presence of the mindful Sentinel, who protects us through active care and wakefulness, is necessary for this journey. The creative person must be flexible enough to make the passage back and forth between the conscious and unconscious realms.

Some people fear to enter the depths of primordial experience because they fear the confusing multiplicity of perspectives and new revelations. Compulsive Doers often occupy themselves with busywork in order to avoid dealing with the vertigo of open possibilities that upsets their practical rational routines. Even the most experienced artists may find themselves doing work they hate in order to escape the horror of the void.

George Delareux, who composed the music for memorable films like *Jules and Jim* and *Women in Love,* has described his horror of the blank page. Before he starts a composition, Delareux says, he tends to do anything to avoid it: reorganize files, clean his studio, and even read junk mail. But once he dares to sit down to compose and listen to the silence, something secret in him takes over and is irresistible. The mysterious Muse wakes him up with new ideas even in his sleep, and he hears the call to go to his piano. This exciting process continues until he has finished the piece. Then after finishing, the anguish of being confronted with the empty page returns, along with the old fear that he won't be able to compose anything new.

Delareux's story is one that many creative people know well. Cleaning closets, sorting out old drawers, accepting work offers that one doesn't really want—all elicit the Compulsive Doer in ourselves to take on so much that we have no time to sit in silence or to face the void. For some artists and composers like Delareux, busywork can be almost ritualistic, a prelude to facing the inevitable emptiness that they know they must enter in order to create. But for many of us, keeping busy remains a mechanical way to avoid confronting inner depths and the strange space of dizzying possibilities.

Those who find themselves thrown into the unfathomable abyss may be seduced to stay there. Like the Sluggard, they resist the struggle and exertion of consciousness required to bring a new work into being. To escape the tension of deciding to actualize even one of the myriad potentialities, they prefer to sink into a sleep from which they do not want to awaken. Sometimes people drug themselves with substances that keep them dulled or with excuses that feed their propensity to be passive.

Still others take the trip into unconsciousness and back to consciousness over and over again. But like the Dilettante, they do not persist in the toil required to embody their discoveries or to complete their work. They dip in and out of exciting possibilities. When they become bored, they do not develop the patience to endure the uncanny tension and acute alertness that creative transformation requires.

The crux of creativity requires courage and conscious commitment to dare to leap into the depths. For this one must be ready and open to receive the revelation and be strong enough and prepared with skills to give it form. Instead of fleeing the call to creativity as the Escape Artist tries to do, the creative person must be willing to face its challenge to transform.

The void that most of us go to any lengths to avoid is the center of transformation and birth. From accustomed perspectives, the leap of faith into the center's depths may strike the ego as perilous, as a foolish act that can overwhelm and ruin us and lead us to death. But the death of old patterns, even those that are comfortable and secure, is prerequisite to creative transformation, which requires a sacrifice of egoic control and plans.

Only if we confront the chaos and the potential for death at the very basis of our being will we be able to uncover the nascent vision and bring it into being. Sooner or later all of us encounter death. The creator knows this and chooses to face death continually as a part of transformation. The call to create beckons us to a death that leads to the capacity for renewal.

For this task, on this journey, the alert and watchful Sentinel, who knows the routes back and forth across the borders, can assist us. The Sentinel watches with a different purpose from Freud's "censor," who stands vigil at the borders between the conscious mind and the unconscious in order to keep out unacceptable thoughts, feelings, and impulses. In Jung's view we must acknowledge these dark parts of ourselves—we must know the "Shadow" so we can transform its energy for creative purposes. In contrast to the "censor," the Sentinel's wakefulness allows us to dip into the unconscious as a creative source and to come out again, and it prevents us from drowning in the depths. The Sentinel is alert to the complexities and risks of creative transformation and is constantly attentive to the various transits between the edges of life and death.

Creative people take the turn of transformation by giving expression to what they find on that journey. The composer Claude Debussy, speaking of music, described this creative challenge: Music is the expression of the inexpressible. The poet Rilke wrote that the call to create summons us "to make the invisible visible." It is the same for creative living.

When we embody growth and transformation in our lives and dare to show it to others, we are like the artist who lifts the primordial image out of the transitory and into the enduring domain. We transmute our personal growth into the evolving development of humankind. Every advance of consciousness, every act of courage, and every gesture of compassion is sown and planted like a seed in the rich and fertile soil of human existence.

6
DISCOVERY

I don't write out of what I know. It's what I don't know that stimulates me. I merely know enough to get started. Writing is discovery; it's talking deep within myself, "deep talking" as you say.

Toni Morrison

THE ADVENTURER CHALLENGES
THE CONFORMIST

To lead a creative life or to create an artistic work, we have to balance all the time with the agility of an acrobat, as if we were on a tightrope stretched across an abyss. On one side the Conformist attempts to restrain us in order to assure security, profit, and safety. On the other side the Adventurer dares us to embark on a journey of discovery—a gamble that is dangerous but can lead to something new.

If we remain only on the Conformist's side, we fail to take the risks necessary to change. If we move solely in the Adventurer's fast lane, we may burn up our energy or fail to acknowledge the social structures that need our input in order to be transformed.

In midlife people tend to search for new professions that challenge them to actualize talents that they never dared to try. Or they may need to make changes in married life to revitalize it or to start anew. Those who try to hold on to the status quo become captive to the Conformist's desire for security and stifle crises in relationships and careers. If they sell their souls to commerce out of need or greed to gain safety and sheer comfort, their lives become deadened. In contrast, those who exclusively follow the Adventurer can collapse in the dizzying possibilities of partners or interests and lose the solid ground upon which to make a choice.

Novelists like Virginia Woolf and Hermann Hesse describe characters who face this dilemma in their novels. In *Mrs. Dalloway* Virginia Woolf describes a woman who is attracted to two very different men. One is a thrilling free-spirited adventurer who offers her the possibilities of independence and freedom and the chance to care for her soul and fulfill their youthful dream to change the world. The other is a good-hearted dependable conformist who offers her security, luxury, and a comfortable social life. In reflecting upon the choice she has made, Mrs. Dalloway learns to differentiate and integrate the Adventurer and Conformist in herself—a task that every human being faces.[1]

In *Steppenwolf* Hermann Hesse describes a man who confronts a similar dilemma. He feels alienated from bourgeois society and condemns it. Yet a part of him yearns to belong to the conventional group that he despises. He suffers from the way he has split these two aspects of himself into irreconcilable opposites, and he discovers that life is complex and requires him to reconcile the many parts of himself.

Creative life requires a dialogue between the Adventurer and the Conformist so that we can bring new visions into being and take action based on them. Creativity challenges us to find the thread of continuity that connects new possibilities with those organic patterns that are inherent to human beings and that are necessary for civilization.

THE CONFORMIST

The Conformist's desire for security leads him to avoid or discourage the risk-taking necessary for discovery and creativity because it might threaten his goals. Eager to lead a normal life, the Conformist is likely to become an anonymous tool of the Tyrant. In such a case the Conformist, who wants to construct a safety system, may actually work for the Tyrant by effectively imprisoning those who threaten the status quo.

If, as children, we are brought up by parents who posit only conventional values and demand compliance with them, we may overvalue the Conformist in ourselves. Conforming to convention is a strategy that a child may develop to protect himself and to be accepted by parents, teachers, and peers.

Political states that coerce obedience to narrow tenets, religious institutions that are inflexible, and socioeconomic milieus that dictate rigid mores and manners—all tend to propel conformity. If we grow up in these structures and become trapped in them, we may "imprison" our own impulses toward creativity and adventure.

The age-old conflict between the artist and society enters here. Creativity is a process of discovery that requires a person to explore new territory and go beyond traditional boundaries. Throughout the generations discoverers in every field risk ridicule and condemnation by the ruling status quo and its adherents. Conformity's repercussions—alienation in a sterile society or a robotlike existence devoid of fun and dignity—have been delineated in classic books such as David Riesman's *The Lonely Crowd* and Simone de Beauvoir's *The Second Sex*.

The deadening consequences of conformity are portrayed in films such as Bernardo Bertolucci's *The Conformist*, James Ivory's *Mr. and Mrs. Bridge*, and most recently, Gary Ross' *Pleasantville*. Artists from Pieter Brueghel the Elder, the sixteenth-century Flemish painter, to the twentieth-century German artist Käthe Kollwitz, have depicted the dangers of conformity in their paintings.

The Adventurer Challenges the Conformist

If we identify only with the Conformist in ourselves, we tend to remain in or regress to the mentality of the "mass man." This leads to a state of unconscious despair because the Conformist neglects to respond to the call to change that is inherent in the human condition.

In *Sickness unto Death*, Søren Kierkegaard understands despair as a dis-relationship to the source of being human. The person who regresses or remains in unconscious despair is out of relation to the deeper Self but is unaware of it. This may be a person whose life is dispersed by the sensation of the moment, or one who goes along with the "crowd." Today we see the media manipulate the masses by commercial advertisements. We also see the rise of inflated gurus who discourage thinking for oneself.

Because people may fear the psyche's creative energy—its accompanying dangers as well as its dizzying possibilities—they try to maintain security and control by denying its existence. As a result their own life-energy becomes listless, mediocre, and dull. Through denial they may succumb to the extremes of fundamentalism, which discourages thinking for oneself.

Although dark moments of boredom and anxiety may signal despair, the Conformist tends to ignore these signs by retreating to the security of collectivized life. The Conformist posits and justifies what is "normal" and criticizes those who dare to go a different way. In family life, for example, a mother might say to a daughter, "Why can't you be like the daughters of my friends, find a nice normal guy to marry, have a family, and settle down?" Or a father might say to a son who wants to be a poet: "Be practical! The only way to get ahead in this world is to make money. Study business or engineering." Daughters and sons of such parents often comply and essentially repeat their parents' lives. Sometimes they rebel to follow the Adventurer.

The Call to Create

The torments of certain artists are a bold illustration of what many of us suffer in ordinary life whenever we dare create. It is the very secret, subtle, or intangible character of suffering, however, that makes it more horrendous. The denial of suffering leads to the doubt of inner feelings and experiences. Films like *Ordinary People, The Ice Storm,* and *Breaking the Waves* address the horror of hiding pain, grief, and rage when confronted with the Conformist.

FREEING THE CONFORMIST'S CLUTCH

The story of Arthur, a man who remained in the grip of the Conformist for many years, is typical of the dilemma that seizes many women and men when they feel afraid to follow their own path. Arthur's story shows how the Tyrant oppresses the Conformist, who in the end becomes his victim. It also shows a way to transform these patterns that hinder creative life.

Arthur was a gifted child with high intelligence; he was avidly interested in the sciences. In his senior year in high school, he won a Westinghouse scholarship—a grant that provided him with the opportunity to become a nuclear physicist—his life's dream.

Arthur's father was a kind but passive man who worked hard and owned a small business. His mother, an active woman bustling with energy and intelligence, conformed to the expectations of her generation like most women born at the beginning of the twentieth century.

Caught in the long line of women who sacrificed creative potential to be at their husband's side, Arthur's mother denied herself her career desire to become a lawyer. Instead, she married and worked with her husband in their business. The energy that she neglected burst forth like a hurricane at home, where she dominated her husband and her only son. At dinnertime she lectured Arthur about the importance of work and money. Arthur's mother became the raging family tyrant who intimidated anyone who opposed her or got in her way.

When Arthur told his parents about the scholarship and his deep desire to become a nuclear physicist, his mother dismissed it as impractical and demanded that he work in the family business. She automatically expected him to conform to her wishes, as she had done with her parents. Arthur's father passively supported his wife in this mandate.

Confronted with his mother's demand, Arthur was afraid to risk her anger by choosing the scientific career path. He complied with her bidding and gave up the fellowship. Instead he studied management, worked in the family business, and continued his parents' pursuit of security. Like his passive father, Arthur became a workaholic. His parents' emphasis on money began to occupy his energy.

Arthur married a woman who had grown up with playful parents who had supported her intelligence and creativity. At first Rebecca conformed to her wifely role by relinquishing serious attention to her musical talents. Soon, however, she became inexplicably depressed. She suffered for several years from depression so severe that she became afraid to venture forth from the house. Rebecca sought help from a psychiatrist, who helped her realize that Arthur's mother dominated the couple in many ways and especially by expecting her son to amass money.

Since Arthur came home from work exhausted, anxious, and depressed himself, Rebecca asked him to go into therapy too. She told him that their marriage was in jeopardy. Acknowledging Rebecca's desperation and the depression that had plagued him for many years, Arthur agreed.

Once Arthur began to examine his life, he realized that his mother became angry with him whenever he wanted to do what he enjoyed. She criticized his playmates and demanded that he stay at home to help her out. Since Arthur did not shine in sports, he grew up assuming he was weak and awkward, a belief that his mother reinforced. When he enjoyed a sailing course in college, his mother reproved him for wasting time—he should work every weekend to help his father run the family business. Ever the dutiful son, Arthur stopped sailing.

In the course of therapy Arthur realized that his mother was a Tyrant. By conforming to her dictates, he had become a Victim, oppressed by his mother's tyranny. As the Tyrant, Conformist, and Victim battled within him, he unconsciously enacted all of these figures in his life and marriage. Arthur began to confront his mother by setting limits on her behavior. But the battle with the Tyrant had only begun; he still needed to confront the despot, Conformist, and Victim in himself to change these destructive life patterns.

At first Arthur became confident enough to initiate small risks of opposition to his mother. He also began to see how his conformity had sabotaged his creativity. After his father retired, Arthur sold the business and enrolled in graduate school to study science. By now he was in his forties.

At home he sometimes acted like a Tyrant toward his teenage children. For example, he expected his teenage daughter to conform to his rules. When she rebelled, he yelled at her just as his mother had yelled at him. Nevertheless, Arthur was learning to look within himself. He began to recognize the times when he repeated his mother's reactions, and he no longer blindly conformed to rules. Although he still had to confront his mother's tyranny, he learned to say no to her by hanging up the telephone whenever she talked disrespectfully to him.

At work, however, Arthur encountered another crisis that challenged him to grow. Funding was cut at the research clinic where he worked, and the clinic was forced to downsize. Older workers were laid off first. Arthur, who had just turned sixty, was asked to retire. The word *retire* sent Arthur into a panic. The inner Tyrant who demanded work and productivity resurfaced, along with the inner Victim, who felt rejected, and the inner Conformist, who didn't want to risk adventuring into a new phase of life.

Although he had planned his family finances wisely so that he and Rebecca could live a quality life with his retirement income, Arthur became severely depressed. During his first year out of work, he desperately tried to find a new job—to no avail. His dreams, however, were revealing. In a series of dreams he was working again at the clinic. The woman administrator, who in reality had harshly laid him off, was criticizing and bullying him. The dreams helped him notice that her nasty dominating manner was like that of his mother.

Arthur consciously saw a connection between his mother, the female boss, and his own inner Tyrant who forbade him peace and serenity, rest and regeneration. He realized that he needed to learn to stand up to this inner bully, represented in his dreams by the female boss.

Instead of conforming to conventional ideas about retirement as the end of life, Arthur realized that he must create his life anew and enjoy the opportunities that early retirement afforded him. He could spend more living time with his wife and children, nourish his soul by the sea, read the books he had longed to read, and be inspired by listening to music, one of his greatest loves. Arthur volunteered to work for social services in his community. He surrendered his tendency to compete with male associates and developed close male friendships that helped heal the distant relationship he had with his father.

The couple began to vacation at the seaside, where they enjoyed swimming and sailing. The ebb and flow of the ocean renewed them. Arthur's forced retirement became an opportunity for him to learn to relax and to be held in the loving arms of Mother Nature—a healing mother that inspired and nourished him instead of bullying him like his natal mother.

Arthur's journey to free himself from the tyranny of his inner saboteurs took more than thirty years, and he continues to give conscious attention to his life. He keeps on developing the inner Sentinel that helped him transform the meek Conformist of his adolescent years into a courageous Adventurer who now can respond to the inner call to create and set out on the path of discovery. Arthur's journey to transform his inner figures is a way we all must travel if we want to respond to the call to create. It is a passage that takes time and becomes part of our lifelong adventure.

THE ADVENTURER

The Adventurer breaks out of the given structure to go in new directions by taking a leap of faith and risking failure. Even as the Adventurer accepts the challenge to create, however, she must learn to be centered and balance on life's tightrope—that is, to exist in the paradox of creation and destruction.

As we have seen, Jung described the energy of the psyche as daimonic—an indwelling force or spirit that calls us to create and that bears within it the tension of good and evil. The Greek origins of the word *daimon* also underscore the paradox contained within it. The daimon is a force containing both divine and diabolical energies. The call to create requires us to live and struggle in this tension with the divine and the diabolical, just as the biblical Jacob wrestled with the angel.

The daimonic energy entailed in creativity can move us toward either the divine or the diabolical. We can relate to this energy in three radically different ways. Like the Tyrant, we can use it in dysfunctional and destructive ways. Or like the Conformist, we can try to deny or suppress creative energy, because we are afraid to live in the disturbances it creates. But we can also accept and embrace daimonic energy by learning to center ourselves so that we can direct it toward creativity, healing, and wholeness. By consciously choosing this third way, we respond to the call to create.

The Adventurer accepts the challenge—the dangers and the responsibility—to live in this tension as consciously as possible. Learning how to survive in the tension of opposites, to move between the finite and infinite realms, and to respect our human practical needs as well as the greater mysteries are tasks of the Adventurer. The call to create challenges us to live resolutely in the paradox of life and death, creation and destruction, and to struggle to bear witness.

One of the greatest directors in modern cinema, Andrey Tarkovsky, accepted this endeavor as the challenge of human existence and noted that the purpose of art is to bear witness to this universal struggle. He said, "The artist cannot be deaf to the call of truth; it alone defines his creative will, organizes it, thus enabling him to pass on his faith to others. . . . The aim of art is to prepare a person for death, to plough and harrow his soul, rendering it capable of turning to good."[2]

The Adventurer is not afraid to struggle with the disturbances that are intrinsic to the call to create. Thus the Adventurer calls us to the clarity of consciousness, along with its inherent dangers, such as egoism. The Adventurer knows that the creative journey requires facing danger and demands toil and struggle. He understands that the process of struggle itself brings special beauty, joy, and meaningful moments that are inherent to creativity.

A pitfall for the Adventurer is to be unaware of, or even to deny, the importance of the period of preparation that is necessary to build up one's strength so that one can consciously meet the dangers of creativity in order to survive.

Heather, an imaginative woman in her twenties, identified with the Adventurer but related a dream in which she was reminded of the hazards in adventuring.

> I am leading an escape from a skyscraper institution. We go upstairs to the top of the building. My followers look uncertain about how we would escape from such a high place. I see the door I know will be there, jump out, and fly to the lawn below. But the woman that follows me

cannot control her flight and is impaled on a statue. I feel completely responsible for her death. I wake up with the realization that I can't expect others to follow me on my adventures if it is not safe for them.

At the time of the dream, Heather had completed her first book—a powerful memoir in which she described her reactions toward her father's recent suicide. In order to write the book, Heather had to leap into an emotional abyss in which she confronted her rage, tears, and overwhelming confusion. During this process, which lasted several years, she confronted her despair, her tendencies to feel hopeless, and her own flirtation with suicide. During this time she suffered physically from a variety of viruses, flues, and fevers.

Writing the book plunged Heather into the dark depths, but the process of putting words on paper and forming her feelings also grounded her and gave her strength, courage, and patience—all requisite to the creative process of self-transformation.

After she had finished, Heather sent her manuscript to her mother, her brothers and sisters, her grandparents, and her aunts, uncles, and cousins. While her immediate family affirmed the book and the courage that it took to write it, her father's siblings did not want the stigma of his suicide to mar their name. Some asked her to fictionalize her account or use a pseudonym; others asked her not to submit it for publication.

It was essential for Heather, however, to put her story out in the open. Using a pseudonym or presenting it as fiction, she felt, would be tantamount to hiding the truth—an act that she knew was emotionally and spiritually lethal and totally contrary to her purpose in writing the book. The dream reminded Heather of the time and effort it took her to deal with this trauma. Instead of dismissing the fears of her relatives as mere conventional ones, Heather set about the difficult task of talking with them about their concerns. She had to learn to balance her need to publish her story and the fears of her father's siblings.

ON THE TIGHTROPE: CAMILLE AND COLETTE

The sculptress Camille Claudel and the novelist Colette both were born in France in the latter half of the nineteenth century into provincial middle-class families. Both Camille and Colette had to struggle with the social expectations to which women were supposed to conform. At that time in France women had no legal rights and barely had access to professional life. Women were expected to marry and have children, and the dowry system was in effect.

Each of these women was an Adventurer who chose to pursue her unique call to creative life, and each eventually became recognized in the twentieth century as a great artist. But Camille Claudel's struggle with the Conformist ended in tragedy. By the time she died in 1943, she had destroyed nearly half of her sculptures; and her life ended in misery in seclusion in a madhouse. Colette, in contrast, was awarded three honors by the French government before she died in 1954—all accolades that had never before been granted in France to a woman. She was made grand officer of the Legion of Honor; she became president of the Académie Goncourt; and she was honored by being given a state funeral that recognized her artistic contribution to

France. By getting to know the story of each of these remarkable women, we can explore some of the complexities of the Adventurer.

THE TRAGIC REVOLT OF CAMILLE CLAUDEL

Camille Claudel was born December 8, 1864, in a small village in the Champagne district.[3] Her father encouraged her to develop her artistic gifts and worked hard to put her through art school. Her mother was rigidly bound to bourgeoisie conventions, however, and opposed Camille's creativity. Camille, the eldest daughter, was high spirited, temperamental, and eccentric. She flourished in her mystical love for art and nature and loved to walk with her youngest brother, Paul, among the strange colossal rocks in the eerie moor land near their home. During his childhood Paul Claudel, who became one of France's greatest writers, was influenced by Camille, who was his muse.

Unafraid of the dark depths of her creative passion, Camille worked with clay. Eagerly she went out at night to dig up the clay for her sculptures. By the time she was fifteen, she had already created three striking works, and her talent was noticed by the sculptor Alfred Boucher, who recommended her to Auguste Rodin as his most gifted student.

Rodin accepted Camille as his first female student, and she worked so attentively on his sculptures that she soon became his assistant, helping to sculpt his great work *The Gate of Hell.* Camille, who developed her own technique, outstripped Rodin in her proficiency to cut marble. Rodin, who was forty and in a dry period of his creativity, was inspired by Camille, who became his muse, model, and lover.

Rodin and Camille met in a romantic studio that he rented for her, and they were lovers for fifteen years. When Camille became pregnant, Rodin told her he was unable to leave his common-law wife, Rose Bauret, to live with her. Angrily, Camille had an abortion. In 1893 she separated from Rodin, moved to her own studio, and broke with his style of art. Soon her love turned to hatred, and she terminated their communication. At the age of thirty her romantic life ended.

While Camille was Rodin's lover, her mother and sister condemned their lawless love affair, dealt with her as if she were a prostitute, and judged her for her disgraceful behavior and her libertine character. It was the turn of the century, and it was still disreputable to be a woman artist living alone. Camille was now dependent upon her parents financially. Although her father and brother gave her money during this period, they had to hide their assistance to Camille from her mother and sister.

After she left Rodin, Camille developed a unique style, through which she revealed people and scenes of daily life in sculptures such as *The Old Blind Singer* and *The Gossipers.* She experimented with her art and regarded Rodin with disdain for commercializing his art and for acquiescing to celebrity. Although her sculpture was exhibited and collectors admired her art, many critics still regarded her as Rodin's student. Camille, who was actively differentiating her art from Rodin's, felt disparaged and began to suspect that he was behind this scheme. Rodin, however, still loved Camille and in his way was trying to support her in her artistry.

Meanwhile Camille became a recluse, living in semipoverty. She began to drink heavily. She gained weight. She began to look unkempt and older than her age. Her studio was chaotic and cluttered. Camille was badgered by creditors to repay the debts she had amassed for the Italian marble that she needed for her sculptures. She was forced to beg her father for the money to pay her rent.

As her condition worsened, Camille became increasingly paranoid. She began to blame Rodin for her torment. She was deluded that Rodin had influenced her mother to refuse to give her money that she needed to live. Camille suspected that Rodin was pilfering her ideas and swaying the minds of her models and workmen against her. She accused him of hiring scoundrels to break into her studio and ruin her work. Afraid that her work would be put next to Rodin's and credited to him, Camille began to refuse offers to exhibit her sculptures.

As Camille's state of mind deteriorated, she started to destroy her own work. In a letter Camille wrote that whenever she became frustrated or disappointed, she would throw her wax models into the fire in a fury, or pick up a hammer and crush a statue.

When her father died in 1913, her mother did not inform Camille, who did not even know about the funeral. Soon after her father's death her conformist and tyrannical mother had Camille committed to an insane asylum, where she was imprisoned for the rest of her life. At first Camille blamed Rodin for this incarceration. But after Rodin died, Camille began to see that her mother had imposed this punishment upon her and refused to release her. Camille spent the next thirty years of her life as a captive in the madhouse. She refused to sculpt again and died ignored and unknown.

After her death Camille's remaining works—less than half of her creations—were recognized for their genius and were acquired by museums. Her luminous sculptures portray feminine intimacy. Critics now acknowledge that they uniquely express the sad and tender fragility of the human condition.

Internally, Camille's creative energy remained attached to Rodin, even though externally she tried to separate herself from him. Since she could not free herself fully from Rodin, it is likely that Camille's love turned to hatred—the animosity that obsessed her and that led her to destroy her own work in retaliation. Resentment is an underlying cause of most acts of self-destruction, whether it is the ruin of one's creations or of one's life.

Camille Claudel lost the direction of her creative energy through her losing battle with conformity. Rejected by her cold, cruel, and conventional mother, Camille fought back through her art. But the power of her mother, supported by society's rigid rules for women, may have been akin to the *Gate of Hell* piece that she had helped Rodin to sculpt. Her mother's abuse and rejection fed the traumatic jealousy and rage she experienced when she felt forsaken by Rodin. In addition, her poverty and her addiction to alcohol, her isolation together with society's stigma, and the absence of the art world's recognition of her creative genius and her unique contribution to culture—all were factors that contributed to Camille's tragic plight.

Perhaps in her own way Camille became as rigid as her mother. By refusing to recognize, work with, and attempt to change some of society's demands and by neglecting the necessary requirements of physical and mental survival, Camille isolated herself and became an outcast. One could say that her Adventurer went too far and was unable to acknowledge and integrate the worthwhile aspects of the Conformist. In the end Camille's extreme rebellion against the Conformist left her without the stability and roots needed for survival.

COLETTE: THE ACROBAT

Sidonie-Gabrielle Colette, who was to be acknowledged as one of France's greatest writers, was born in Burgundy on January 28, 1873.[4] Her father, a captain in the army, was wounded in action and his left leg was amputated. As a result, he was made a chevalier of the Legion of Honor. He then retired to the post of tax collector in the provinces, where he met and fell in love with Colette's mother, Sido, who was widowed.

Sido had inherited a large house from her first husband. The house was replete with a carriage entrance, a yard, and a small garden concealed from the road by a high wall. As a child, Colette played with her sisters and brothers in the secret garden, an earthly paradise of trees and flowers, birds and animals.

Sido and the captain were unconventional parents. Both loved to read. The captain had a passion for politics and hoped to be a writer. Sido was a freethinker who taught the children about plants, animals, and gardening. She encouraged them to read the classics and play the piano. She allowed the children to go to church so that they could experience for themselves what religion was about. Sido tried to create an idyllic atmosphere for her children to compensate for her own unhappy childhood and for her unfortunate first marriage to an alcoholic. Despite her attempts to shield her children, however,

Sido's eldest daughter showed signs of autism and later committed suicide.

Sido was especially possessive of Colette, her youngest child, and refused to allow her to go away to boarding school. She was described by Colette as warm, wholesome, and intelligent. But she dominated the family emotionally in a subtle, nonauthoritarian way. Meanwhile the captain withdrew into fantasies of writing and spent most of his time in the upstairs library. Colette later learned that the bound books that supposedly contained his work held nothing but blank pages. Sido left the finances to her husband who, through lack of interest, mismanaged the estate. By the time Colette was sixteen, the family was in debt. The house, along with its wonderful garden, was sold by order of the court, and the family went to live with Colette's stepbrother Achille, a country doctor.

Leaving the magical house and garden was traumatic for Colette. But she admired her stepbrother. Both shared a curiosity about the natural world and spent time together in nature searching for mushrooms and collecting butterflies. Colette also accompanied her brother while he visited patients and sometimes helped him dress wounds.

When Colette was nineteen, a son of a former military colleague of the captain came to visit. Henri Gauthier-Villars, called Willy by his friends, lived in Paris, where he worked in publishing and moved in literary circles. Willy was urbane, witty, and amusing and flattered Colette with his attention. Although Colette did not have a dowry, he proposed marriage, and her parents consented.

Sido, however, was reluctant to let go of Colette and became gloomy. Sido had not had a dowry and had been "sold" to her first husband. She felt that the institution of marriage was barbarous.

Moreover, Colette was her "jewel of gold," the "golden sun" that lightened up her world. Sido tried to discourage Colette from marrying because she didn't want her daughter to leave her. But Colette needed independence from her mother and sought escape through marriage.

In the marriage, however, Colette soon felt disillusioned and lonely. Willy was not the brilliant writer she had imagined him to be. Instead, he was a shrewd man always seeking money. He arranged to have others write the books that he signed as his own. With Willy, Colette found sex to be laborious and exhausting. She lamented her loss of happiness. She missed her mother and craved to be with her again. Yet she could not admit to Sido that she had been right about the marriage; nor could she confide in Sido and tell her about her unhappiness. Colette became depressed to the point of illness. Learning of the illness, Sido came to Paris to nurse her.

Colette eventually resigned herself to the marriage. But she refused to be Willy's literary hostess—a social role allowed to women at that time. Colette was uninterested in social advancement and detested artificial, hypocritical, or calculated behavior. To others, she seemed shy and almost afraid to meet people.

Colette was unhappy in contrived social situations, but she was also unhappy to be left alone and forgotten in the apartment. Most of the time she read and played with her cat. Occasionally she went to the theater, and she enjoyed making friends with some of the women and the young gay men who came to visit.

Finally, Willy began to consider Colette as a possible ghostwriter, and he suggested that she write down impressions of her school life in detail. Like a schoolgirl passively following the teacher's orders, Colette applied herself to the task. When she showed her writing to

Willy, he told her it wasn't good and put it in his desk drawer. Colette felt liberated and went back to reading on her divan and playing with her cat. Two years later Willy found the notebooks while clearing his desk. This time, as he glanced through them, he realized their worth and took them to a publisher.

The book, *Claudine à l'école (Claudine at School)*, was an instant success and sold more than fifty thousand copies at the first printing. It was an amusing description of the lesbian behavior of schoolgirls and their teachers in a country village. Colette, as it turned out, had a gift for writing entertaining stories, and the experience had allowed her to express her nostalgia for her lost childhood.

Willy demanded that she write more books. According to Colette, he even locked her in a room for several hours a day to be sure she wrote. Colette confessed that she was afraid of Willy, and she obeyed his orders. Although she claimed that she did not like to write, this activity allowed her to escape the reality of her marriage and her artificial life and to begin to discover her authentic self. The *Claudine* books allowed her to express different aspects of herself and mature through that process.

During the next several years Colette wrote a number of novels always with Willy's signature at the end of the book. She had signed a contract with him. In 1904, after several of her books were published, Colette finally fought for permission to sign her books herself. Willy refused, but Colette was allowed to keep the publication rights for herself. Later, in 1909, Willy sold the exclusive rights to the *Claudine* books to the original publisher.

In 1906, after thirteen years of marriage, Willy and Colette separated. Always the impresario, Willy had arranged for Colette to take lessons from an actor-mime. Colette, with her close friend Missy, began to act in mime dramas and finally performed onstage. Colette appeared in men's clothing and in erotic costumes; and sometimes she revealed her breasts onstage. If the drama required it, she and Missy would exchange a long passionate kiss.

The relationship between Colette and Missy has been described as *amitié amoureuse*, an amorous friendship with emotional and physical depth. With Missy, Colette felt content, confident, and happy. She wore bracelets engraved with the words: "I belong to Missy." Around this time Colette wrote a lyrical prose piece, *Nuit Blanche*, in which it is revealed at the end that the two people who share a bed are two women. Drawn together by passion, the women seek both mother and daughter in each other. Colette felt comforted with Missy and allowed herself every luxury. Later Missy bought and furnished a villa in Brittany for Colette, who loved the sea.

When Colette danced nude onstage, it was scandalous—bold and daring for the time. Yet she also conveyed the impression of naïveté, acquiring the image of an "innocent libertine." The title of her novel *La Vagabonde* was a description of herself. Its protagonist, an unhappy actress disillusioned by marriage, searches for love, yet cannot receive it when it is given.

Then Colette met Henri de Jouvenel, editor of the newspaper *Le Matin*. She began to write articles for the paper and fell in love with him. When Jouvenel's mistress, known as "Panther," learned of his affair with Colette, Panther threatened to kill her. Jouvenel had Colette kidnapped to protect her. Meanwhile Missy became jealous of Jouvenel. It was a melodramatic time, during which Colette's divorce became finalized.

Colette's mother, displeased with the divorce, was disturbed by her daughter's plan to marry again. Although Sido acknowledged that other "arrangements" were considered scandalous, she told Colette that anything would be better than marriage. Sido preferred Willy, since with him Colette had written novels. Sido criticized Colette's journalism, saying it would kill the novelist in her. She warned Colette that a woman in love gives away her most priceless gifts.

Colette hoped for happiness, however, and moved in with Jouvenal. They were in love, but their relationship was stormy. Colette did not want to feel dominated again; she wanted control in her emotional life. She felt that Jouvenel needed her too much. For example, he didn't want her to visit Sido, whose health was failing, for more than three days. Then, three weeks after Colette's last visit, Sido died. Colette felt bereft and became ill from grief. She was tormented because she could no longer write letters to her mother.

Two months after Sido's death, Colette discovered that she was pregnant. As a consequence, she married Jouvenel, and their daughter was born in July 1913, just before her fortieth birthday. That year Colette finished another novel, *L'Entrave*, which described the paradoxes of relationships—the twisting of roles and the mixture of motives. In this novel love was dangerous for the protagonist, who longed for it yet shunned it.

During the war years Colette continued to write journalistic articles. She also volunteered to work as a night nurse in Paris. Under a false name, she followed her husband to the front at Verdun to be near him. In 1915 Colette was sent to Italy to write about the war. In 1917 she was sent as a delegate to a peace conference held by the Allies in Rome.

By the 1920s Colette was famous. Her novel *Mitsou* had moved Proust to tears. Gide admired *Chéri*, the novel many consider to be her masterpiece. Although she valued herself and her work, Colette took her fame lightly. Always in need of money, she felt obliged to work continuously. She remembered her sixteenth year, when bankruptcy forced her family to leave their country home. The fear of poverty remained with her.

Tired of Jouvenel's affairs, Colette divorced him in 1924. Soon she met Maurice Goudeket, a younger man with whom she found passion, love, and companionship. They lived together in Paris and married ten years later.

The 1930s was an active decade for Colette, who published seven books, including three novels, nonfiction books, and a collection of short stories. At Maurice Ravel's request she composed a libretto for one of his operas. She also wrote a scenario for a film directed by Max Ophuls. Next Colette began a business in which she opened a beauty institute, made and sold her own cosmetic products, and traveled to French provincial towns to give presentations in the art of makeup. In one of her letters she wrote: "at the age when others finish, I am presuming to begin." During this time she was invited into the Belgian Academy of Royal Literature.

Following the German invasion of France in 1940, Colette and Maurice left Paris to stay with her daughter. They returned to stay in the Palais-Royal apartment that she had purchased. It was wartime. Maurice was arrested and put in a prison camp; later he remained in the unoccupied zone.

In 1944 Colette published her last fictional work, *Gigi*, a novella based on a true story. *Gigi* is the tale of a young girl who, by refusing to be a "kept woman" for a rich admirer, later becomes his wife. The novella's happy ending shows that young love can win over money and the custom of kept women. When she saw the young actress Audrey Hepburn in person at a film festival in Monte Carlo, Colette knew she was the right Gigi for America. The musical comedy *Gigi*, starring Audrey Hepburn, was a hit on Broadway. Later Leslie Caron portrayed Gigi in the movie, which became one of Hollywood's most beloved films.

In her seventies Colette was forced into a limited state of relative immobility due to the war years and to arthritis in her hip. She struggled with her habit of writing and her desire to stop. Colette accepted pain as a "new companion" and old age as offering her the leisure to try out new techniques in writing.

She said:

> With humility, I am going to write again. There is no other destiny for me. But when does one stop writing? What warning is there? Do one's hands tremble? I thought in the past that the work of writing was like other tasks; the tool is laid down and one cries out in delight, "Finished!" . . .
> It is then that you read in the outlines traced by the grains of the sand the words, "To be continued . . . "[5]

Colette was the first woman elected to the Académie Goncourt, in 1945. Later she became its president. In 1953 she received the Grand Cross of the Legion of Honor. When Colette died a year later at the age of eighty-one, she was honored with a state funeral and buried in the celebrated cemetery, Père-Lachaise, although the Church declined its approval.

"I belong to a country I have abandoned," Colette once wrote. With this poignant sentence Colette described her devotion to the Adventurer in herself. She risked writing about unconventional subjects that seemed daring to many at the time—the tensions in love relationships, including those that were heterosexual and homosexual, affairs between older women and younger men, ménages à trois and polygamy, women's ambivalence about marriage, and their search for independence.

Although she always claimed that she did not enjoy writing and that it was a slow and painstaking task, Colette wrote from her personal experience with talent and perseverance to find the exact words that would express both physical sensations and ideas. She described life's surfaces as well as its deeper essence.

Colette was adventurous in both her writing and her life. Yet she remained connected to her roots and was able to "dance" with whatever was required to conform to the necessities of publishing. She lived in the tension between the polarities of the conventional and the unconventional and acquired the agility to be an acrobat, able to balance on the tightrope of both worlds.

Both Camille Claudel and Colette responded to the call to create. Both women struggled with the Conformist and the Adventurer. And both are now recognized for their creative genius in their fields. In contrast with the tragic end suffered by Camille Claudel, however, Colette was honored.

Camille's fiery, impulsive, and impetuous temperament may have made it more difficult for her to survive in her revolt against the period's emphasis on cultural conformity, which relegated women to dowried marriages. In contrast, Colette's ability to live with a sense of aesthetic distance despite such tensions may have enabled her to persist and receive the recognition due to her.

Although Camille's father supported her emotionally and financially, her bourgeoisie-bound mother's rejection, abuse, and cruelty gave her little ground upon which to stand. Moreover, the battles between her parents did not provide her with a model of harmony. In contrast, Colette's parents' lack of conventionality in the midst of French provincial life—even though this led to financial ruin—must have influenced her. And possessive as it was, her mother's love gave her a necessary developmental foundation as well as a desire to break free to independence. Colette's memories of her childhood spent in the family's secret garden amidst nature's paradise supported her throughout her life. And her love of animals and plants gave her solid roots in the earth.

THE CREATIVE CHALLENGE

The Adventurer fails the creative challenge if she does not learn from experience, or if she neglects the task of applying and embodying what she has learned from her ventures. She must take responsibility to plant and tend to creativity in daily life. In order for the Adventurer to successfully challenge the Conformist, she must be aware of the values that the Conformist has to offer. The Conformist knows that essential social structures are the products of years of civilization, and she honors and marks these essential and proven predictable patterns for others. Just as our bodies have certain organic requirements for survival, so does all of life. The Conformist knows the importance of adapting to the earth and its necessities. At best the Conformist affirms the worth of stability, consistency, persever-ance, and endurance in creative life.

But the Conformist impedes creativity when she absolutizes these principles into a static system with rigid rules that are closed and that fend off openness, growth, and dialogue with others who have different viewpoints. Like the Adventurer, the Conformist must learn to take risks. Indeed, life is a continual process of growth and change that requires us to venture into the unknown.

Thus, the call to create requires the Conformist and the Adven-turer to acknowledge each other, to cooperate, and to work together to sustain and to forge new life.

7
TOIL

I think it's dangerous to concern oneself too damned much with "being an artist." It's more important to get the work done.

Maya Angelou

THE ARTISAN TEACHES
THE STAR HUMILITY

A formidable temptation for the creative person is the insatiable longing to be a Star. The Star has a shining beauty and is often charismatic, attracting others to her. But if the Star succumbs to egoism and becomes inflated with success, fame, and power, she loses humility. If she lords it over others, she threatens the creative process because she wants to take all the credit for creating.

The Star has a need to be the "special one"—to be the prince or princess we know from fairy tales. This desire may derive from feelings of inferiority that have been internalized as the result of a deprived childhood, as in the case of Marilyn Monroe. Or conversely, it can stem from adoring parents who place their son or daughter on a pedestal. This position isolates the child because it does not accord with the exigencies of ordinary life. Emily Watson's portrayal of the cellist Jacqueline Du Pré, in the film *Jackie and Hilary* shows how isolated a Star can be.

As the special one, the Star believes she deserves the best. The Star presumes she is extraordinary and feels entitled to the recognition of others. To convince others and herself of her exalted image, the Star often resorts to name-dropping to show that she is in the "special" circle. She wears designer suits and does whatever is "in" at the moment to gain the prestige so necessary to her image. Her presumed superiority may exist only in her fantasies. Or it may be augmented by actual worldly success.

The Call to Create

In external life the Star might be a celebrity in the creative arts, a guru in the spiritual arena, a wealthy businessman, a TV personality, a junior executive on the rise, a socially elite hostess, someone who has made the best-seller list, the wife or husband of an influential person, or a political leader.

In contrast, the Star may also exist only in our daydreams. In daily life people who fantasize stardom may work as taxi drivers, waitresses, salesmen, secretaries, laborers, housewives, or maintenance men or even be on welfare. The Brazilian film *Hour of the Star* shows the tragedy that often engulfs the would-be star.

Whether the Star appears in worldly life or only in our fantasies, she is a figure in ourselves with whom we have to reckon. Yearning to be a Star is part of the human condition. It is an expression of our longing for the infinite. If this desire is balanced in ourselves by accepting our finitude, it can serve the creative process, which requires both human endeavor and divine inspiration.

But if the Star insists on being first, identifies with power, denies the participation inherent in creativity, and competes to be highest on the pinnacle, her rise may be her downfall. Then the Star's need to shine and be the "special one" begins to obstruct creativity.

The Star's need to keep going higher on the list of fame colludes with the insatiable desire for more and more in the form of praise and material reward. Then the Star's ravenous appetite can capture her energy. As a result she is likely to become too busy (the Compulsive Doer) or too lazy (the Sluggard) to heed and care for her inner life. The fantasies that feed the Star's inflated egocentric attitude and appearance tend to alienate her from her body. Her attention to clothes and cosmetics may supersede attention to her health.

If the Star hardens in her psyche, she may lose access to her heart.

The Artisan Teaches the Star Humility

The Star's emphasis on outer image can confine her to the surface and keep her away from the demanding depths of soul-work. Moreover, she is likely to confuse the genuine inner need for love and self-esteem with a pretentious sense of self-importance. Instead of love, the Star is more likely to experience envy and rivalry. People who are impressed by her rise may secretly wish for her fall because her arrogant and self-serving behavior offends them.

The egoist in us can succumb to fantasies of greatness. Secretly we may long to win the Nobel Prize or an Oscar or to be on the best-seller list, or we may have pretensions to be a guru. If we fall prey to grandiosity, we lose sight of the process. Self-aggrandizement and ego-inflation are a pitfall because they lead us to concentrate on the resulting product rather than on the constant toiling care that goes into creative life. In this way we succumb to "bad faith," a form of false consciousness through which we objectify and sell ourselves as if we were a finished thing, that is, as a commodity. If we see ourselves as an object, we deny our fundamental consciousness and choice. In this way we disregard the paradoxical complexities inherent in human existence.

When we are in "bad faith," as Jean-Paul Sartre has described it, we objectify our identity. We see ourselves as though we were static things, thereby denying the possibility to change and grow—a process that is inherent in human consciousness. Sartre actually refused the Nobel Prize, to avoid what he considered to be false consciousness. Bad faith ignores human limitations, the reality that we all have "dirty hands," a title that Sartre gave to one of his plays. Jung acknowledged the proclivity to "bad faith" when he emphasized that we must be aware of our "shadow" side if we want to become healthy, integrated, mature persons. It is the shadow side—the part of us that we don't like and would rather forget because it upsets an inflated self-image—that can throw the Star off the pedestal.

The old adage "nothing fails like success" is an important reminder to heed. William Hamilton, professor at the Wharton School of Business, reminds his students of this adage by pointing out that the arrogance that tempts the Star to neglect the constant work of craft is an everyday risk for business people involved in designing or implementing products, processes, or strategies.

To transform the egoism of the Star, we must turn to the humble Artisan, who acknowledges that creativity is a gift. The Artisan feels responsible to cherish and use this gift appropriately, knowing that it is not something that can be possessed or to which one is automatically entitled. Artisans stress the importance of the constant work and struggle to develop the craft that goes into a creative work or life.

Dostoyevsky emphasized this when he wrote that a poem is like a precious stone buried in the ground. A poem is a gift that the writer finds hidden in the soul. The poet must be like a jeweler who works to set this diamond that the creator has placed in the soul.

SUNSET BOULEVARD

Hollywood, that special place where a Star can be born, knows the star syndrome intimately and has portrayed the rise and the fall of the Star in an array of films. *Sunset Boulevard*, *A Star Is Born*, and *Boogie Nights* are just a few of the multitude of films that depict the Star.

Billy Wilder's classic film *Sunset Boulevard* shows the interactions between the Star, who is possessed by delusions of grandeur, and the Cynic, whose enthusiasm for creativity has withered under the conformist and profit-ridden Hollywood system.

A script writer (portrayed by William Holden) can no longer support himself by his writing and makes a last effort to sell formula screenplays. To avoid having his automobile repossessed, Joe tries to escape with his car by outracing the auto company agents.

During the chase Joe's car gives out, and by a fluke he is able to turn up the driveway to an old run-down mansion while the agents speed by. Joe thinks that the mansion is deserted and hides his car in the garage. But a servant, Max (played by Erich von Stroheim), sees Joe and summons him into the mansion. It is the residence of a formerly famous silent film star, Norma Desmond, who is played by Gloria Swanson. Norma, who lives with the relics of her past and waits for another great film to come her way, mistakes Joe for a funeral director whom she has called to the house to bury her pet chimpanzee.

When she learns that Joe is a screenwriter, she pulls out her own script, *Salome,* in which she hopes to star. Norma offers to pay Joe to help her edit it. Although Joe detests the imperious, demanding, faded star who lords it over him and is repulsed by her excessive crumbling mansion, he accepts her offer since he needs the money and thinks he has nothing to lose. He hopes to make the money that will help him keep his car.

Time passes, while Joe suffers Norma's derision and goading remarks by reacting with clever cynical repartee. One day he sees his car being towed away by the men who want to repossess it. He makes a feeble effort to stop them from taking the car, which represents his freedom, but fails. Without the car he feels paralyzed, as if he has lost his true self. But he does not leave to retrieve it. Joe has become a hostage to Norma's wealth and power.

That night Joe has a nightmare in which he sees a chimpanzee dancing for pennies to the tune of an old organ grinder. He has become like the pet chimpanzee who hops to Norma's commands. She dresses him in elegant clothes, which she buys to replace his threadbare garb. She prescribes how he should behave. When she tells him to stop chewing gum, he obeys.

Meanwhile Norma falls in love with Joe; with him her life and her mansion do not seem so empty and deserted. But she continues to act like a sleepwalker on the giddy heights of her diminished celluloid self. She brags to Joe that she receives fan letters every day and boasts: "I am big; it's the pictures that got small. Have they forgotten what a star looks like? I'll be up there again, so help me."

On New Year's Eve, after a wrenching evening with Norma, who wants him to romance her, Joe slips out to go to a friend's party. He reencounters Betty, a young writer and script reader who had rejected his formulaic plays but who finds the seeds for a great script in one of his old manuscripts. But Norma's servant, Max, has Joe followed and phones him at the party. Norma has slit her wrists. Joe returns to the suicidal Norma, who says, "Great stars have great pride."

When Joe finishes *Salome*, Norma sends it to Cecil B. DeMille, expecting him to call her immediately. A few days later, when DeMille's assistant calls, she feels slighted. In the old days directors returned her calls personally on her demand. "Without me there wouldn't be a Paramount Studio," she says. "I've waited twenty years for that call. Now DeMille can wait."

But Norma soon gives in and goes to the studio. Most workers there don't remember her; the ones that do are amazed that she is still alive. Nevertheless, they are excited to see the old star and surround her like the fans of yesteryear. When an old cameraman recognizes her and turns the spotlight on her, Norma feels the glory of being the Star again.

Surprised to see her, DeMille comes over and holds her hand; then he calls his office to find out who phoned her. He learns that his assistant wanted to use her antique car in a movie scene. Sorry for the aging actress, DeMille covers up the mistake and tells her there will be a film for her soon. He remembers her as a talented young actress with courage and spirit.

Max learns the truth and confesses to Joe that he was the first of Norma's many husbands and the director who made her a star. Still devoted to her star image, now acting as her servant, Max secretly directs her life. He upholds her image by writing the fan letters she receives every day and feeds her grandiosity with flattery and veneration for her past.

Thrilled by the possibility of acting once more, Norma undergoes excruciating beauty treatments and counts calories to get ready for the cameras that will never turn. Meanwhile Joe sneaks away each night to work with Betty, whose enthusiasm has convinced him he can still write a good script. Joe begins to rediscover his original passion for writing, and he and Betty fall in love. Joe becomes intent on finishing the script with her. Facing the fact that he has become Norma's prisoner, Joe hopes that he can escape the old star's clutch.

Max keeps tabs on Joe for Norma, however, and tells her of his betrayal. In retaliation Norma phones Betty. She informs Betty that Joe lives in her mansion and is dependent on her. Joe intercepts the call and asks Betty to come to the mansion to see for herself.

Stinging with humiliation, Joe shows Betty the mansion. Then cynically he tells Betty that he is tied to these possessions. Betty replies that he still has a choice. He can leave with her to continue their writing life together, and she will forget what she has seen. But Joe says that he can't give up the lifestyle Norma offers. Betty leaves in tears.

Joe packs his suitcase, planning to leave Hollywood and return to write for his hometown newspaper. Norma sees him pack and, in a frenzy, says she can't live without him; she will give him anything he wants. Joe confronts her with the truth. Filmgoers don't know her anymore: It is Max who has been writing her fan letters. "You're a woman of fifty," he says. "Grow up. There's nothing tragic with being fifty unless you want to be twenty-five."

As Joe crosses the patio to leave, the crazed Norma shoots him in the back of the head with the gun that she had intended to use to shoot herself. Joe falls dead into the swimming pool, floating face-down in the pool that he had admired on his first day there.

The press arrives and surrounds the confused actress, anticipating the gory story and the killing headlines: "Aging actress, yesterday's glamour queen, famous star of yesteryear." In a daze and in the delusion to which she has clung for so long, Norma believes that she is still the Star as she stands in the spotlight of the flashing cameras. As the police escort her from the mansion, Max tells her that she is the greatest star of all. Norma replies: "This is my life. It always will be. There's nothing else. Just me and the cameras and those wonderful people watching in the dark. Let the cameras roll. I'm ready for my close-up."

Joe's fate is a metaphor for that of the Cynic. He loses his original passion for writing through disillusionment with Hollywood's commercial, conventional demand for success. His cynicism traps him along with Norma in the peculiar prison of the Star. He becomes like the many jaded people who surround the Star, jeering at her yet hoping that her fame and her wealth will rub off on them. Unable to surrender his character as Cynic and open himself to the Muse and Sower, whom Betty represents, Joe rejects the possibilities for love and creativity that he has found with Betty.

Betty represents the Muse who finds the creative seed in Joe's writing and the Sower who plants it. Betty sows the seed of inspiration and enthusiasm and tends it as they write together. As the Sower, she offers him the hope to change his life. She rejects the role of Star when she tells Joe she prefers to stay behind the scenes and write.

Norma symbolizes the Star who clings to the delusions that destroy her. Underneath her image she is cynical, like Joe, but has covered it with self-deception so that she no longer knows the truth. As a young actress she was enthusiastic, like Betty, but became hardened in the shell of her image as Star.

As Star, Norma has become a Tyrant, directed by an even more powerful Tyrant, Max, who poses as her servant but commands her life. And let's not forget the audience, the admirers who, in conformity to the star system, sit watching in the dark as they unconsciously fan the flames that burn up creativity.

THE ARTISAN

The Artisan teaches the Star to value patience, listening, and mindfulness as she develops her craft. The Artisan knows that nature is greater than our attempts at sophistication and humbles us all at death. Thus this adept can ground the Star by pointing out her place as part of the whole.

The myth of Daedalus and Icarus shows the wisdom that the Artisan can teach us and the pitfall that awaits the rising Star. Daedalus is a brilliant inventor and artisan who has been trained by Athena, the goddess of arts, crafts, and wisdom. His skills include architecture, sculpture, and mechanics, and it is said that he constructs robots—animated statues that can perform many actions of living beings.

Despite his brilliance, Daedalus is not free from jealousy. When his apprentice, Talos, invents the saw, Daedalus becomes envious and hurls him from the heights of the Acropolis. Daedalus is punished for this murderous act. Exiled, he flees to the court of King Minos of Crete. There he designs and builds a labyrinth that Minos uses as a palace prison. Later, when Minos becomes displeased with Daedalus, he imprisons him and his young son, Icarus, in the horrendous maze.

Escape by land or by sea seems impossible. As he looks down on the ground, however, Daedalus has a brilliant idea. He picks two feathers from the ground. Then, by threading them together, he fashions them into wings. With some wax that he finds, Daedalus attaches one set of wings to Icarus and the other to himself; they can fly out of the labyrinth like birds.

Since he has formed many new things from matter, however, Daedalus knows their limits. He counsels Icarus to use the wings with moderation. If they fly too high, the blazing sun can melt the wax; but if they fly too low, the force of gravity can pull them into the ocean. Daedalus flies ahead as a guide and tells Icarus to follow him. But Icarus becomes so intoxicated by the flight that he forgets his father's words about the limits of the wings. Lost in the ecstasy of flight, Icarus soars too close to the sun. The wax that holds the wings together melts, and Icarus falls into the sea and drowns.

Icarus is like the Star who becomes so inflated with the excitement of new creation that he loses all sense of boundaries. Like Icarus, many stars rise before they have the maturity to know how to cope with success and its dangers. As a result, they fall to their deaths. The tragic stories of James Dean, Elvis Presley, and Kurt Cobain are reminders.

Knowing and abiding by the limits inherent in creation takes the hard-won knowledge of a seasoned, accomplished artisan like Daedalus, who himself succumbs to wanting to be a Star. As we have seen, Daedalus' inflation—wanting to be the number-one craftsman—results in his jealousy of Talos and culminates in murder and his exile.

Perhaps this is why mature cinematic artists, who have experienced and understand the inherent seductions and dangers of stardom, emphasize the importance of the Artisan. They concentrate on craft and not on themselves. Despite the star system that drives the movie business, film is an expensive and complex medium that requires patience and cooperation from its participants. Notable actors like Joanne Woodward, Paul Newman, Jessica Lange, Dennis Hopper, Holly Hunter, Harvey Keitel, Glenn Close, and Anthony Hopkins—all interviewed by James Lipton in the television series *Inside the Actors Studio*—stress the importance of craft to the students they teach.

For example, Paul Newman has remarked that his popular image as a youthful, handsome sex symbol could have trapped him into the fixed and static identity of an idol. When the public wants the Star to repeat himself in his roles, they fail to appreciate the craft and skill that serious actors want to develop. After the first flush of fame, committed actors must work diligently to find roles that challenge them. Like Newman, they know they must continue to refine their acting skills and broaden their scope. If they allow themselves to become trapped in star roles, it may keep them from accepting new creative challenges.

In her memoir *Changing,* the Swedish actress Liv Ullmann writes that her need for love often resulted in a desire to please, a fear to hurt, and a trepidation before authority. But whenever she suppressed her authenticity by doing what she believed others expected of her, she felt ashamed and guilty. Once, flattered by an interview that promised to "immortalize" her, she later felt humiliated and alone. She realized that she had not expressed her true convictions. Ullman says that one of the healthy gifts of her profession is the chance to break oneself into pieces so that wounds can't fester.[1] She is an artisan who gives thanks for the opportunity to be on a continual journey of self-discovery and the chance to express something about humanity through work.

Eminent directors, like Krzysztof Kieślowski (*Blue, White,* and *Red*) and Ingmar Bergman (*The Seventh Seal, Persona,* and *Fanny and Alexander*), refer to themselves as artisans. Bergman points to the numerous medieval artisans who worked anonymously building the cathedrals as examples of the patient, humble, communal work required to create. Hillary Rodham Clinton makes the same point in her book *It Takes a Village.*

THE CRAFT OF CARE: KRZYSZTOF KIEŚLOWSKI

The Polish filmmaker Krzysztof Kieślowski is considered by many to be one of the greatest directors of all time. Despite all his accolades, Kieślowski prefers to call himself an artisan rather than an artist. Creating, Kieślowski emphasizes, is an arduous and continual process of small steps that take him nearer to his goal: to capture on film that which dwells within us—a goal that he considers rare, perhaps impossible, to reach.

The artisan finds knowledge within the confines of his skills, Kieślowski once told an interviewer.

> For example, I know a lot about lenses, about the editing room, I know what the different buttons on the camera are for. I know more or less how to use a microphone. I know all that, but that's not real knowledge. Real knowledge is knowing how to live, why we live . . . things like that.[2]

In a description of the daily work of filmmaking, Kieślowski deflates the overblown, exaggerated image of the Star and the dramatic events that go with it:

> Filmmaking doesn't mean audiences, festivals, reviews, interviews. It means getting up every day at six o'clock in the morning. It means the cold, the rain, the mud and having to carry heavy lights. It's a nerve-racking business, and,

at a certain point, everything else has to come second, including your family, emotions, and private life. Of course, engine drivers, business men or bankers would say the same thing about their jobs. No doubt they'd be right.[3]

Like the artisan that he considers himself to be, Kieślowski believes that the elusive spirit of a film is born in the editing room. Shooting the film—an act that filmgoers sometimes mistake for the entire art—is only a first stage in which the director collects material and creates possibilities. Craftsmanship requires him to attempt to cut out everything that is not necessary to the film.

Kieślowski's hope in directing is to try to create films in which a person may find him or herself. In his films he attempts to reveal emotional states and moods of the soul. He constantly searches and attempts to hone his skills, hoping to come as close as he can to illumine the soul's complexities in a way that speaks to other human beings. Kieślowski *cares* for the audience's spiritual life and hopes that his films can illumine someone's fate or help them to change something in their life. In the following story, he describes what makes the arduous process of filmmaking worthwhile for him.

Once a fifteen-year-old girl approached him in Paris and said that she had gone to see *The Double Life of Veronique* several times. She only wanted to thank him. Seeing the film enabled her to realize something she hadn't known before—that the soul does exist. Kieślowski said

> There's something beautiful in that. It was worth making *Veronique* for that girl. It was worth working for a year, sacrificing all that money, energy, time, patience, torturing

yourself, killing yourself, taking thousands of decisions, so that one young girl in Paris should realize that there is such a thing as a soul. It's worth it.[4]

Another time a woman about fifty recognized him in Berlin, where *A Short Film About Love* was being publicized. She told him that she had seen the film with her daughter. Although they shared an apartment, neither mother nor daughter had been able to talk with each other or to share their real feelings for several years. They had been quarreling and could talk only about superficial things. After seeing the film, the daughter suddenly kissed her mother for the first time in five years. Kieślowski surmised that whatever they had seen in the film helped them realize the real reason for their conflict. "It was worth making the film for that kiss, for that one woman."[5]

Kieślowski was born in 1941 during the war years in Poland, a country disrupted by Hitler and Stalin. His family was poor. His father, a civil engineer, suffered from tuberculosis. Unable to work, he was sent from one sanatorium town to another. His mother supported the family by working as an office clerk and moved frequently to be with her husband. Kieślowski admired both parents and especially his father for his wisdom. But it was for his mother that he later persisted in applying to film school.

Throughout childhood Kieślowski was sickly and in danger of contracting tuberculosis. Partly due to his sickliness and also because his mother earned too little money, he and his sister were sent to sanatoria for children. Although he was able to play with the other children when he was well, he spent much time in convalescence, when books became his friends. Because there was no money, he was rarely able to see films.

The Call to Create

Like many young artists, Kieślowski was bored at school and didn't like to study. At his father's suggestion, he attended a school to train to be a fireman. Three months was enough, as his father had intuited. Kieślowski was now ready to study. By chance he was accepted to an arts school in Warsaw, where he was exposed to theater and the cinema—a world with different values from the everyday world that emphasized money and comfort. Kieślowski fell in love with theater and wanted to be a stage director. Determined to study at film school in Lodz, he applied three times before he was accepted; he graduated in 1969.

Although his film career was threatened continually by political and economic change within Poland, Kieślowski made black and white documentaries, including an astounding series of ten films based on the Ten Commandments, made for Polish television. *Decalogue* brought him to the attention of international audiences.

In Poland he had to contend with political censorship. Then, after political censorship was abolished, he had to contend with the economic crisis and the lack of funds in Poland to make films. Kieślowski has pointed out that in many ways it was easier to trick the censors than to deal with the profit-ridden mandates of commercial filmmaking. Nevertheless, his elegant, intimate, and spiritual films, *The Double Life of Veronique* and his trilogy, *Three Colours: Red, White,* and *Blue,* have received an array of international awards.

In addition to his emphasis on the importance of craft, Kieślowski's advice to young filmmakers is to examine their own lives and to develop themselves by looking within to see what brought them to direct a particular film. If the artist doesn't understand his own life, Kieślowski asks, how can he understand the lives of the characters in the stories and the lives of the audience?

Known for his modesty and awareness of the many pitfalls of getting to the top, Kieślowski says that he doesn't like the word *success*. It suggests a static state in which we are likely to forget human pain and what it means to suffer and to hurt. This results in failing to care about ourselves and others. Kieślowski's wisdom about the importance of humility and cultivating the Artisan is shared by many artists of living—people who know that developing the dexterity to live is essential to mature creative life.

Cultivating Care

Because the creative process requires the courage to enter the unknown and to live with chaos until we find the threads of meaning that can help us weave the new work, we must learn, like the Artisan, to cultivate the care, patience, and strength to dwell in paradox. This is as true for the person who is consciously striving to lead a creative life as it is for the artist struggling to create a new artwork. Learning to live in the tension of opposites, like the ones we have been exploring in this book, is inherent to the human condition and is part of the challenge of the call to create.

Let us return to our mythic heroine Psyche, who had to learn to contain the opposites in order to recover her relationship with Eros. Psyche's tasks are tasks that must be completed within the psyche of the creative person. You will recall that Psyche's first task was to sort and separate into appropriate piles an infinite and chaotic mass of seeds. Psyche fell into despair when faced with this impossible task that no human alone could perform. But help came from an unexpected source when some worker ants appeared to assist her with this task.

Sorting is a task essential to any creative process, as the Artisan well knows. For example, a film director must sort out and select from a multitudinous number of images; an artist must choose the colors and shapes for a painting and decide where to place them on the canvas; a writer must sift out and order which words to use and how. Similarly, any person endeavoring to lead a creative and spiritual life must sort out the emotions and thoughts that have been obstacles to growth and choose from a myriad of possibilities the values by which to live.

Psyche's second task shows a way to deal with the raving energy released by the sorting process. She must gather the fleece from raging solar rams so ferocious that no mortal human risks to go near them. Faced with this terrifying task, Psyche is about to quit and jump into the river when a reed growing nearby the river's edge whispers to her the secret way to do it.

It is too dangerous to approach the rams head-on in daylight, the reed tells her. But if she can wait until nightfall when the rams are asleep, then she can gather the fleece that has caught on the bushes through which the rams have stormed. The rams' fleece is akin to the fiery energy that we encounter when we create.

Stories abound of artists who have been consumed by the creative fire when they do not understand how to approach it. Many are consumed by addictions or by attempts at suicide, as we have seen in the cases of the rise and fall of Stars.

The way to approach this energy, the reed advises Psyche, is to be patient and to wait until the right moment, when it is possible to gather a small amount of fleece at a time. This is the way of the Artisan, who knows the importance of patience in trying to harvest and contain creative fire.

Learning to contain creative energy is the brunt of Psyche's third task—to procure and collect the water from the river that flows between the peak of a mountain, surrounded by menacing serpents, and the bottom of the underworld. Once more the task feels impossible to Psyche, who is about to give up. But an eagle appears from nowhere and assists her by flying to the mountaintop and delivering water in a crystal bowl.

The crystal bowl is an image for containing the waters of spiritual life—the waters of the soul for which the creative person thirsts in the depths of deflation and the heights of inflated aspirations. In order to create, we must be able to contain the emotional energy that flows between the heights and the depths—that is, the agony and the ecstasy of creation.

Like Psyche, the artisans of life must learn to form the crystal container within themselves to hold the tension of these opposites in creative consciousness. And as artisans who work together understand, in that process we must be able to accept the love and help of others as Psyche accepted the aid of the ants, the reed, and the eagle in the myth.

Accepting the challenge to create ourselves and our world means that we must be ready and willing to embrace the agony and ecstasy inherent in creation. This means learning to acknowledge and live with the anxiety, frustration, discomfort, restlessness, depression, boredom, and loneliness that can seize us in the act of creation. We must also be able to greet the ecstasy, thrills, and joy that are part of this process. Paradoxically, some people find containing the rapture and bliss of creation as hard as bearing its torments.

The Artisan of life knows that instead of trying to be the special

Star, she can look up in the night sky and see the stars all shining together in the galaxy. Each one of us is like a beautiful shining star amidst the multitudes that light up the world. Accepting oneself as a part of the whole creative cycle takes the wisdom to know that each person sparkles with a unique light that can combine with others in harmony to illumine and enlighten life.

Part III
THE BLOSSOMING

. . . all progress must come from deep within and cannot be pressed or hurried by anything. Everything is gestation and then bringing forth. To let each impression and each germ of a feeling come to completion wholly in itself, in the dark, in the inexpressible, the unconscious, beyond the reach of one's own intelligence, and await with deep humility and patience the birth-hour of a new clarity; that alone is living the artist's life; in understanding as in creating. There is here no measuring with time, no year matters and ten years are nothing. Being an artist means, not reckoning and counting, but ripening like the tree which does not force its sap and stands confident in the storms of spring without the fear that after them may come no summer. It does come. But it comes only to the patient, who are there as though eternity lay before them, so unconcernedly still and wide. I learn it daily, learn it with pain to which I am grateful: patience is everything!

Rainer Maria Rilke

8
PLAY

An artist is a child always and sees things with childlike wonder. That is what makes him an artist.

Federico Fellini

THE DUMMLING SHOWS THE PERFECTIONIST HOW TO PLAY

When the Tyrant finds he cannot bully us into submission, he steps aside for the Perfectionist. The Perfectionist sabotages creativity by projecting an absolute standard that we cannot hope to reach. It says, "You'll never measure up; you'll never do it right; you'll never be effective; you don't have the right stuff." This leads to feeling like a failure and to the fear that one is a fraud, which then paralyzes us.

In the workshops I have given on creativity, an overwhelming number of people say that the major obstacle to seeing themselves as creative is that they feel like a fraud. Over and over I hear the following words of despair: "I feel like a fraud when I try to create, when I express my values, and when I expose my creations to the world."

Since I have experienced the same inner indictment, these replies do not surprise me. In response I always ask, "What obstructs your creativity?" For example, a university professor in her forties said that she had stopped writing for two years after she had received an overwhelmingly positive response from her publisher to the first part of her book. Although she was a competent scholar, she was afraid she would be exposed in public as a fraud. Inside her head a voice kept nagging her with the following reproach: "Who do you think you are to try to write a book?" Upon hearing this woman's worry, an editor from a large publishing firm acknowledged her fears and added, "I can write a book, but I feel like I have nothing to say."

The Dummling Shows the Perfectionist How to Play

In one group, a wife and mother talked about the following common obstacle to creativity. She said, "I need permission from others to express myself." She, too, felt blocked by fear and said, "If I expose my creative work, I'm afraid I'll get criticized and rejected." A psychiatrist added, "I fear people will ridicule me every time I stand up to give a public lecture." Then a dancer, who had already performed in public, reported the following doubt: "My first show was successful, but can I do it again? I always feel I need to top myself."

A physician spoke of a difficulty that plagued many people. "About halfway through starting a project," he said, "I quit. I can't seem to finish anything." To this remark a talented artist, who had dared to show her work to a group, said, "I can finish my paintings, but I'm afraid to put them out into the world and risk rejection." Then an executive secretary voiced a feeling shared by many: "I'm not really good at anything." A lament common to most of the men and women in the workshops was related by an accomplished CEO: "Although I am a successful businesswoman and earn a lot of money, I don't see myself as creative. I'm just an ordinary person. Who am I to create?"

Doubts such as these undermine creativity. They are voiced in the clever, caustic, and controlling words of an inner saboteur who obstructs people from starting, finishing, or showing their creative lives and work to others. Shame, guilt, and feelings of being an impostor accompany this syndrome and promote depression, low self-esteem, and even self-abuse. Frustration, resignation, and impotence feed these feelings of illegitimacy that stifle inner authority and suffocate creative life.

At bottom these feelings of mistrust and self-doubt come from the Perfectionist—a character in ourselves whose ideals and private goals derive from a comparison to an absolute standard that is impossible for humans to reach.

THE PERFECTIONIST'S PLAGUE—FEELING LIKE A FRAUD

Since I, too, have experienced feeling like a fraud, I began to ponder its origins. Feeling like a fraud—what is its source, and how does it prevent creativity? I believe these feelings of illegitimacy stem from our personal histories, which in turn are shaped by the hierarchical value system and the linear rational structures embedded in Western society. The challenge to create requires that we transform these feelings of illegitimacy in ourselves and in society.

When we compare our own accomplishments to those of others, or when we measure them against our own prior achievements, we are caught in the Perfectionist's artificially constructed ideals. The Perfectionist ranks enterprises, achievements, and even personal life according to a preconceived hierarchical criterion that subverts creativity. Envy results, splits us against one another (or ourselves), and cuts us off from creative conversation and collaboration.

The irony is that we can do this to ourselves. Just as external inquisitors denounced Joan of Arc as a witch whose visions came from the devil instead of God, our inner inquisitors can twist our words and distort our perceptions so that we cease to believe in ourselves and begin to feel like we are fraudulent.

Feeling like a fraud can overwhelm us with despair if we measure ourselves against perfectionist expectations that are impossible to reach. Up against the Perfectionist, we feel inferior because, as finite human beings, we can never measure up to ideal absolute standards. To transform the Perfectionist and the feeling of fraudulence, we need the hope of the Dummling.

On the personal level, I believe my own feelings of fraudulence stem from the sense of shame that I felt as the child of an alcoholic father who was publicly humiliated as he staggered home through the neighborhood streets. If the neighborhood kids were mad at me, they mocked me because my father was a drunk. Sometimes grown-ups—neighbors and shopkeepers from whom my father borrowed money—shamed me because I was his daughter. If my mother was angry with me, she would say, "You're just like your father." For years I struggled with this identification and worked hard to detach from it. I attempted to counter my feelings of disgrace by studying hard to get good grades and to escape my past through reading and learning.

My mother worked hard to survive and to support our family at minimum wages and had no time for extra activities like writing, reading, or scholarship. She chose to quit high school and considered my attempt to educate myself as impractical. My mother was bound by her generation's collective images of the feminine, and she expected me to mirror her own sense of duty and practicality. She often asked me why I couldn't be like the other girls in the neighborhood. When I headed down the path of the bohemian intellectual, romantic writer, and dreamer, she was shocked. But despite her fears for me, she loved me. I remember her telling me to stand up straight, hold my head high, and feel proud of myself even when others belittled me. My mother helped me to learn to be a survivor.

The Call to Create

Even though I became successful as a teacher, therapist, and writer, feelings of shame haunted me for many years. While the accusation "fraud" did not torment me when I wrote in private, it tortured me whenever I appeared in public to present my work. This fear was reflected in recurrent dreams of a rational and ridiculing "attacker" in the audience. I believe the fear of feeling like a fraud was directly linked to that inner conspirator, the Perfectionist. In order to compensate for my father's failure, I wanted to be opposite to him. At the time this seemed to require being perfect and adapting to the academic system.

It was when I wrote my first book, *The Wounded Woman,* that I discovered that the low sense of self-esteem and lack of personal authority that I felt in public situations came from a secret desire to compensate for my father's failure by becoming a paradigm of perfection and success. I also began clearly to see that I was not alone.

Feeling like a fraud is bound in Western culture's yoke of perfectionism, which stems from the dualistic, linear, patriarchal value system we have adopted. In *The Wounded Woman* I explored the injuries to women and men resulting from the wounds of the personal and societal fathers. In a later book, *Meeting the Madwoman,* I continued to look at ways in which imbalanced patriarchy affects and restricts women's lives.

I am convinced that it is important for women and men to speak from the heart. As I began to do this myself in lectures, my fears subsided. I decided that I spoke best when I sat, told stories that illustrated my ideas, and talked conversationally with the audience. I like to weave visions and ideas with people's comments and to stimulate them to reflect and express their own thoughts and feelings.

Lecturing from behind the podium is not consistent with my personal teaching style. But colleagues suggested that I stand up and speak with command to enhance my image as an author. People were surprised to see that I was a small woman and not the tall blond amazon they had expected. I learned that many people want the author to be an expert whom they can place on the pedestal and idolize. But I feel it is "fraudulent" to accept this role, for it runs counter to the spirit of being human and separates us from one another.

Shortly before this book was about to go to press, a friend showed me a stimulating article on this very subject by Peggy McIntosh, program director at the Wellesley College Center for Research on Women.[1] In it she made a very interesting point about feeling like a fraud. Feeling like a fraud, she suggested, is an internalized destructive feeling that works against us. But, it can also be a genuine feeling that points to the fraudulence of dishonest public roles and behaviors that an artificial, hierarchical, power-based system imposes upon us and expects of us. If we recognize this as true for ourselves when we feel like frauds, we can reap the wisdom to see and expose inauthentic authority. We can also resist disempowering hierarchies by establishing peaceful communities in which creative conversation can take place.

ANNE-MARIE'S INNER INQUISITOR

Anne-Marie, a French-Canadian woman in her forties, shared the following story. She had grown up in an environment in which well-known artists frequently came to her home to visit her parents. Her father was a prominent professor, and her mother enjoyed hosting salons for the creative people who gathered at their house. Because the energy of both parents was directed toward their famous friends, they tended to slight their children. At the same time both parents expected great things of their sons and daughters.

Anne-Marie remembered that when she was eight years old, her mother had disparaged her childish paintings of water lilies by degrading them in comparison to the work of Monet. If Anne-Marie was not a genius, how could she be an artist? Anne-Marie stopped painting the water lilies that she loved.

Throughout Anne-Marie's childhood and adolescence, her perfectionist mother continued to compare Anne-Marie's artwork to that of well-known artists who came to their salons. Unconsciously Anne-Marie adopted her mother's standards of greatness and judged her own efforts by them. Her major fear was to appear foolish in her mother's eyes or those of anyone else. For a while she turned to making jewelry. But she felt her work was not good enough, and so she quit.

Anne-Marie decided not to go to the art school where she wanted to study. Instead she enrolled in law school and became a corporate lawyer—a field in which she could defend herself against her mother. Although Anne-Marie continued to paint, she regarded it as a hobby, thereby unconsciously slighting its value in her life. After her fortieth birthday she started to suffer from a deep depression and sought the help of a therapist. In the course of her therapeutic work, she realized that she was applying her mother's perfectionist standards to herself.

The Perfectionist had taken over in her psyche whenever she started to draw. After she had finished a drawing, she would look at it in despair, assuming that it couldn't measure up to the work of other artists. Scoffing at her own artwork, Anne-Marie hid it in the bottom drawer of her desk. She ceased to enjoy drawing, yet she felt a compulsive need to continue doing it.

One day when Anne-Marie went for an appointment, her therapist suggested she do a sandbox during the hour. The therapist led Anne-Marie to an adjacent room and showed her an empty box filled only with sand. Next to the sandbox were shelves of tiny toylike figurines. The therapist told her that she could choose whatever she liked from these shelves, put them in the sandbox, and play with them.

Hesitant at first, Anne-Marie picked out a brown ostrich and put it in the box. Then she chose a brightly colored peacock. Soon Anne-Marie lost track of time as she chose the figurines with delight and created a unique world within the sandbox. Together she and her therapist admired what Anne-Marie had created. Anne-Marie liked making the sandbox so much that she continued this throughout the course of her therapy. As she designed the sandboxes, Anne-Marie discovered that she was able to play in a way that had been discouraged during childhood. Moreover, her therapist also delighted in Anne-Marie's creative compositions.

In this playful atmosphere there were no comparisons, no standards to meet, no judgmental feedback to fear. By experiencing the freedom of creating in this way, Anne-Marie returned to painting with the joy and bliss that she felt during her sand play sessions. Now she was able to bring this spirited attitude to infuse her life.

The interior Perfectionist that promotes doubts of the kind Anne-Marie experienced promotes unhealthy attitudes toward creativity.

For example, the British writer Jean Rhys was publicly honored when her novel *Wide Sargasso Sea* won highly esteemed British awards for service to literature. Inwardly, however, Rhys felt like a fraud. She was so obsessed that her books should be perfect that her agent-husband forcibly took away her manuscripts to send them to her publisher. Rhys was unable to let them go because she felt her work had flaws. Although Rhys tried to work through her feelings of failure and imperfection by writing, she used alcohol to flee from her pain and to find the perfect ending for her novels.

Rhys's inner Perfectionist was probably formed in girlhood by a combination of factors. She always felt like an outsider. She was viewed as a foreigner on Dominica, the Caribbean island where she grew up. Her intuitive bent of mind was dismissed as far-fetched by conservative teachers and schoolmates. To them she was an anathema.

Rhys believed that her romantic and sensitive nature was so alien to that of her practical and emotionally distant mother that she failed to win her mother's love. Her father, a Welsh country doctor, was rarely home; he traveled around the island for his practice. This family pattern of a rejecting mother and an absent father frequently leads to an excruciating sensitivity to rejection and to the "Ghostly Lover" syndrome. Rhys later believed that she had fabricated an idealistic and romanticized view of her father due to his absence. She continued this pattern later in England with her first and greatest love, Lancelot. She idealized this unavailable man, who remained a lifelong "Ghostly Lover" in her fantasies.

Longing for the perfect love that is impossible for finite human beings to obtain, Rhys became overly susceptible to rejection. Rebuffs overwhelmed her. At the end of her life she wrote that she felt "cold" and lonely. Rhys's story is similar to that of many women and men whose desire for the perfect partner leaves them feeling like failures in love relationships. Often they become bitter and complain that they can't meet the "right" person. But developing a healthy relationship, like any other form of creativity, requires a long-term, continual process of discovery. We must find how to communicate effectively, acknowledge weaknesses and strengths, and learn from failures and feats in ongoing dialogue with our partners.

If we let the Perfectionist rule our lives, we allow ourselves to be controlled by autocratic goals set by a despotic tyrant. Whether measured against a model of perfection set by an outer authority or by our own inner compulsion to be best and first, we secretly feel like impostors. In bondage to the Perfectionist, we cower in fear and apprehension that we will be exposed.

Western society fosters this reaction by relegating creativity to a corner of human existence rather than understanding that it is central to life. Dualistic ways of thinking—black/white, right/wrong, creative/not creative—are split into irreconcilable oppositions. When we sever reality into either/or factions, we split off imaginative expression from ordinary daily life. For example, if we sever the creative process from its product and judge ourselves by the success or failure of the outcome, we ignore the excitement, joy, and wonder of the unfolding process.

The Perfectionist is an inner saboteur that stems from a cultural and educational milieu that tends to give precedence to the linear way of learning. Its formula emphasizes competition, comparison, and a hierarchical model that can discourage uniqueness and innovations that depart from the established norm. Many under the sway of this model have ridiculed the originator throughout the history of science and art.

For example, the Norwegian artist Edvard Munch was ridiculed by critics of his work along with the impressionists before him. Munch's paintings were mocked and belittled in comparison to those of preceding artists. No wonder that he expressed his feelings by creating the powerful painting *The Scream.* This painting was devalued in Munch's lifetime. *The Scream* is now worth millions of dollars and is coveted by art collectors all over the world.

This experience is familiar to many creative people. Consider the "failures" of Van Gogh and Gauguin in their own time, or the derision that Stravinsky's *The Rite of Spring* received when it was first performed. The inventor Thomas Edison was also called a fraud by his colleagues.

Edison experimented laboriously for more than a year to develop the electric light. Even when he succeeded and throngs of people came to witness the new wonder, a former colleague protested "in behalf of true science" that Edison's experiments were "a conspicuous failure, trumpeted as a wonderful success. A fraud upon the public."[2] Even though they saw the results with their own eyes, his fellow scientists did not believe it. Edison's critics, like those of Munch, were caught in the conformist trap of the status quo.

Our creations, like our lives, are never all good or all bad—they are works in process. This is why many artists prefer not to look back at former works but rather would continue with their next projects. They do not regard their artworks as mere products; the process of creating is what excites them. Many filmmakers like Buñuel and

Tarkovsky say that once they finish a film, they don't want to look at it again. The call to create summons them to their new project. Like Picasso, who once said that he was more interested in the art that he had not yet painted, they move on to new and different periods in their creative work.

In a society that is product- and market-oriented we can be tempted to think that the end result is all that matters. The emphasis of product over process lures us to forget that it is the act of creating that gives us a sense of wonder, ecstasy, and awe. We ignore what creative people tell us: The *process* of giving birth to something new is what they enjoy. They create to discover new forms of expression, to perceive new meaning, and to reveal fresh aspects of life.

If we do not believe that creativity is a process essential to our human search for meaning, or if we believe that creativity exists only in the rarefied atmosphere of great art and not in the pursuits of ordinary life, we are in danger of retreating when confronted with the call to create. This was Jane's experience, as she related it in the following story.

JANE'S DISCOVERY

The story of a gifted woman who humorously calls herself "Jane Citizen" illustrates the view of creativity that has influenced many of us. Jane grew up in a small town in the Midwest. She remembers a time in kindergarten when the teacher asked the children to draw pictures of themselves on a brown bag by filling in some outlines. It was near Halloween, and the children were told they could use the bags as masks. Jane made a portrait of herself with bushy wild hair. Her drawing extended beyond the lines of the prescribed fill-it-in model. She used the crayons in the box to paint her hair in many different vibrant colors—various colors she had seen in her own hair. Jane loved drawing her "wild child" so much. She was happy with her portrait and looked forward to showing it to her teacher.

When the teacher saw Jane's painting, however, she was shocked and punished her for not following directions. In the teacher's view, blond-haired girls were supposed to paint their hair yellow, and the brunettes to paint their hair brown. Instead of seeing Jane's drawing as a creative venture, the teacher thought she was rebellious and had mocked the assignment. First the teacher criticized Jane and humiliated her before the class. Then she punished the five-year-old girl by sending her out of the classroom to stand alone in the hall.

Later, as an adult, Jane reflected that the teacher may have falsely assumed that the little girl was threatening her authority; she had accused Jane of scribbling colors and not following directions. Jane traced her feeling that she was uncreative to this and other "educational" experiences. At school she was expected to repeat the standard prescribed model rather than to find her individual way of learning. This led her to think of creativity as a "noun" rather than as an ongoing process.

At home Jane's parents praised her brother for his artistic talent. But when Jane created something, she felt that they ignored it or compared it to her brother's output. When she took piano lessons, she remembers, both her parents and teachers pointed out what she did wrong rather than encouraging her for what she did right. Jane had been excited to learn how to play the piano. But after this experience she became disillusioned, and her enthusiasm and playfulness were dampened.

"I didn't consider myself good enough or creative enough because teachers always pointed to what was wrong with my playing. I became frustrated and felt guilty because I was supposed to do it right," Jane recalled. Twenty years later she had the same experience as an adult playing in an orchestra. The conductor emphasized only the flaws of the musicians. When he singled out Jane, she felt humiliated, guilty, and shamed. Many of the other musicians shared her experience.

One time when Jane came home with an A-minus grade, her father asked her why she didn't get an A plus. She was expected to be the best in her class. Jane was beginning to encounter the Perfectionist critic at home and at school. Yet when Jane's essay won first prize in an English class, her father accused her of not writing it herself. No matter what she did, it seemed, she was taken to be a failure or a fraud. Jane began to feel that she was a failure at home and at school. She felt she was a loser as a person because she failed to be "good enough."

Many years later, as an adult in therapy, Jane began to realize that her father was threatened by smartness in women. He hadn't gone to college, while her mother had graduated with honors. In her family her mother was also the creative one. Jane realized that her mother was bound by perfectionist standards, which she imposed upon her daughter. During Jane's adolescence her mother was especially critical of Jane's appearance. If Jane looked different in any way—especially when her hairstyle seemed too sensuous or when she looked sexually attractive—Jane's mother would criticize her. She would say to Jane, "That tight sweater makes you look too fat" or "Your hair is too wild and unkempt." Meanwhile her father focused on his son's achievements, neglecting his daughter.

Despite Jane's intellectual accomplishments (she now holds a doctoral degree and works with innovation in her profession as an elementary school teacher trying to encourage students to create) and her artistic practice (she is a musician in an orchestra), she still tends to exclude herself from the list of creative people. Jane expressed it this way: "I am not only not creative; I feel I have a genetic lack. I'm not even true to myself because I'm in bad faith about creativity. I'm not committed to all that I can be because I tend to be lazy and cowardly." Instead of giving herself credit for all that she does, Jane tends to devalue herself—a basic attitude that negates and undermines the creative work that she has accomplished and is still accomplishing.

The notion that the call to be human entails the call to create was a revelation for Jane. When she understood that choosing to become conscious and to develop through life's crises *is* a creative challenge, Jane began to think about herself differently. It also soothed her to discover that in other cultures, such as Bali, every person and every activity is considered creative. Sewing, cooking, carving, planting, dancing in rituals to honor the divinities—all are valued as creative acts.

As Jane began to realize that her view of creativity had been limited to a rigid cultural standard, she allowed herself to explore. She took a course in process painting that encourages the painter to relax, to let go, and to follow where the brush and colors take her. As she surrendered to this process, she began to enjoy the act of painting for itself.

Jane read this account of her story about a year after she first related it. As she read it, Jane said, she realized that today she feels quite different about her creative potential. With her broadened view, she now experiences herself as creative and acknowledges it. She takes responsibility for her creative potential.

By consciously differentiating her own views from the opinions she had taken automatically from her parents and her teachers, Jane gained the confidence, self-esteem, and courage to take a leap of faith into her own process rather than pursue a model approved by others. Now that she focuses on the process in both her painting and her life, instead of on a product, she feels free to allow the Dummling in herself to explore.

Jane felt inspired by movies such as *Stand and Deliver, Dangerous Minds, Mr. Holland's Opus,* and *Dead Poets Society*—all films that portray inventive, resourceful teachers who dedicate themselves to fostering the uniqueness and individuality of their students. Such films support Jane in her belief that Eros in education is essential for creativity and help her appreciate her own creativity as a teacher.

CARL GUSTAV JUNG'S SCHOOL DAYS

Accusations of cheating can accompany censure for being different from the prevailing standard or for doing something new. Gifted children, as in Jane's case, often suffer from such accusations. The psychiatrist Carl Gustav Jung recounts such an incident in his autobiography, *Memories, Dreams, Reflections.*[3]

Jung was like any gifted child who is sometimes more intelligent than his teachers. He was bored in school because the assigned themes seemed shallow and silly to him. He tended to be careless in his work and slipped by with average grades. Inwardly, however, he felt different from his classmates, because he was interested and engaged in facing fundamental human questions concerning good and evil and the relationship between God and the devil.

Jung felt like an outsider for many reasons. He was the son of a poor country parson and had to go to school with holes in his shoes and wear worn-out clothing, and he had no pocket money to spend like the other boys. In contrast, most of his schoolmates came from wealthy families. They were well dressed and had been taught refined manners. When they told of their vacations in the Alps or their trips to the seaside, Jung was astonished and felt envious. The grandeur and power of his classmates and their rich families overwhelmed him. He felt shy and ashamed of his humble origins.

Mathematics classes became a torture that he dreaded because he was unable to manipulate equations unless he understood the fundamental nature of numbers. His intense need to understand the foundations of whatever he was studying made him seem strange to most of his peers and teachers. Jung also got poor grades in drawing. Although he could draw what stirred his imagination, he was unable to copy from prints. He hated gymnastics because he abhorred practicing senseless acrobatics. As a result, his teachers thought that he was stupid and wily. Whenever there was a commotion in school, the teachers tended to suspect and blame Jung.

Feeling like a scapegoat, Jung became so intimidated by the accusations, the fear of failure, and his sense of smallness when compared with his classmates that he began to have fainting spells. For a while he was allowed to stay away from school.

While this reprieve relieved him, since it freed him to plunge into his imagination, to enjoy his solitude, and to immerse himself in the wonders of nature, he also feared he might be fleeing from himself. One day Jung overheard his father express his worry: The doctors thought Jung might have epilepsy. Jung's father also feared for his son's survival in case he couldn't earn a living. Jung was shocked.

For the first time Jung seriously started to work at his studies. He learned Latin. He also began to read the books in his father's library. In particular he was fascinated by Goethe's *Faust*, which ponders the eternal questions of God's existence, the paradox of good and evil, and the power of the devil.

About this time Jung had a series of overwhelming dreams that surprised and astounded him. The vivid dreams, his awe of nature, and the questions confronting him about the meaning of existence gave him a sense of purpose and direction. But these experiences also increased his feeling of isolation from his schoolmates and his teachers. He hid his rich inner life, slid through school with average grades, and tried not to be conspicuous.

Then one day at school he received an assignment that interested him. He worked hard to produce a well-written, thoughtful paper for which he expected to receive a high mark. The teacher, who discussed the compositions in the order of their excellence, spoke first to the prize student of the class. Then he discussed the work of all the other boys except Jung, who couldn't believe his composition was that bad. Finally the teacher turned to Jung and said that his composition was by far the best and deserved first place. "But," the teacher added, "unfortunately it is a fraud. Where did you copy it from? Confess the truth!"

Furious, Jung protested, but the teacher insisted he was lying. Jung was singled out as being a cheat, an accusation that offended his moral sensibility. He felt dishonored, and his grief and rage almost erupted out of control. Since Jung was introspective, he reflected on his reactions. When he looked within, he realized that the teacher's misunderstanding and mistrust of him was like his own distrust of himself and others. This insight freed him to see that the teacher was limited.[4] Once Jung understood the psychodynamics of this event, he was able to let go of the injustice and continue privately on his unique quest for wisdom.

By comprehending that the accusation of fraud came from a teacher who judged him from a limited perspective that allowed no differences beyond conventional standards, and by understanding that the teacher's suspicion corresponded to an inner mistrust of himself, Jung was able to free himself from the inner shame and fear of being a fraud.

If, like Jung, we reflect introspectively and identify the Perfectionist that denounces us as fraud, we can prevent ourselves from taking on false projections that sabotage creativity. By recognizing the damaging dualism that results and detecting the way it operates in ourselves and society, we can transform it. Then we will find the freedom to explore and express the great wealth of creativity in our lives.

THE DUMMLING

In view of his experience as a schoolboy, it is not surprising that Jung, in his description of archetypal patterns in the human psyche, pinpointed the Dummling as an important character for creative transformation.

Jung is not alone in his experience of being accused as stupid and recalcitrant. As we have seen in the example of Jane's story, gifted children are frequently considered to be rebellious, stupid, or foolish simply because they seem different from other children.

The Nobel Prize winner for literature Hermann Hesse is an example. When he was a schoolboy, Hesse was regarded as so clumsy and dumb by his teachers that his parents placed him in a school for retarded children.

Janet Frame, the New Zealand writer whose life is portrayed in Jane Campion's film *An Angel at My Table,* seemed awkward, shy, and inept to the male supervisors who came to judge her teaching at school. They relegated her to a mental asylum. Despite electroshock and insulin treatments given to her while she was in the asylum, Frame was able to write short stories, which she smuggled out to her sister when she came to visit. Frame's sister gave the stories to a publisher, who admired them. When her first book was published and the public discovered that the gifted writer was incarcerated in an asylum, her admirers protested. Frame was released and became one of New Zealand's most admired and respected authors.

The Dummling is a figure in many fairy tales—for example, the Grimm brothers' "The Golden Goose" and "Three Feathers." Shakespeare portrays Dummling figures in his plays. One example is the Fool who offers wisdom to the patriarch in *King Lear.* Cervantes's *Don Quixote* depicts another example of the Dummling in literature.

In movies Buster Keaton, Charlie Chaplin, and Peter Sellers enact the Dummling—a sympathetic simpleton whom we find endearing.

Several years ago the Oscar-winning film *Forrest Gump* raised the Dummling figure from the cultural unconscious of the contemporary Western world to public attention and acclaim. *Forrest Gump* shows the instinctive, joyful creativity of the Fool that can help us in our struggle with the Perfectionist. But many critics viewed this modern film tale on the literal level; thus they overlooked its symbolic significance as a parable.

In *Life Is Beautiful* the 1999 Italian film that won several Oscars, Roberto Begnini plays the part of a Dummling whose spontaneity, naïveté, and trickster qualities help him shield his son from the horrors of the Holocaust. You will recognize the character that Begnini plays in the following description of the Dummling.

In fairy tales a typical Dummling story goes like this. The Dummling is the youngest son and is so naïve that he is ridiculed by his father. In contrast, his older brothers are clever, practical, and act rationally according to calculated egoistic plans. The father and brothers mock and sneer at the youngest because they believe he is stupid and a bumbler.

In the typical tale a perfectionist father assigns his sons the task of fetching some wood or finding a specific treasure before nightfall. On the appointed day the father gives a good lunch and a fine bottle of wine to his eldest son, who sets forth in the forest with enough food and a thought-out plan to reach his goal. On the way a hungry animal stops the eldest brother and asks him for food. This brother refuses to give the animal anything because he wants to keep all the food and drink for himself. He is determined to let nothing divert him from his goal. Despite his calculated formula for success, he has an accident and at nightfall returns home hurt and empty-handed.

The Dummling Shows the Perfectionist How to Play

The next day the father asks his second son to find the treasure and gives him a hearty lunch to take on his journey. The second son approaches the task just as his elder brother did. He, too, has a rational plan. He refuses the hungry animal in the forest and keeps his food for himself. Like the elder brother, he returns home at the end of the day empty-handed. Disappointed, the father complains about the ineptitude of his sons.

When the youngest brother, the Dummling, asks his father to let him try to find the treasure, his brothers smirk and sneer. "How could such a simpleton do anything?" they jeer in derision. "Especially if we couldn't succeed." Dummling's father doesn't think his youngest son can succeed at anything. But when Dummling continues to beg him, his father lets him attempt the task to find the treasure. The father gives Dummling the only food that is left—some crusts of bread and sour beer. Dummling enters the forest without a plan. Soon he is lost and sits down by a tree to eat his meager lunch. When a woodchuck approaches and asks him for some crumbs, Dummling smiles and shares his food with the little creature. The woodchuck asks him what he is doing in the forest. As the woodchuck leaves, he thanks Dummling, who proceeds on his way.

After a long time Dummling, still lost, sits down on the ground to cry. A little voice from some bushes nearby calls out to the Dummling to comfort him and asks what is troubling him so much. The comforter is the creature with whom Dummling shared his lunch. The grateful woodchuck knows the forest well and guides Dummling to find the treasure. When Dummling returns home before nightfall with the prize, his brothers gape at his success. In amazement his father congratulates the son he has disparaged.

If the Dummling thinks he cannot perform the impossible task set by the father, he is likely to sit down and weep instead of trying to prove himself. His tears often save him because he is not ashamed to acknowledge his weakness and vulnerability. The Dummling is able to be patient and wait because he trusts that help will come. Since he has a good heart and shares whatever he has, the creatures of the forest befriend and help him. Because the Dummling surrenders control, approval, and traditional ego orientation, he appears unsuccessful, naïve, and foolish to the collective eye. But when all the familiar and known ways fail, the Dummling bumbles and stumbles into a new discovery because he is not rigid. The Dummling's receptivity and openness to the unknown allow the creative element to enter.

At one time or another on the journey to create, most of us have felt like the Dummling who does not know his way. But if, like the Dummling, we trust our hearts and instincts to guide us, we may blunder into new possibilities. When we create, we need the naïveté to wander in the mystery of the forest. We need to have the trust and courage to allow ourselves to become lost, and the compassion and generosity to help and feed others who are on the journey. In this way we reach beyond ourselves and become part of a bigger whole.

Sometimes, like the Dummling, we simply need to sit down and cry, because tears allow us to be vulnerable and ask for help. Tears also lubricate our eyes so that we can see in a new way. Tears reveal the vulnerability and openness that soften us. In this way tears allow the breakthrough of fresh insight or a new way of relating that has been missing.

In contrast to the Perfectionist, the Dummling proceeds without a plan, without knowing the way or the outcome—and stumbles upon wisdom. This is the way of creative people who follow the path of discovery rather than paths that are already known. We can choose between echoing the Perfectionist's voice or joining the Dummling, whose spontaneous movements and generous heart can ease and encourage us along the way.

THE POWER OF PLAY

Early in his career Jung was negatively portrayed as a Dummling by his colleagues. Jung's explorations of the psyche—particularly in such areas as extrasensory perception, precognition, parapsychology, telepathic phenomena, and the significance of synchronistic happenings—were mocked as fool's play by his "elder brothers."

Jung's claim that nonlinear and nonrational modes of perception such as intuition and feeling are valid ways of knowing was ridiculed. His notion of the "collective unconscious," a sphere of the psyche that is universal for people of all cultures, was dismissed as foolish. Western psychologists scorned Jung when he contended that learning about images and symbols by studying mythology, anthropology, and the world religions can help us to understand more about our dreams, our own lives, and modern society. When he suggested that the rituals and way of life of so-called "primitive peoples" might give us understanding of nature and psychological knowledge that the Western world lacked, many thought he was mad.

When Jung contested the absolutism of Freud's sexual theory and noted the spiritual significance of incest as a symbol, Freud clung to his literal interpretation and broke off their friendship. Freud could not go along with the spiritual direction that Jung affirmed as inherent in the psyche. Most of Jung's friends and colleagues followed Freud and declared that Jung's work was "rubbish." He was rebuked as a "mystic," which, to his critics at that time, implied that his approach was irrational and antithetical to empirical science.

At first Jung suffered from inner uncertainty and felt disoriented. But then, in 1912, during the Christmas holidays, he had a dream that helped him. In the dream Jung found himself in a magnificent Italian loggia, set high in the tower of a castle. Jung sat on a gold Renaissance chair. In front of him was a rare, exquisite table made of green stone, like emerald. Jung's children were sitting at the table too. A white dove suddenly descended and rested on the table. The dove unexpectedly changed itself into a little girl with golden blond hair, about eight years old. The girl ran off with Jung's children and played with them while Jung sat musing about what he had seen. Soon the girl returned and placed her arms tenderly around Jung's neck, then vanished. The dove took her place. Speaking slowly in a human voice, the dove told Jung that she could transform herself into a human being only during the first hour of the night, while the male dove was busy with the twelve dead. Jung awoke as the dove flew off into the sky.

Although Jung could not fathom the entire meaning of the dream, particularly the last part, it left him with a feeling of awe and wonder. Still under the sway of his sense of disorientation, he began to reflect on his childhood. He remembered that when he was ten years old, he used to play passionately with building blocks and stones, assembling houses and castles. Along with this emotional memory, Jung realized that as a small boy he had experienced creative life with a vitality that he found missing as an adult. Although at the time he felt it was humiliating to turn toward childish games, the dream helped Jung realize that it was necessary to reestablish contact with that period in his boyhood.

Jung was wise enough to acknowledge his own ignorance, and he said to himself, "Since I know nothing at all, I shall simply do whatever occurs to me."[5] And so he consciously surrendered to impulses that sprang from the unconscious. Jung started to gather stones from the water and the lake shore near his home. With the stones he built an entire village, including cottages and a castle. Finally, he constructed a church with an altar, an act that led him to recall an important childhood dream that had changed his life.

Jung continued with his building game at lunchtime until his afternoon patients arrived. Sometimes he continued in the early evening after they had left. While Jung was building, his thoughts clarified and released a flow of fantasies, which he recorded. He understood that returning to childhood play was a necessary part of the process of discovering the myth by which he lived. He also envisioned that this myth might be the myth of modern man as well. Moreover, the physical contact with the water, earth, and stones helped him regain his stability.

Throughout his life and into old age, Jung constantly returned to play—to drawing, painting, and building with stones. In the course of this play he built a tower with stones that he gathered in a solitary place at the upper end of the Zürichsee—a place that became his haven. To the outer eye of the Perfectionist, Jung may have looked naïve and foolish. But inwardly Jung had recognized the creative power of the playful Dummling.

To counter the obstacles that the Perfectionist within ourselves places in our way and to transform and heal the feelings that we are frauds, we must allow ourselves to be humble and to enjoy the simple appreciation of the creative act itself. And, although it may seem contradictory and puzzling, the way for us to reclaim self-respect and self-esteem from the Perfectionist's domination is to accept, as Jung did, a certain naïveté and even foolishness in ourselves—like that of the Dummling who stumbles into creativity.

The creative challenge for those of us who are caught in the stranglehold of perfectionism is to admit that we are mortal humans; it is necessary to surrender our wish to be gods. One important key here is humor. Humor is healing. If we can laugh kindly with ourselves and others when the frustrations and failures that accompany discovery arise, we will experience the joy of play—a delight that every child experiences while creating castles in the sand or forming fortresses in the mud—that is, unless an adult Perfectionist criticizes the child and subdues his or her imagination. And then we must turn to our inner Dummling, who can heal us again with play and laughter.

9
COMPASSION

You are working for the whole, you are acting for the future. . . . Know the measure, know the times, study that. When you are left alone pray. Love to throw yourself on the earth and kiss it. Kiss the earth and love it with an unceasing, consuming love. Love all men, love everything. Seek that rapture and ecstasy. Water the earth with the tears of your joy and love those tears. Don't be ashamed of that ecstasy, prize it, for it is a gift of God and a great one.

Fyodor Dostoyevsky

THE LOVER OPENS
THE CRITIC'S HEART

Each of us can destroy our creative work and kill ourselves in little ways that lead to loss of soul—a tragic story that I have heard many times in the course of my work in the field of creativity. An inner character that typically plays a part in such ruin is the Critic.

The hurtful voice of the Critic ensues from the cruel collaboration of the Cynic, the Tyrant, the Escape Artist, the Star, the Conformist, and the Perfectionist—all actors at play in the interior theater of the psyche. When these characters collude surreptitiously in our minds, they can tempt us to disregard the call to create as shrewdly as Mephistopheles seduced Faust.

In order to avoid becoming hostage to these characters, we need to become alert to their verbal bait. We can do this by identifying their lingo and by detecting the distinct moods and tones of their voices. This conscious work will help us recognize the times when they deluge us with destructive discourse that obscures our capacity to discriminate.

The Cynic, who says no to life, may mock us by sneering, "Why bother to create? Nothing will come of it." The Tyrant, who seeks power, threatens us by ordering, "Don't speak without my permission! Don't create unless I tell you to!" The Perfectionist argues, "Whatever you do must be flawless. If you can't be perfect, it's not good enough." The Conformist warns, "Beware of risks. Be cautious. Don't rock the boat." The Star, presuming to be special and feeling entitled to lord it over others, may neglect the task of craft by whispering, "You're at the top. No need to work so hard." The Escape Artist can avoid the challenge of creativity by whining, "I'm so tired," or, "I have too much work to do." Or he might seduce us by saying, "Enjoy yourself now. Tomorrow is another day."

The presumptions and power of these characters inside us often culminate in detrimental edicts from the inner Critic, who uses the different ploys of these detractors. For example, the Critic might ask, "Who do you think *you are* to create?" Or he might accuse, "Don't be selfish. You should do things for others instead of spending time on yourself." Internally the Critic might play on our guilty feelings by insinuating, "You're crazy to waste all that energy on a mere 'hobby.' Be practical and put away your daft dreams." Another harmful device of the Critic is to suggest, "You're a failure. It's not good enough. Forget this. Put it away before others laugh at you."

We cannot completely dismiss the Critic, however, because we need its help in order to create. The Critic's clarity and insight can help us make decisions in our lives and in our work. It is important to recognize and differentiate when the Critic's voice hinders us from when it helps us.

If we hear the voice of a self-righteous figure, an expert at self-justification who has an answer to everything, we can detect the destructive Critic. The illusion of perfection often underlies the Critic's rationale and masks a hidden agenda to gain dominance, power, and control in the psyche. If the emphasis is on competing, comparing, and end results instead of discovery and process, we know that we are face to face with the hostile critic.

One way to recognize whether the critic's commentary is helpful or harmful is to take note consciously whether compassion and respect inform its comments. Creativity requires that we learn to make discerning judgments that consider the unique tone, style, and being of each person. Compassion and respect celebrate the dignity inherent to the person searching for creativity.

Some Causes of the Harmful Critic

Injurious judgments from the Critic arise inside people from various causes and in diverse ways. Parental reproaches, barbs from siblings, censure from teachers, cruel remarks from peers, and rigidly restrictive cultural norms all combine to influence the voice of the inner Critic. Criticisms accumulate inside ourselves. Whether they are blatant or subtle, asserted overtly or conveyed by neglect, they tend to influence the way we treat ourselves.

Even great artists are plagued by menacing verdicts of the Critic—decrees that echo in their inner ear. We have seen how the sculptress Camille Claudel and the opera singer Maria Callas each killed her inner creative children when the Critic inside berated her. Both suffered from critical and rejecting mothers, and both felt rejected by their lovers. Callas's mother rejected her daughter when she did not live up to her demand for perfectionism and fame, while Claudel's bourgeois-conformist mother rejected her by disapproving and disrespecting her daughter's adventurous artistic temperament.

The writer Franz Kafka suffered all his life from the condemnation of his tyrannical, critical father. A self-made prosperous businessman, Kafka's father disregarded and frowned on his only son's aspiration to write; he rebuked him for his failure to succeed in the business world. Throughout his life Kafka sent his father his short stories and novels. But his father never read the stories and threw them away. Even though Kafka finally became acclaimed as one of the world's greatest novelists, his father continued to berate him for having nothing worthwhile to show for his life.

In his classic novels *The Trial* and *The Castle*, Kafka describes the absurdity and helpless horror of entrapment in a bewildering system of institutionalized judgment. His characters are caught in a maliciously constructed maze from which they can never free themselves. They experience horrendous guilt for an inexplicable "crime" that is never identified or named. Kafka's protagonists suffer from a loss of fundamental trust and faith in the predictability of the world around them. Their uncertainty makes them particularly vulnerable to outer judgment and to the Critic inside of them.

Adult victims of abuse and children of alcoholics or mentally ill parents frequently suffer from sadistic inner Critics who burden and batter them with a baffling sense of guilt and shame. If they cannot recognize and understand them, the chaotic feelings continue to perpetuate prior abuse that makes them feel helpless before the Critic. They must confront the abusive and often faceless Critic, however, in order to overcome their role as Victim. If they want to transform, they must identify, name, and counter the harmful internalized Critic so they can reclaim and rebuild their lives. Kafka consciously met this challenge through his writing, which he considered to be an art of self-preservation and healing.

The detrimental talk of the Critic tends to be passed down in families throughout the generations. The Swedish director Ingmar Bergman shows how this vicious chain of criticism is passed down from mother to daughter in his film *Autumn Sonata.* In this film Charlotte, a concert pianist who is acted by Ingrid Bergman, unconsciously undermines her daughter's efforts and self-esteem. Charlotte's drive for perfection, her desire to be the center-stage Star, and her critical aloofness contribute to her daughter's feeling that she is unlovable.

Although she has been dreading her mother's visit, Eva, acted by Liv Ullmann, has invited her mother to visit in the hope of reconciliation. When Charlotte asks Eva to play the piano, Eva plays a piece by Chopin with passion and feeling. Eva senses her mother's condescension, however, and presses her for a genuine reaction. Charlotte answers professionally, without giving Eva the encouragement that she needs. Charlotte coolly explains that technically the Chopin piece requires emotional restraint instead of fire.

Finally Eva breaks down. She succumbs to hysterical rage, during which she rebukes her mother with the injured feelings of anger and resentment that she has stored up for years. Eva's outburst breaks through her mother's icy exterior and punctures her self-defensive mask.

In a flash of self-recognition, Charlotte realizes that she has never learned to love. She confesses to Eva that her own parents had responded to her in the way she now treats her daughter. She pleads with her daughter to forgive her and to teach her how to love—a potential her parents had never shown her how to develop. But Eva is so angry that she can neither forgive nor respond to her mother.

Unable to cope with her daughter's feelings, Charlotte decides to cut short her visit, on the pretense that her agent has arranged a concert for her. Charlotte leaves with the cognizance that she is isolated and depressed and longs for rapprochement with Eva. But she feels unable to face the emotional confrontation that creative relationship requires. Charlotte's inner Critic tricks and deceives her, cheating her out of her flash of insight, as she justifies herself: "I can't be bothered about self-knowledge. I'll have to live without it."[1]

Meanwhile, Eva's rage abates. She recognizes that her mother has been injured by a vicious cycle of criticism transferred down through the generations. Eva realizes that her mother's cool composure masks her fear, and she forgives her mother. She knows that someone must break this brutal chain of criticism.

Eva hopes to rid their relationship of the toxic criticisms that have plagued it. She writes Charlotte a letter saying that the redemption of their relationship is possible if they care for and help each other by expressing their affection. In this way Eva transforms the inner Critic that has held her hostage in a bell jar of resentment. She transfigures the Critic into a Lover by affirming that mercy and love offer the only genuine chance for human transformation and survival.

The harassing critic can develop also if a sibling berates, lords it over, or even abuses their sisters or brothers. Whenever verbal, physical, sexual, or emotionally abusive criticism violates the dignity of the other, it thereby sets up a power hierarchy of sadism and masochism. Later in this chapter we will see an example of the way a sibling's criticism becomes internalized and undermines a person's confidence, in the story of the Canadian artist Emily Carr.

Merciless inner Critics are spawned in adolescence, when confused teenagers either attempt to conform to the standards of their peers in order to obtain social acceptance or rebel against the social norms, only to find themselves categorized as society's outcasts. Novels like Carson McCullers's *The Heart Is a Lonely Hunter* and *A Member of the Wedding*, J. D. Salinger's *The Catcher in the Rye*, and Hermann Hesse's *Demian* show the struggles of young people trying to separate from the collective Critic so they can live authentic lives.

Films like Peter Weir's *Dead Poets Society*, John Singleton's *Boyz N the Hood*, and Allison Anders's *My Crazy Life (Mi Vida Loca)* are just a few examples of the multitude of modern-day films that portray the tragic struggles that adolescents incur with the cultural Critic.

THE CRITIC AS VOYEUR

A common temptation that seduces people to the bondage of the Critic is to become a Voyeur who retreats to the sidelines. Observing from far away gives them the safety to criticize everything they see. The Critic can become a Voyeur who destructively objectifies life by becoming abstract, distant, and cool. In this way the Critic undermines passion and enthusiasm.

If this passive pattern continues, the Voyeur can freeze the flow of life within himself. Jean-Paul Sartre described this syndrome in his novel *Nausea*. Albert Camus portrayed it in *The Stranger*. Hermann Hesse depicted the dilemma of wanting to participate in life, yet shrinking back through cynical criticism, in his novel *Steppenwolf.*

The Voyeur is a well-known figure in films such as *Monsieur Hire* and *The Conversation.* Francis Ford Coppola's 1974 film *The Conversation* portrays a Voyeur who works as an electronics surveillance expert. The protagonist, played by Gene Hackman, lives alone in a bare, indistinguishable apartment. His only human contact is with his mistress. But their relationship is utilitarian and impersonal; he meets her only when he has a physical urge.

His existence is as mechanical as the equipment that he uses to bug other people's relationships. He is proud to be the "chief" of electronic surveillance and attributes his expertise to the fact that he has divested his life of all personal connections. He relates to others only in his work as a Voyeur.

When Hackman is hired to tape a couple's conversation, he begins to project his own alienated, lonely, and desolate isolation onto the woman with whom he becomes intrigued and infatuated. Obsessed, he begins to play the tapes repeatedly and adjusts the sound levels so that he can piece together its fragments. Imagining a terrible tragedy from the words he can retrieve, he feels compelled to circumvent it and intervenes to shield the woman, with whom he has fallen in love.

But he has been tricked by his voyeurism. It is the woman who is guilty of the murder plan that he has recorded. Through his inexperience with women and his voyeuristic infatuation with imagined love, he has misconstrued the situation and contributed to the tragedy. In a flashback he remembers a similar betrayal by his mother, who had left him alone.

In despair that he has been tricked and betrayed, he is horrified that he has exposed his soul. Shattered by madness, he thinks that it is he who has been bugged. Crazed and in excruciating emotional pain, he tears up his room in an attempt to find the surveillance device. At the end he is a broken man who slumps to the floor, defeated by his voyeurism.

The Conversation shows how the Voyeur can be possessed by his shadow—in this case, a repressed longing for love that causes him to lose control and to fall into madness and self-destruction. The film portrays the tragedy that results when the Critic-Voyeur loses contact with a healthy inner Lover.

By standing apart from the flow of life, the Voyeur shirks conscious responsibility and can lead a person to destroy what he or she has composed at any point in the creative process. Or the Voyeur's voice can tell a person not to create at all for fear of exposure. Gregory, a photographer who stands on the sidelines of life, suffered from the Voyeur's proclivity to distance. Afraid to show his work, he disguised his fear with the cynical cliché that to be successful an artist must sell his soul—a view common to many trying to make it in the arts. Since Gregory began to believe there was no place in the commercial world for his creativity, he withdrew from the marketplace.

Gregory's Critic most probably developed from the constant criticism of his father, an educator who was more interested in trying out his principles on his son than in relating to him. His mother conformed to his father's comments, backing everything he said. Gregory unconsciously continued this pattern of parental criticism in his adult relationships when he married a woman as cold and critical as his father. Gregory felt like an outsider in his natal family, in his marriage, and in the world.

Because he didn't know how to bring his interests into life, Gregory became depressed and unable to work. His marriage broke up. He was unhappy and alone for several years. One day, still feeling isolated and alienated, he was looking at a photography album in a bookstore when a woman standing next to him suddenly asked him if he was interested in the arts. They began to talk and learned that they shared mutual interests in photography and the arts, so they decided to meet again over coffee. Kimberly's lively spontaneity and openhearted zest for life pierced through Gregory's reserve. Now, a year later, he is glowing from the care and love in their relationship, and he has begun to court the Lover in himself. Although he is still tentative, Gregory has started to show his photography work to others and has submitted it for consideration in several upcoming exhibitions.

Gregory learned what Nietzsche pointed out about creativity— active participation is essential to the creativity process. Nietzsche observed that the great poet Goethe did not retire from life but rather put himself into the midst of life because he wanted to be whole.

TRANSFORMING THE CRITIC

The Critic is an inner figure who can find fault with everything we do and thus discourage the creative process. But if we can elicit the Critic's constructive ability to discriminate, he can help us make the crucial decisions required to lead a healthy and creative life.

Like midwives who help mothers bring new life into being, editors, teachers, therapists, and parents help writers, students, patients, and children to create and to love. They need to be constructive judges who decide for life. In our inner lives, too, it is necessary to develop a reliable judge who is able to make sincere and honest decisions with respect to creativity and destruction, life and death. If we can learn to transform the Critic into one that judges fairly, appreciating and encouraging the fruits of creative effort, we will have developed the maturity that enables us to be birth-givers.

To this end, in order to open the Critic's heart, we must call upon the Lover within us. As in the case of Gregory, the Critic-Voyeur who withdraws from life and condemns it from a distance must be countered by compassion and passionate participation in life's flow. The Lover assumes an active role in response to creative life, joining and sharing with others in its struggles and in harvesting its fruits.

We cannot expect an outer lover to do this work for us. Even if we are fortunate enough to encounter a loving person in our external lives, we still must learn to develop the Lover in ourselves. Acting from the heart, the Lover can fire the Critic's passion and call others to creative communion. The Lover can help us develop an honorable, compassionate inner judge who helps us decide whether to cut, add, or reorder things in our lives and artworks.

JENNIFER'S WORK WITH THE INNER CRITIC

Jennifer, a single working mother, learned this lesson when she decided to go to graduate school while her children were away studying at college. In a psychology course she was assigned to create a three-dimensional portrait of the figure inside herself who continually berated her. This Critic, as Jennifer consciously envisioned it, was a judge who wore a black robe. She decided to make his portrait in the form of a papier-mâché doll.

The first time Jennifer attempted to construct the Critic in black, the figure did not look like the man she had in mind. She tried again and again. But each time the figure persisted in looking like an old woman. Finally she allowed herself to go with the unconscious flow of the process. She found herself using the color pink instead of black. When she was finished, the papier-mâché Critic turned out to be an older woman who looked remarkably like her mother.

Jennifer began to recall old memories of her mother, who had criticized her during her childhood and adolescence. She remembered her mother's sly reproaches that she was not the dutiful debutante daughter that her mother, a social climber, wanted her to be. She could still see the looks of disgust and hear the grudging tone of her mother's voice when she scrutinized Jennifer and said, "How could you?" This happened whenever Jennifer did not look and dress in accord with the social rules required by her mother. Her mother had continually criticized her manners, her behavior, her goals, and her adventurous spirit.

In her mother's eyes, Jennifer believed, she had made a "mess" of her life. She had not succeeded in entering a proper respectable profession, such as law or medicine, as her sisters had done. Nor had she married into the right social circles. Jennifer believed that she alone, of all her siblings, had been singled out, and that her mother had never found fault with her sisters. But years later, during late-night discussions, both sisters revealed that they, too, had experienced their mother's critical voice. Each complained, along with Jennifer, that her mother had paid no attention to who she really was.

In Jennifer's mind, her mother's prediction that she would never be successful had chiseled away at her self-esteem over the years. She began to see that her rebellion and her acting out had been proportionate to the feelings that she could not express or communicate to her mother. At least, Jennifer thought to herself as she examined the papier-mâché figure in her hand, she was not merciless and critical like her mother. Certainly in this one count Jennifer felt superior to her mother.

As Jennifer continued to hold the pink papier-mâché doll and to dialogue with it, a surprising thought occurred to her. She recognized that her feeling of superiority over her judgmental mother was no better or worse than her mother's disapproval of her. Each, in actuality, was a Critic judging the other. In this respect she and her mother were alike. Jennifer realized that the inner voice that berated her was actually her own.

Although the critical comments that prevented Jennifer from allowing herself her full range of creativity and self-esteem may have derived from her mother's censure, Jennifer suddenly understood that she had incorporated these demeaning words and made them her own. Jennifer grasped that only *she* could change this. As long as she clung to the Critic's words, she would be their victim. Jennifer began to laugh at herself, and her healthy sense of humor began to heal her own inner Critic and to transform it. The process of making the inner Critic's papier-mâché puppet had opened the Critic's heart.

With this unexpected emotional insight, Jennifer felt a surge of love for her mother. Probably her mother had inherited a pattern of criticism from her parents and social milieu and had suffered in her life too. Like Eva in *Autumn Sonata*, Jennifer understood that she and her mother had the same task—to transform the Critic that paralyzed each of them. Indeed, when she had seen this film many years ago, she had identified with it. Perhaps, Jennifer surmised, her mother was doing the best she could, given her history and circumstances. In any case it was only through compassion for each other, Jennifer reflected, that they could help one another.

Jennifer now consciously focuses on compassion, integrity, and equality—values that she esteems and has imparted to her children. Only an unhealthy Critic would promulgate a rigid, unrealistic hierarchy that leads to being judged as better or worse than others, Jennifer has concluded. In contrast, a healthy inner Critic would acknowledge both difference and unity, uniqueness and harmony, and would encourage each person to develop toward their personal best—a goal that is not to be confused with perfection.

THE DIVINE LOVE OF EMILY CARR

The discouraging voice of the inner Critic plagued the eminent Canadian painter Emily Carr, who once bemoaned the flaws she perceived in her painting *The Mountain.* Upon uncovering the canvas, she wrote in her journal, "It makes me sick. I am heavy in spirit over my painting. It is so lacking. What's the use: Sometimes I could quit paint and take to charring. It must be fine to clean perfectly, to shine and polish and *know* that it could not be done better. In painting that never occurs."[2]

Nevertheless, Carr had a great love that nourished her and that was stronger than the Critic's caustic comments. She felt awe before the majestic mountain wilderness of western Canada, and she embodied her spiritual reverence for nature in her paintings. Despite the inner Critic's prattle, her "inner self" said, "Start again and profit by your experience."[3] So Carr covered the first canvas under a layer of white paint and began to paint the mountain anew. She felt the seed of the painting sprout with vigor.

Although after further attempts she felt *The Mountain* was still incomplete, Carr was comforted with the knowledge that she had wrestled with this painting honestly. She was ready to proceed to her next painting because she knew that the learning and growth attained through her previous efforts would carry on to the next. Carr expressed her faith in development as follows: "Oh, the glory of growth, silent, mighty, persistent, inevitable! To awaken, to open up like a flower to the light of a fuller consciousness!"[4]

Carr's inner Critic most likely developed as a result of her unhappy childhood and, later, by the lack of recognition from the art world. She was born in 1871 on the Canadian island of Victoria in British Columbia. Twelve years later her mother died. Her father, who had expected her mother to serve him, was a rigid authoritarian who ignored his children until they were old enough to admire him and to buckle under his will. When she was fourteen, two years after her mother's death, he died. After her father's death she suffered under the hard discipline of the domineering sister who took charge of her.

When she was young, Carr's inner critic caused her to burn up her journals. One New Year's Eve she recorded her feelings of failure about the past year along with her hopes for the coming year. When her big sister found and read what she had written in the journal, she shamed and ridiculed Emily by throwing her secret thoughts at her. Emily was so angry, hurt, and humiliated that she broke all of her

New Year's resolutions. She burned her diary and buried her thoughts. She began to feel angry and hurt about the meanness and underhandedness in the world. After that she soon destroyed what she wrote in order to keep her privacy.

As with many of us, Carr's inner Critic developed from and reacted to a cruel Critic: in her case one that she had experienced in relationship to her big sister and her father. Even after she received acclaim in the art world, her early experience remained with her. But an encounter with a fellow artist helped her transform the Critic in herself.

When Carr learned that a colleague, with whom she had exchanged letters, had shown her letters to others, she became upset. She found that she could no longer write letters freely, recording her innermost thoughts, if unchosen people might read them. She regarded her personal thoughts as important to her painting.

But Carr did not remain a victim of this event. She knew that writing to this colleague was important because it alleviated her isolation as an artist. These letters with a fellow painter were the first real exchange of ideas about art that she had experienced. The letters enabled her to clarify her thoughts and helped her discover her aims and beliefs.

When Carr confronted her correspondent with her feelings of betrayal, she asked him never to show her letters to anyone again without her permission. He understood her point of view and agreed with her. He apologized and promised to keep all her letters in confidence. His response enabled her to trust him and to write openly again.

This experience helped Carr to recognize the harmful power of the inner cynical Critic that held her hostage to fear. She deplored the censure that causes people to be terrified or to hide their serious side due to dread of ridicule. If people are ashamed to show their best, Carr once wrote, they hide their authentic selves behind a facade of superficiality.

Carr escaped the external criticism of her sister when she left her home in Victoria in order to study painting in San Francisco, Paris, and London. The beauty and magnificence of the mountains drew her back to the island of Victoria, where she devoted the rest of her life to painting the grandeur and transcendence of the wilderness.

Although Carr never married, she had sweethearts and received a proposal of marriage from one of her lovers, an offer that she declined. She knew that he would demand more than she could give him. Although he might not admit it, underneath he, like her father, wanted worship. Forty years later he wrote her a letter saying that although he had married, he still loved her. He felt that she had made a great mistake in not marrying him. But Carr knew that her independent spirit and her devotion to art would have been unpalatable to him. Moreover, she knew that marriage to him would have bored her and deadened her spiritual life. Although she remained single, she felt close to her family, especially to two of her sisters in later life.

Carr was eccentric and high-spirited—an adventurer at heart. When she was a child, she pledged to herself to go everywhere, to be active, and to experience all that she could. She wanted to have a fund of meaningful memories upon which to reflect when she became old. In later years she bought an old caravan and drove great distances so she could camp for days in the wilderness, which thrilled and inspired her.

Despite her isolation from the art world and its neglect of her talent, Carr continued to paint steadfastly and faithfully. Although she criticized herself for shirking the chore of selling herself and for dodging publicity, she was embarrassed by the role of marketing herself, a role that she considered to be a selfish conceit. Carr's primary dedication to art was neither merely to paint pictures nor to become recognized as a great artist. She felt called by a dynamic force within her to paint and to make visible all that stirred her soul in nature.

Carr recognized that male painters tended to despise their female counterparts and secretly resented a woman who got honors in a field they considered their own. After a critical review of her work described her as a "Canadian painter" because of her subject matter and her approach, she realized that her work also was neglected because she was Canadian. But Carr was proud to be a woman and felt privileged to live in the inspiring rugged wilderness of Canada. She felt honored to feel a part of a land that revealed such sublime and primeval power. She felt graced with the gift to respond, express, and share this beauty through her art.

When Carr was in her fifties, the Canadian Group of Seven recognized her artwork. This eminent group of male artists dedicated themselves to expressing the spiritual beauty of nature. They recognized that Carr's rhythm and style of painting, which was ardent, devoted, and impregnated by nature, was like their own. Eventually the critics concurred. In her sixties Carr's gifts and contributions to art were widely acclaimed.

By this time, however, her health was failing. As a consequence she had to reduce her painting. So she turned to the journal she had begun in her fifties and spent more of her time writing. She began to write her autobiography, *Growing Pains*, along with books for children.

Toward the end of her life, Carr wrote that life had been good to her, particularly in its second half. She considered herself to be a late developer. Despite the difficulties she had experienced in childhood, she felt that intrinsically she had a happy nature. The fact that her sensitive temperament was tinged with a tragic vein due to her vulnerability to hurt did not diminish her thankfulness for life.

The ultimate creative challenge of life, Carr said, is to face death and old age. For Carr this meant accepting to be an example for younger women rather than a rival. Women who cannot or will not accept aging's adventure succumb to stupidity and selfishness, often ending their years in grudging resentment. Instead, aging women must learn to dare to face old age and acquiesce to its decline of energy and strength. Their spiritual task, Carr emphasized, is daring to discover how to channel their energy so they can continue to create as long as possible and to pass on wisdom to others.

Carr was not a Pollyanna. She thought that old age without spirituality must be ghastly, and she abhorred its ugliness. To look in the mirror and see only "broken down feet, bent knees, peering eyes, rheumatic knuckles, and withered skin" requires supreme patience and tolerance, she wrote. Carr foresaw that it is of the utmost importance to converse intimately with contemporaries about the issues of spirituality and death. She lamented the reticence to do so among others of her age.

Her philosophy and spirituality were based upon her experience in nature. As she painted in the wilderness, she saw nature's cycles in their extremity. She knew the terrors of the wilderness as well as its ecstasies. Even near the end, when she had suffered a stroke and her heart was giving out, Carr wrote: "There is a lot of life in me yet. Maybe I shall go out into the woods sketching again, who knows?"[5]

Accepting nature's greatest mystery—the cycles of the seasons—Carr made the final entry in her diary on March 7, 1941. On this day during World War II—a day toward the end of winter yet near the beginning of spring—a companion took her for a drive in the country. Carr noted the beauty of the day while reflecting on the war. She wrote:

> The war is staggering. When you think of it you come to a stone wall. All private plans stop. The world has stopped; man has stopped. Everything holds its breath except spring. She bursts through as strong as ever. I gave the birds their mates and nests today. They are bursting their throats. Instinct bids them carry on. They fulfill their moment; carry on, carry on, carry on.[6]

Carr's call to create was fed by a larger sense of purpose and passion that sustained her, even though she spent most of her life ignored by the critics. True art, she believed, does not exist without faith in something greater. Even the artist who denies religion or who does not believe himself to be spiritual is sincere when he creates. Sincerity *is* religion, she maintained. Carr was confident that the attempt to create stems from a faith that something greater surges in the soul. The artist tries to express what she has seen through her vision and the earthly materials that she uses. The very act of creating attests to both the longing and the search for something beyond what one can see or reach.

How Critics Love

The healthy function of the Critic has been described by the film critic David Denby in his article "The Moviegoers: Why Don't People Love the Right Movies Anymore?"[7] What Denby says of the movie critic is true for the well-being of the Critic inside us whose role is to serve creativity.

The movie critic, Denby writes, "can seize, loverlike, on the particulars, the tone, the succulent difference between one movie and another."[8] The critic's job is to evoke and to arouse us and not to be a crank or a huckster who merely drowns us with opinions. A critic's sense of excitement can provoke us to refine our tastes and sensibilities and to open to new insights.

Denby maintains that while part of the critic's task is to elucidate and analyze, the critic also can "celebrate art and pleasure and applaud new talent." One of the critic's key contributions is to nurture a "conversation" with movie lovers who care about stories and their characters with passion and emotion. "Movie love," Denby points out, helps people to feel their instincts, and it can lead to transformation and to self-reconciliation.

Love is the critic's resource, the reservoir from which the critic can foster hope, point to new visions and sensibilities, and record and help us remember the steps in a creative person's development. A critic's love can encourage dialogue that leads to discovery and reflection about values, and it can confront the cynicism and ridicule that undermines and extinguishes creative effort. "And only as lovers," Denby concludes, can critics "re-create the fervent connection with bodies, faces and stories that drew so many people to movies in the first place."[9]

With Denby's remarks in mind, I would like to share my love for Kieślowski's film *Red*, which shows the relationship between the Critic and the Lover.

THE CRITIC AND THE LOVER WED

Kieślowski's haunting film *Red* can be seen as a "spiritual romance" about the strange meeting of two contrary characters who embody the seemingly irreconcilable traits of the Critic and the Lover. *Red* presents the story of a synchronous meeting between a cynical judge-voyeur (played by Jean-Louis Trintignant) and a woman with heart, the Lover (played by Irène Jacob). The film draws the viewer to experience how the encounter of these two characters effects a transformation in each and illumines the inner dynamics and process of the wedding within the soul of the Critic and the Lover.

Valentine, a young model, is seen at work as an object of allure and beauty for the camera and the fashion show runway. She lives alone in her Geneva apartment, where she spends most of her time and energy struggling to communicate by phone with her jealous but distant boyfriend. She is also beset with worry about her younger brother, a teenage drug addict.

On the surface Valentine's life reveals neither her spiritual depth nor her authenticity. Yet as her name suggests, Valentine is a Lover. She is ardently honest and intensely compassionate—a person of integrity and strong moral fiber. But her worries about her brother and her boyfriend bewilder and confuse her. She wants to help but is unclear about what action she should take, so she tries to bear up under her conflicts.

One night, as she drives home in the rain, she accidentally hits a dog. Valentine jumps out of her car, takes the dog in her arms, places it gently in her car, and drives to the address on the dog's collar. She arrives at a dark and gloomy house in a suburb of Geneva. Although the house seems empty, Valentine pushes open a creaking door and finds the dog's owner. He is a bitter and isolated man who has abandoned his dog, Rita, and does not care about its fate. Valentine leaves the house in anger and takes the dog to a veterinarian, who treats its injuries and tells her it is pregnant.

Valentine takes the dog home to care for it. One day when she takes Rita out for a run, the dog suddenly disappears. Valentine drives to Rita's previous home to find the dog. She observes Rita's former owner eavesdropping on his neighbors' phone calls with electronic equipment. Valentine confronts him. She tells him that spying is disgusting. In response he agrees. Then he cynically says that his activity is illegal.

During this encounter Valentine learns that he is a retired judge. Instead of apologizing for his actions, he interrogates Valentine. Although he seems hard-hearted, the judge recognizes Valentine's purity of heart and intuits that she feels troubled. At last Valentine breaks down and exposes her soul to him.

Despite their contrasting temperaments, the judge and Valentine are mysteriously drawn to each other. Valentine challenges the judge to give up his spying. Provoked by his refusal to participate in life, Valentine pierces through his cynical despair by saying sharply, "Then stop breathing."

Valentine's spiritual beauty reawakens the judge's capacity for love.

Her direct, natural way of relating to him bids him to reengage in life. The judge exposes the relentless heartache that has haunted him and that has led to his embittered, voyeuristic retreat from life. He reveals to Valentine the transgression that he perpetrated—the sin that has driven him to the perversity of voyeurism and the guilt for which he needs expiation.

The woman with whom he was in love deceived and betrayed him by taking another lover. Her treachery devastated him, and he felt overpowered by a hateful craving for revenge. By coincidence, her new lover was put on trial for a crime before him as magistrate. The judge knew that it would be unethical to take on this case, but he chose to do so nonetheless.

After this breach of justice, known only to himself, he retired from his judicial position and from life. Consumed by bitterness and self-hatred, he condemned himself to stagnate in the despicable role of misanthropic Voyeur. Like Dostoyevsky's "underground man," he took perverse delight in reducing himself to this repulsive character.

When Valentine unexpectedly enters his life, she confronts him with his depravity and challenges him to change. She does not censure him to hopeless doom. Instead, she presents the judge with a fresh, candid, forthright embodiment of the Lover—a figure that the judge had been seeking all his life and had mistakenly projected upon his unfaithful lover.

The judge knows deep within himself that Valentine is like the ephemeral sunlight that enters his dark room, and then will vanish as the sun moves across the sky. As they talk, he lapses into silence for this moment so that she can see the beauty of this light as it enters the room in which they converse. In this tender way he reveals to her the inner light that illumines and reflects her soul—a wordless way that allows her to embrace her inner loveliness. He understands that Valentine's beauty has been captured and objectified externally in her role as a model, and that she needs to recognize her interior light so she can feel empowered in herself.

Just as Valentine viscerally elicits the judge's capacity to love, so he subtly guides her to discover the authenticity in herself so that she can grow fully into maturity and wisdom. The light they both see also symbolizes the gift he can offer her—the inner clarity and discerning judgment that Valentine must learn to exercise in order to disengage from her uncaring boyfriend, to deal effectively with her brother and family conflicts, and to embark on her own voyage of self-discovery.

The judge does not fall into the Critic's trap of lecturing, for this would cheat her of the chance to perceive the truths that she needs to discover for herself. Instead, the judge's wisdom, generosity, and sense of justice prevail, and he offers her the still and spacious moment. He understands Valentine's inner significance for him and comprehends that their meeting symbolizes a soul-encounter for each of them. He resists projecting his soul-image upon her, knowing that by attempting to possess her, as he did the woman who betrayed him, he would avoid the call to develop his own capacity to love. Hence he encourages her to go out into life to discover her own path.

In *Red* the Critic and the Lover are inevitably drawn together because they need each other. The Lover needs the Critic's strength and discernment, while the Critic needs the Lover's good will and purity of heart. The healthy Critic, who values truth, integrity, and compassion, guides us with beneficence, charity, and compassion—with love. For example, to develop creative relationships, we need to hear the truth spoken with respect and discernment by a compassionate Critic infused with the grace of a Lover.

The Lover needs the discriminating capacity of the Critic in order not to dissipate her energies and give herself away at random or haphazardly in an aimless way. Without the discerning eye of the Critic, the Lover can exhaust herself by giving herself away purposelessly. If she does this, she betrays her authentic self by allowing her integrity and her energy to become dissipated and used up. Thereby she becomes a victim of her own lack of substance. She becomes that dreaded codependent caretaker figure, "the woman who loves too much," whose unboundaried and unlimited love becomes destructive. This vampire love, which drains and is draining, is quite different from radical, unconditional love, which heals. The latter love is guided by something greater than mere mortal desire. Unconditional love is directed by the transcendent, generous, and redemptive power of love, which is informed by the arrow of longing for the divine. This is the inexplicable wondrous love that mystics call *agape*. It is this love that informs creativity. Awakening to the creative call means embracing life. This entails I-Thou encounters of the kind we see in *Red*.

Creative living requires that we learn to discriminate between two types of criticisms—those infused with love and care that help us honor the mystery of creation and those cynical critiques that ridicule and lead us to scorn ourselves and all of existence. The former regenerate us and help us to grow, while the latter drain our energy, deplete our self-esteem, and sap our passion.

The constructive function of the inner Critic is to illuminate, to clarify, and to help us sort out the welter of thoughts, feelings, images, and experiences that go into creating. When motivated by the inner Lover, the Critic can foster the creative conversation within us that nurtures imagination and originality.

If the Critic weds the Lover, their marriage can give birth to the Celebrant, who seeks beauty and truth and who sees, appreciates, and praises existence. The Sower helps plant and care for the seeds that bring growth to fruition. The Sentinel awakens us to consciousness. The Witness affirms truth and integrity, guiding us to record and remember our positive experiences as well as the impediments to development. The Dummling encourages us to laugh at ourselves and to play so we can be open to discovery. The Adventurer encourages the risk-taking that leads us to explore new paths. Throughout this entire process the Artisan teaches us craft and faithfully affirms the care, humility, and effort that it takes to bring a seed to bear fruit.

Part IV
THE HARVESTING

To praise is the whole thing!

Rainer Maria Rilke

10

TO PRAISE IS THE WHOLE THING

The art I have practiced since my childhood has taught me that man is capable of love and that love can save him. That, to me, is the true color, the true substance of art. It is as natural as a tree or a stone. All my works here and there are reflections of all I have seen, as in a sky, and felt every day in my soul. I have tried to keep all that in my heart.

Marc Chagall

THE CELEBRANT

As we celebrate the creative process, we give and we receive. We receive inspiration from the Muse and respond to the call to create. We accept the risk and responsibility to venture into the unknown in order to return with the new vision, and we struggle to embody it in an art form or actualize it in our lives. Then, by putting forth our new creation into the world, whether it is the creative transformation that shines in our lives or the gleaming artwork, we give to others who can consciously choose to continue this cycle of creativity.

If others appreciate the newborn work or transformed life, they experience a similar activity in themselves. Those who respond to the newborn work or life are inspired to explore, encounter, and struggle with undiscovered parts of themselves—a process that leads to creative transformation.

Appreciation of creativity is itself a celebration. In order to appreciate a work of art, we, too, must be creative to experience it. By appreciating the work of other artists, creative people are inspired to create their own work, and they in turn inspire others in a cyclical chain of creativity.

The same process occurs in self-transformation. We are inspired by others who have transformed. And as we ourselves transform, we continue the process of inspiring others. We shall see this process in the following story of Rachel.

The Art of Appreciation — Rachel's Story

Many of us forget to cultivate and cherish the interior "appreciator" that is so central to the nature of creativity. How can we sing a hymn to the blessings of life, of the earth, and of others if we cannot celebrate them in ourselves?

Appreciation has become the keynote in the life of Rachel, a wife and mother who is now in her mid-fifties. Rachel grew up in a low-socioeconomic-class immigrant neighborhood in New York City. Her father was a baker, and her mother took care of the family. They were hardworking people who were satisfied to sit down at the end of the day and to have the luxury to rest. Rachel felt loved by her parents and siblings, her large extended family of aunts, uncles, and cousins, and especially her grandmother.

In adolescence, however, Rachel started to feel like an outsider with her peers. She was not adept at athletics, and she felt like a klutz. She felt tall and ungainly and somehow "not good enough." She felt unpopular because she was never "chosen" for anything. But she got top grades, studied chemistry in college, and planned to go to medical school.

Soon after she graduated from college, she fell in love and married. The couple went to Europe, where her husband entered medical school. Rachel got pregnant and became involved with raising her family. When her husband finished medical school, the family returned to the States.

Rachel loved being a mother. Cooking for her family was both a creative act and a great joy. She especially enjoyed creating new recipes.

Like many women, however, Rachel felt a vacuum when her children left home for college. She was in her forties, had not developed a profession, and needed new challenges in her life. Old feelings of inadequacy like those she had experienced in adolescence resurfaced. Rachel felt at loose ends and became depressed. She realized that over the years she had become subservient to her husband and was caught in the role of caretaker.

Rachel took a creative step; she decided to join a women's consciousness group. The intimate exchange with other women in her situation helped her to see her own strengths and gave her new perspectives. With the group's support Rachel realized she needed to acknowledge and accept her strengths and to change her pattern of subservience. This meant transforming the unhealthy aspect of being a codependent caretaker. Instead, she wanted to be a woman who could serve as a model for her community.

Rachel also began studying with a spiritual teacher—a Hindu philosopher. At about the same time her husband discovered the path of Buddhism. The couple realized that they shared a new passion—the search for spirituality. Their relationship deepened as they exchanged the insights and discoveries of their spiritual practices with each other, and they began participate together in meditation retreats. Rachel's relationship also deepened with her grown children.

Rachel was developing the art of appreciation for herself as well as others. The opportunity of raising children had given her important skills such as discovering and responding to the needs of others. "When your child screams at you," Rachel said, "you must find out what she needs; you learn that different cries mean different things." Rachel appreciates these strengths in herself and now sees them as creative. The art of listening and doing what needs to be done, Rachel realized, was an art that she could bring into service for the community.

Rachel started to use these skills by volunteering at a nonprofit women's resource center that aimed to help women to become emotionally and financially independent. She learned how to be a peer counselor and worked part time at the center. She also created meetings for older women who felt lonely and alienated, and she started communal dialogues between women from different ethnic backgrounds.

Rachel also began to appreciate her creativity in the art of cooking, a way that she could give people love and make them feel comfortable. The creativity she finds in cooking is not merely to make a flavorful meal. Cooking is also the art of serving others; it entails the act of respecting and honoring the fruits of the earth.

When she cooks, Rachel feels the responsibility to present a growing fruit of the earth. The fruit goes through the birth process just as we do. As she bakes an apple pie and her hands go through a cup of flour to make the crust, she thinks about the people who have participated in the creation of the flour and the growth of the apple. She wants her cooking to give homage to their lives. While preparing a meal, Rachel dedicates it to everyone involved. Whenever people appreciate a meal, they celebrate all those who contribute to it. Rachel remarked that she experiences a "high," a feeling of ecstasy, as she participates in this process of creation that includes the sower, the cultivator, the harvester, the nourisher, the lover, and the recipients of the meal.

The Celebrant, who sees, appreciates, and praises life, is now Rachel's inner companion, and she tries to be mindful of this timeless part of herself. Rachel shared her philosophy of creativity as follows: Creating means to be awake, to be thankful and open to the new day without prejudging it, to see whatever passes by, whether it is pain or joy, and to learn about compassion. If you see that a person is lonely or suffering, you can reach out to show them that they're not alone. Witnessing people helps them to value themselves and their existence as part of the whole. Whenever we appreciate others, we appreciate ourselves.

THE COMMUNITY OF APPRECIATION

Whether we are in a concert hall listening to a symphony, a dark womblike room in which we view a film, a museum where we see a painting or a sculpture, alone at home reading a book, in conversations with others, or outdoors in awe of nature's changing wonders, we must surrender our habitual expectations if we want to be open to the new marvel happening before us. Opening to a creative work excites, awakens, and unites us in its call to join in an astonishing communal adventure of appreciation.

The painter Georgia O'Keeffe expressed this when she observed that to really see and experience—especially something small like a flower—takes time, just as it takes time to develop a friendship. O'Keeffe said, "I'll paint what I see—what the flower is to me, but I'll paint it big and they will be surprised into taking time to look at it—I will make even busy New Yorkers take time to see what I see of flowers."[1] Her paintings became magnificent celebrations of beauty that stir people from all over the world and bring them together in a shared sense of wonder.

The Russian film director Andrey Tarkovsky believes that creative gifts offer spiritual awakening and community to their recipients. He wrote:

> Touched by a masterpiece, a person begins to hear in himself that same call of truth which prompted the artist to his creative act. When a link is established between the work and its beholder, the latter experiences a sublime, purging trauma. Within that aura which unites masterpieces and audience, the best sides of our souls are made known, and we long for them to be freed. In those moments we recognize and discover ourselves, the unfathomable depths of our own potential, and the furthest reaches of our emotions.[2]

What Tarkovsky wrote about the energetic relationship between artist, artwork, and beholder is true of every creative act, whether it is embodied in an art form, a relationship, a worldly deed, a prayer, a ritual, or an interior awakening in a person. An atmosphere of transformative energy emanates and inspires all those who are ready to receive it. Sometimes it affects those who least expect it.

The Buddhist bodhisattva's generous gift of compassion, Martin Buber's notion of the I-Thou relationship that honors the holy in the other and generates the mystery of love, indigenous peoples' ceremonies of healing and thanksgiving—all these and more issue from the celebration of creativity that circulates to others.

The Call to Create

The Celebrant gives thanks for the new creation and praises its birth. Creative people like the novelist Dostoyevsky and the poet Maya Angelou all emphasize the importance of giving thanks and acknowledging the chain of creation. They also thank each other.

For example, the novelist Henry Miller wrote a letter of thanks and appreciation to Somerset Maugham for the gift of the novels he had written. Miller, who had read Maugham's novels years before, said that it was a joy to discover his work again when he chanced to reread *The Razor's Edge.* Miller was touched by the "simple soul" of Larry, the protagonist, and asked Maugham if he had actually known such a man or whether he had invented this character. Miller added that on his jaunts around America he had met such "simple souls" who moved him as people of wisdom. He wondered whether in a previous existence they had tackled and resolved the problems that plague most of us today. The "anonymous" figures like Larry, Miller wrote, struck him as "the holy figures in America."[3]

Miller ended his letter to Maugham with the following gift of gratitude: "Wherever you are may fortune be kind to you! Before I had written a line I read *Of Human Bondage.* It was one of the books which formed me. We owe so much to others and we acknowledge so little. God speed!"

Giving thanks is central to creative life. Indeed, thankfulness for the gift of life is a bond that unites every human being regardless of color, race, creed, gender, economic status or the way a person chooses to create. The gift of creation calls us to celebrate the cycle of life and death. Sowing, waiting, cultivating, harvesting, thanksgiving—and then beginning this cycle anew—is central to existence.

Honoring each part of the cycle is a sacred testimony to the gift of life.

After reaping their first harvest in the new land, the pilgrims celebrated by giving thanks. They gathered the fruits of their work, savored them, and acknowledged this gift of grace with appreciation and gratitude. Without the celebration of thanksgiving, the cycle of creation is unfulfilled.

The poet May Sarton noted this in *Journal of a Solitude*, when she wrote:

> There is only one real deprivation, I decided this morning, and that is not to be able to give one's gift to those one loves most. . . . The gift turned inward, unable to be given, becomes a heavy burden, even sometimes a kind of poison. It is as though the flow of life were backed up.[4]

LIFE'S WONDERS

The flow of life is like a rivulet running down from a mountain spring—like the font where the ancient muses were said to live and play. The small waterway separates into different streams that course down and return to their flowing sources somewhere on the earth. The sun attracts the waters from their resting places in the rivers, lakes, and seas, while the winds move the moist air high toward the heavens where it cools into mist and settles in the clouds.

If we look up at the clouds as they drift across the sky, we can see them reveal heavenly wonders—the moon, the sun, the stars—then cover these celestial splendors again as the air currents stir them onward. When the clouds burst, they discharge the waters in the form of snow, hail, or rain that drops down to bathe the earth and refresh the thirsty flowers, grasses, and trees, whereupon the wondrous water cycle begins again.

The marine biologist and poet Rachel Carson gave thanks for creation's natural gifts, like the water cycle and the splendors of the sea, in her books *The Sea Around Us* and *The Sense of Wonder.* She was a pioneer of ecology who braved attacks of ridicule and threats of lawsuits from chemical companies and trade associations when she exposed the destructive hazards of chemical pesticides to our environment in her revolutionary book *The Silent Spring.*

Carson maintains that the sense of wonder for the natural beauty of creation is central to spiritual life and healing. The sense of wonder is a key deterrent to our destructive tendencies. Carson celebrates both actual and symbolic beauty in the migration of birds, in the ebb and flow of the tides, in the folded bud ready for the spring. She affirms: "There is something infinitely healing in these repeated refrains of nature—the assurance that dawn comes after night, and spring after the winter."[5]

Acts of thanksgiving and celebration for the gifts of creation offered by creative people like those mentioned in this chapter— Georgia O'Keeffe, May Sarton, Rachel Carson, Boris Pasternak, Andrey Tarkovsky, and Rainer Maria Rilke—contribute to the communal resource from which each of us draws and to which each of us gives whenever we praise creation.

To be in awe before an infant's smile, to marvel at wild columbine on a mountain path, to wonder at the sunflower that grows from a small seed planted in the ground, to thrill at the fleet deer springing through the forest, to admire a needlework design embroidered on blank cloth, to relish a meal cooked with love in the company of friends, to see the light of love in another's eyes, to stir to the trill of a songbird at dawn or the croak of a frog at dusk, to see beauty in the face of the dying as they pass from this world to the unknown—all are creative acts of response and celebration.

During our early years of life we sometimes remember the moment when we first responded to a seed of creativity planted in our souls. Georgia O'Keeffe said that her first memory was of the brightness of light surrounding her. Later, when she was in the eighth grade, she remarked, "I am going to be an artist." Although she didn't know where the idea to be an artist came from, the urge to make something beautiful moved her to paint. She especially hoped to celebrate the beauty that she saw.

After she had worked for years to hone the craft of painting, she described some of the sources that inspired her to paint so she could share the beauty of seeing and offer it to others.

> I have picked flowers where I found them—have picked
> up sea shells and rocks and pieces of wood. . . . When I
> found the beautiful white bones on the desert I picked

them up and took them home too. . . . I have used these things to say what is to me the wideness and wonder of the world as I live in it.[6]

Henri Matisse said that it was in the first moment in which he had a box of colors in his hands that he experienced the feeling that his life was his own. Although it took him years to find his unique style, he felt that he had set foot on his true path. He used the colors to tell artistic truths—for example, the way light affects us.

In 1902 Matisse said, "Slowly, I discovered the secret of my art consists of a meditation on nature." The sea was his great inspiration. When he was too old to swim, he brought the sea inside his home by decorating his house with the cutout, *The Swimming Pool.* Matisse said that since he adored the sea but could no longer swim, he surrounded himself with it through his art. Matisse did not experience "outside" and "inside" as two different worlds; rather he experienced both as a continuum of wholeness. Like Matisse, we can also do this with our imagination.

Throughout the course of life we experience the cycles of struggle and silence, grace and rejoicing. Virginia Woolf noted that the creative power "brings the whole universe to order. I can see the day whole, proportioned." She celebrated the excitement and ecstasy of creativity despite the depression, despair, and anxiety that accompanied her work. After she had written down the final words of her novel *The Waves,* during a flurry of intensity and intoxication that had sent her reeling, she finally sat down feeling glory and calm amid her tears.[7]

The Celebrant

DEATH AND REBIRTH

Especially when faced with death, we are brought before the mystery of creation. After recovering from a malady that threatened his life, the Russian poet and novelist Boris Pasternak wrote that in his last moments he wanted to thank God so that he could praise all visible things. "Dear Lord," I whispered,

> I thank you for applying the paint so richly and that in your creation of life and death you speak to us in splendor and music. I thank you that you have made me an artist, that creativity is your school, and that all my life you have been preparing me for this night.[8]

Creativity calls both the artist and recipient to enter an extraordinary time and space in which they set aside conventional concerns and customary modes of perception in order to be open to the new event. Viewing things anew requires a readiness to sacrifice the ego-interests that hold people in habitual patterns. We must prepare ourselves to die symbolically if we are to be open to the possibility of transformation. The creative process calls all of us to encounter death in order to embark on the journey to seek the treasure of rebirth. Facing death consciously is an inevitable aspect of the way we grow and unites us on our spiritual paths.

Although I fall into the chasm of despair whenever I face the death of old ways to enter a new phase of transformation and creativity, I am graced with this memory: I have been in this black hole many times before. And each time I have received a spiritual awakening that has given me the energy and the courage to create.

The Call to Create

I recall the words of the poet Theodore Roethke: "In a dark time, the eye begins to see." His poetic predecessor Rilke exclaimed that if we seek creative and spiritual transformation, we must leap into the abyss and learn to survive there. Only by learning to dwell in the crater of divine darkness will we be ready to receive creative vision.

Creativity, like all growth, requires endurance and waiting time in the valley of the soul. The mystics know the terror of creation's abyss. During a dark period between creative bursts, the composer, artist and visionary Hildegard von Bingen cried out in terror: "O mother where are you . . . Where is your help now?" She had already experienced the deep ecstasy of divine creation. But once again she was suffering through the dark night in which the soul is emptied and dried up. Like a lost wanderer in the desert wasteland searching for an oasis, she thirsts for the waters of life. But remembering her prior experience of divine illumination, she endures the time of despair with prayer and hope.

The "dark night of the soul" is essential to creative and spiritual metamorphosis. Mystics understand the dark night as a continual cycle of purification that purges obsolete ways of being that hinder and threaten growth. The dark night is intrinsic to the transformational and spiritual threshold that opens to creative insight and is akin to nature's cycle: dusk, night, dawn, and day. Artists, visionaries, and people seeking growth learn they must pass through these portals too.

Facing loss and death is shown in the classic myth of Orpheus and Eurydice. Orpheus, the legendary poet and musician, was the son of the Muse Calliope. The Muses cared for Orpheus and taught him how to play the lyre, which Apollo had given him. Orpheus played so beautifully that he could enchant wild beasts and persuade the trees and rocks to move from their places to follow the sound of his music. He could even transfix the gods of the underworld.

When his wife, Eurydice, died from a snakebite, Orpheus descended into the underworld to try to save his love. His music enraptured the underworld gods, who allowed him to lead Eurydice back to earth. They set only one condition: Orpheus could not look back to see if Eurydice was following him. At the last moment Orpheus lost faith and looked back to be sure she was behind him. As a result he lost Eurydice, who was returned to death. Even though he failed, however, he resolved to return to earth singing, as a survivor and Celebrant for life.

Although Orpheus was in despair over the loss of his beloved, he continued to sing and play the lyre. Orpheus accepted his failure but still praised life through his music, thereby embracing the unity of life and death. Although the maenads, angry at Orpheus for losing Eurydice, tore him into pieces, the muses rescued Orpheus' singing head and built a shrine to him on the isle of Lesbos. Later a mystery religion honored Orpheus by celebrating him as a divinity of creative rebirth and as a mediator between the realms of life and death

Just as Orpheus descended into darkness to retrieve his beloved, so must we descend into chaos if we want to bring new potentialities into being. Many of us stop at just this point—the descent into the unknown. As we have seen in the previous chapters, fear of that which is beyond our control and fear of failure to find or give birth to the new vision can prevent us from this venture. Or like Orpheus, we may forget to trust at the last moment.

Life itself entails facing death. As soon as we are born, we are already on our way to death, which is a part of the human condition. The ultimate human challenge is to endure and find the courage to hope and love in the encounter with death. Creative life and transformation call us to affirm this venture.

When I was in my own despair while trying to enter a new phase of my life and to overcome my block to write this book, I found inspiration by watching the film *Blue* many times and by listening to its soundtrack each night before I went to sleep. I love Kieślowski's film *Blue* and would like to share it with you now because it shows the creative challenge facing all of us. *Blue* is a life-affirming act of celebration that illumines the courage it takes to overcome despair by choosing hope and love.

Blue presents us with a woman in despair after the death of her loved ones. The film is a passionate search for hope. It shows her failed attempt to escape her fate, and her hard-won discovery that she needs to let go of her resentment. Her surrender gives her the courage to risk a leap of faith, hope, and love so she can participate in cocreation.

Julie, the protagonist portrayed by Juliette Binoche, is the victim of a car accident in which her composer husband and her five-year-old daughter have been killed. The color blue is the colored filter through which the viewers experience the mood of despair into which Julie falls.

When she wakes up in the intensive care unit of a hospital, Julie can hardly see; her vision is a blur. She is shocked when she learns about the tragedy. In torment her grief turns to fury, and she breaks a glass window in the hospital. Then she tries to kill herself by swallowing pills, but she cannot go through with it. After Julie is released from the hospital, her anger turns into resentment and self-pity.

Only Julie has the capacity to complete her husband's unfinished work, *Concerto for a United Europe*, a piece commissioned to celebrate the inauguration of a reunified Europe. Julie was her husband's muse, and rumors hint that she is cocreator of the music. Bitter at her fate, Julie refuses to complete the concerto. She wants nothing to do with life and creation.

Caught in the despair of defiance, Julie decides to cut herself off from all her former links to life. She arranges for the sale of her house and for the continued care of her invalid mother, who is in a nursing home. She gives life annuities to her servants. Her longtime maid, Maria, tells Julie that she must shed the tears that Julie cannot. Julie's tears are frozen and congealed in cold anger.

Before she moves to a remote district of Paris where she wants to be anonymous, Julie throws all her photos and the unfinished concerto score in the trash to be shredded. She takes with her only the blue glass lamp that hung in her daughter's room.

Day after day Julie broods alone in despair in her bare apartment or over coffee in a neighborhood café. One day while she stares outside into space from within the café, she unexpectedly hears a street musician playing a theme from the concerto on his flute. Although she tries to flee from what she has heard, the music haunts her, plaguing her with her feelings of loss and loneliness. She cannot avoid the street musician, who reappears unexpectedly playing the concerto motif. The flute player is reminiscent of Orpheus, who can enter and return from the underworld realm of the dead by virtue of his music.

A series of other synchronistic events follow. A young woman from her apartment house sees Julie crying in secret and tries to console her. Julie denies the tears but later responds to the girl, who needs to talk to someone. Julie goes to the strip joint where the girl works and, by chance, sees an interview with her husband's assistant on television. He shows the photo that she thought she had discarded, including a snapshot of her husband with another woman. In shock, Julie realizes her husband was having an affair.

Thrown out of her malaise, Julie decides to meet her husband's mistress and learns that she is pregnant with his child. The encounter is Julie's turning point. She realizes she must revive her former generous self. Julie decides to befriend her husband's mistress and to help her in the birthing process by giving them her home. With this choice she responds to the call to create by embracing new life—an act that is redemptive and gives her hope and meaning.

Having chosen life, Julie decides to work with her husband's assistant to attempt to finish the concerto. As they labor to create the music, Julie is spiritually renewed; she sees the transformed faces of her mother, her maid, the people in her life.

The concerto becomes an ecstatic celebration of life and love as the chorus sings the final stanza, a quotation from Saint Paul's Letter to the Corinthians: "Though I speak with the tongue of men and angels, and have not love, I become as sounding brass or a tinkling cymbal . . . now abideth faith, hope, and love, these three; but the greatest of these is love."

Julie's story describes the dark night of the soul through which all of us pass on our journey to create. The color blue symbolizes the depths of the soul's dark night and is also the color of the heavens, of the spiritual heights. Julie's call to create requires her to unite the depths and heights within herself by living in the tension of the opposites. Blue is also the color of liberty and symbolizes the freedom to choose how to live and to direct life toward creativity or destruction. Like Orpheus, Julie descends into the underworld but chooses to emerge singing. For us she can be a model of the Celebrant, who learns the value of suffering and returns to life to create with compassion.

As with Julie in *Blue,* Rilke's call to create required him to write through his despair and transform it into affirmation. After all of his struggle and waiting, he finally was able to affirm that suffering is a season of our interior year and that sorrows are part of our growth, in his great poetic cycle the *Duino Elegies.* In the *Elegies* he transfigured his lament into poems of praise. And as we have seen, he received an unexpected gift from his muse, *The Sonnets to Orpheus,* songs of celebration.

Rilke came to see that the essential thing in life is to affirm and passionately celebrate existence—to appreciate the entire cycle of creation. His celebration of the relationship between nature and creativity echoes that of the *I Ching,* the ancient Taoist text for spiritual life that is based on the elements and follows the cycles of nature.[9]

The *I Ching* emphasizes life's creative cycle by ending with hexagram 64, "Before Completion." This hexagram presents a parallel to spring that leads out of winter's descent toward the promising fruitful time of summer. The ending is actually a hopeful time of transition to the next cycle of change, in which the creative process starts all over again. It emphasizes that every end embodies and carries a new beginning within itself. The end is the threshold into the period of inspiration that precedes the new birth, the new creative work. It emphasizes the surrender necessary to return to our roots in the earth, to be in the deep ground so we can open ourselves to the whole creative process that give birth anew. When we fight the seasons instead of being in tune with and following their rhythms, we obstruct the natural cycles.

Rilke expressed this as follows:

> Ah, we count the years and make occasional cuttings of them and stop and begin again and hesitate between both. But actually everything that befalls us is of one piece, in whose correlations one thing is kith and kin with another, fashions its own birth, grows and is educated to its own needs, and we have ultimately only to *be there*, simply, fervently as the earth is there, in harmony with the seasons, dark and light, and absolutely in space, not demanding to be cradled in anything but this web of influences and powers in which the very stars feel safeguarded.[10]

I invite you to continue on this great creative cycle by ending with Rilke's words:

> To praise is the whole thing.

NOTES

Preface: Creating from the Wilderness

1. Athol Fugard, "On South Africa and Hope: A Conversation." *New York Times*, December 10, 1995, p. 4.

Introduction. Adventure of the Soul

1. The notion of the "daimon" has been discussed in ancient times by Plato and others. More recently, it has been discussed by Rollo May. *Love and Will* (New York: W. W. Norton, 1969). Linda Leonard. *Witness to the Fire: Creativity and the Veil of Addiction* (Boston: Shambhala Publications, Inc. 1989), and James Hillman. *The Soul's Code: In Search of Character and Calling.* (New York: Random House, 1996). Hillman has also discussed the notion of "genius" in detail.

Chapter 1. Inspiration: The Muse of Nature

1. See Robert Graves, *The Greek Myths,* vol. 1 and 2 (Middlesex, England: Penguin Books, 1986).
2. Quoted in Amanda Haight, *Anna Akhmatova: A Poetic Pilgrimage* (New York: Oxford University Press, 1976), p. 36.
3. W. H. Hudson, *Green Mansions* (New York: Dover Publications, 1989), p. 130.

Chapter 2. Commitment: The Sower

1. Athol Fugard, *Valley Song* (New York: Theatre Communications Group, 1996).

2. The word "coloured" refers to people of mixed color in South Africa as distinguished from all white or all black.

3. Rainer Maria Rilke, *Duino Elegies*, trans. J. B. Leishman and Stephen Spender (New York: W. W. Norton & Co., 1963), p. 21.

4. See Erich Neuman, *Amor and Psyche* (Princeton, N.J.: Princeton University Press, 1971).

5. From an exhibition note for the painting "The Mulberry Tree" by Vincent Van Gogh. Norton Simon Museum, Pasadena, California.

6. Rainer Maria Rilke, *Letters to a Young Poet*, trans. M. D. Herter Norton (New York: W. W. Norton & Co., 1963), p. 74.

7. Ibid., pp. 29–30.

8. Toni Morrison, interviewed in *Black Women Writers at Work*, ed. Claudia Tate (New York: Continuum Publishing Co., 1988), p. 120.

CHAPTER 3. DOUBT: THE CYNIC

1. Fyodor Dostoyevsky, *Notes from Underground*, trans. Constance Garnett (New York: Dell Publishing Co., 1960), p. 56.

CHAPTER 4. COURAGE: THE WITNESS CONFRONTS THE TYRANT AND THE VICTIM

1. For a detiled account of Akhmatova's life, see Amanda Haight, *Anna Akhmatova: A Poetic Pilgrimage* (New York: Oxford University Press, 1976).

2. Ibid., p. 96.

3. Groups that help people work with obstacles to creativity include the twelve-step group Arts Anonymous and Artist Way groups,

modeled on Julia Cameron's book *The Artist's Way: A Spiritual Path to Higher Creativity* (Los Angeles: Jeremy P. Tarcher, 1992).

CHAPTER 5. CONSCIOUSNESS: THE SENTINEL AWAKENS THE ESCAPE ARTIST

1. Anton Chekhov, *The Major Plays* (New York: Penguin Books, 1964).
2. J. E. Cirlot, *A Dictionary of Symbols* (New York: Philosophical Library, 1962), p. 285.
3. Thomas Wolfe, *The Autobiography of an American Novelist*, ed. Leslie Field (Cambridge, Mass.: Harvard University Press, 1983), p. 45.
4. Ibid., p. 28.
5. Ibid., p. 55.
6. Rainer Maria Rilke, *Duino Elegies*, trans. J. B. Leishman and Stephen Spender (New York: W. W. Norton & Co., 1963), p. 33.
7. Wolfe, *Autobiography*, p. 86.
8. The sand play technique is discussed in chapter 8.

CHAPTER 6. DISCOVERY: THE ADVENTURER CHALLENGES THE CONFORMIST

1. Virginia Woolf, *Mrs. Dalloway* (New York: Harcourt, Brace & Co., 1997).
2. Andrey Tarkovsky, *Andrey Tarkovsky: Sculpting in Time*, trans. Kitty Hunter-Blair (New York: Alfred A. Knopf, 1987), pp. 42–43.
3. For a more detailed account, see Reine-Marie Paris, *Camille: The Life of Camille Claudel, Rodin's Muse and Mistress*, trans. Liliane Emery Tuck (New York: Henry Holt, 1988).
4. See Margaret Crossland, *Colette* (New York: Dell Publishing Co., 1973).
5. Ibid., p. 173.

Notes

CHAPTER 7. TOIL: THE ARTISAN TEACHES THE STAR HUMILITY

1. Liv Ullmann, *Changing* (New York: Bantam Books, 1978).
2. See *Aspen Film Fest Notes,* Fall 1994.
3. Krzysztof Kieślowski, *Kieślowski on Kieślowski,* ed. Danusia Stok (London: Faber & Faber, 1993), p. xxii.
4. Ibid., p. 211.
5. Ibid., p. 210.

CHAPTER 8. PLAY: THE DUMMLING SHOWS THE PERFECTIONIST HOW TO PLAY

1. Peggy McIntosh, Ph.D., "Feeling Like a Fraud" (Stone Center Colloquium. Wellseley, Mass., 1984).
2. Robert Conot, *A Streak of Luck* (Norwalk, Conn.: Easton Press, 1920), p. 164.
3. Carl Gustav Jung, *Memories, Dreams, Reflections,* ed. Aniela Jaffe, trans. Richard and Clara Winston (New York: Random House, 1963).
4. Ibid., pp. 65–66.
5. Ibid., p. 173.

CHAPTER 9. COMPASSION: THE LOVER OPENS THE CRITIC'S HEART

1. Ingmar Bergman, *Autumn Sonata: A Film,* trans. Alan Blair (New York: Pantheon Books, 1978), p. 79.
2. Emily Carr, *Excerpts from Hundreds and Thousands: The Journals of Emily Carr* (Clarke, Irwin & Co., 1966), in *Revelations: Diaries of Women,* ed.

Mary Jane Moffat and Charlotte Painter (New York: Random House, 1975), p. 383.

3. Ibid.

4. Ibid., p. 384.

5. Ibid., p. 390.

6. Ibid. , p. 391.

7. David Denby, "The Moviegoers: Why Don't People Love the Right Movies Anymore?" *New Yorker,* April 6, 1998.

8. Ibid., p. 96.

9. Ibid., p. 101.

Chapter 10. To Praise Is the Whole Thing: The Celebrant

1. Georgia O'Keeffe, (New York: Viking Press, 1976), # 23.

2. Andrey Tarkovsky, *Andrey Tarkovsky: Sculpting in Time,* trans. Kitty Hunter-Blair (New York: Alfred A. Knopf, 1987), p. 43.

3. Henry Miller, letter to Somerset Maugham quoted in *New Yorker,* August 24–31, 1998, p. 106.

4. May Sarton, *Journal of a Solitude* (New York: W. W. Norton & Co., 1992).

5. Rachel Carson, *The Sense of Wonder* (New York: Harper & Row, 1967).

6. O'Keeffe, # 71.

7. Virginia Woolf, *A Writer's Diary, Being Extracts From the Diary of Virginia Woolf* (New York: Harcourt Brace Jovanovich, 1989), excerpt July 27, 1934; in *Revelations: Diaries of Women,* ed. Mary Jane Moffat and Charlotte Painter (New York: Random House, 1975), p. 234.

8. Boris Pasternak, *Pasternak: Selected Poems,* trans. Jan Stallworthy and

Peter Frame (Middlesex, England: Penguin Books, 1984), pp. 38–39.

9. Rainer Maria Rilke, *Selected Letters,* trans. R. F. C. Hull (London: Macmillan & Co., 1946), pp. 157–58.

INDEX

Adventurer, 10, 14–15, 148–67, 246
  challenge to Conformist, 140–41,
    143, 148–53, 156–57,
    166–67
Aeneid (Virgil), 25
Aeschylus, 88
Afternoon of a Faun, The (poem and
    musical work), 30–31
Akhmatova, Anna, 24, 26–27,
    96–102, 103
Allen, Woody, 29
Anders, Allison, 226
Andersson, Harriet, 29
Angel at My Table, An (film), 211
Angelou, Maya, 2, 168, 256
Anna Karenina (Dostoyevsky), 69
Antonia's Line (film), 49–50
anxiety, 18–19, 46, 107–8
Aphrodite, 45–46, 51, 52
appreciation, 17, 140–41, 249–59
Après-midi d'un faune, L' (poem and
    musical work), 30–31
Aristophanes, 25
Aristotle, 88
art and artists, 6, 29, 142, 150
  Muse depictions, 25
  muses, 29–30
  Tyrant's abuse of, 87
  See also specific artists
Artisan, 10, 15–16, 172, 177–88,
    246
Athena, 25
Auden, W. H., 108
Autumn Sonata (film), 224–25, 232

bad faith, 171–72
Balanchine, George, 29
Beatles, 28
Beauvoir, Simone de, 142
Beethoven, Ludwig van, 6, 24, 108
Begnini, Roberto, 212
Bergman, Ingmar, 29, 60, 108, 180,
    224–25
Bergman, Ingrid, 28, 224
Berry, Wendell, 6, 41
Bertolucci, Bernardo, 142
Binoche, Juliette, 28, 264
Birdman of Alcatraz, The (film), 5
blocks, creative, 12, 42, 53, 56, 61
Blok, Alexander, 97
Blue (film), 264–67
Book of the Dead, 212
Boucher, Alfred, 153
Brahms, Johannes, 29
Brancusi, Constantin, 24
Breaking the Waves (film), 144
Brodsky, Joseph, 99
Brothers Karamazov, The (Dostoyevsky),
    41, 62–63
Brueghel, Pieter, the Elder, 142
Buber, Martin, 254
Buck, Pearl S., 6
Buddhism, 6, 255
Buñel, Luis, 29, 202–3

Cage, Nicolas, 70
Callas, Maria, 87, 117–19, 222
Calliope, 26, 262
Campion, Jane, 211

Index

Camus, Albert, 6, 226
care, 79, 181–88
Carr, Emily, 225, 233–39
Carson, Rachel, 31, 59–60, 258
Casablanca (film), 28
Castle, The (Kafka), 223
Celebrant, 10, 17, 250–68
censorship, 84, 99, 100–101
Central Station (film), 69
Cervantes, Miguel de, 211
Chagall, Marc, 248
Changing (Ullmann), 180
chaos, 185
　bringing order to, 46, 47, 137
　prisoners of, 114, 115
Chekhov, Anton, 116
Chéri (Colette), 162
Cherubini, Luigi, 118
circadian cycles, 7
Claudel, Camille, 29, 87, 152,
　153–57, 166–67, 222
Claudel, Paul, 38, 153
Claudine stories (Colette), 160
Clinton, Hillary Rodham, 29, 180
Clio, 26
Close, Glenn, 179
Cobain, Kurt, 179
Colette, 152–53, 157–65, 166
collective unconscious, 135–38,
　215
commitment. *See* Sower
compassion, 17, 219, 255
Compulsive Doer, 14, 113, 115, 117,
　119, 123–26, 135, 136, 170
concentration camp inmates, 95–96
Conformist, 10, 14, 68, 140–48
　Adventurer challenge to, 140–41,
　149–53, 156–57, 166–67
　as Critic collaborator, 220

Conformist, The (film), 142
consciousness, 14, 112, 114, 135–
　38, 171. *See also* unconscious
Conversation, The (Ford), 227
Coppola, Francis Ford, 227
courage, 27, 95–96
craft. *See* Artisan
create, definition of word, 3
creativity
　appreciation of, 17, 140–41,
　　250–59
　blocks in, 12, 42, 53, 56, 61
　as craft, 177–88
　cycles, 5, 11–18, 38–39, 54–55
　dramatis personae, 11–18
　as gift, 172
　life as, 20
　nature as nurturer of, 2–7, 59–60
　phases of, 8–10
　process of, 203–7
　seeds of, 41–44, 46, 47, 246,
　　259–60
　self-tolerance and, 16
　unconscious-conscious border of,
　　14
　wilderness analogy, xii-xv
Crime and Punishment (Dostoyevsky),
　75
Critic, 11, 16–17, 220–46
　causes of harmful, 222–26
　healthy function of, 240–41,
　　245–46
　transforming, 229–33
　wedded to Lover, 240–46
Curie, Marie, 108
cycles, 7–18, 38–39, 54–55
Cynic, 10, 12–13, 16, 17, 53,
　59–78, 173
　confronting, 73–78, 97, 98

Index

as Critic collaborator, 220
healing, 70–73
psychological roots of, 63–66,
   71–73
Star and, 173, 176–77
Tyrant and, 83, 84, 100

Daedalus and Icarus, 178–79
daimon, 4, 88, 149
dance, 29, 30–31
"dark night of the soul," 76–77, 100,
   262
Dead Man Walking (book and film), 28,
   108–10
Dean, James, 179
death and rebirth, 260–68
Debussy, Claude, 30, 31, 138
defenses, 89, 102–3
Delareux, George, 135–36
DeMille, Cecil B., 174, 175
Demon Lover, 87, 89
Denby, David, 240
Deneuve, Catherine, 29, 41
De Niro, Robert, 29
despair, 13, 53, 67–69, 261–63
Dickinson, Emily, 108, 126
Dilettante, 14, 113, 115, 118,
   123–26, 136–37
DiMaggio, Joe, 30
discouragement, 53, 73
discovery, 139. *See also* Adventurer
disillusionment, 59, 60
distractions, 113–14, 115, 123–24,
   126
Dolce Vita, La (film), 68
Don Quixote (Cervantes), 211
Dostoyevsky, Fyodor, 28, 41, 54, 60,
   62–63, 67, 69, 75, 91, 172,
   219, 256

as Witness, 90, 96, 102
Double Life of Veronique, The (film),
   182–83, 184
doubt, 13. *See also* Cynic
Duino Elegies (Rilke), 42–43, 128,
   267–68
du Maurier, Daphne, 53
Dummling, 10, 16, 195–96,
   210–17, 218, 246
Du Pré, Jacqueline, 169

Edison, Thomas, 202
ego inflation, 15, 30, 85, 169, 171,
   172
Einstein, Albert, 108
Emerson, Ralph Waldo, 3, 59
Erato, 26
Eros, 42, 44–47
   and Psyche, 44–47
Escape Artist, 10, 13–14, 68,
   113–38
   Compulsive Doer vs. Dilettante,
      123–26
   as Critic Collaborator, 220,
      221
   ploys of, 113–14
Euripides, 118
Eurydice, 262–63
Euterpe, 26
Eyre, Jane (Brontë), 54

fairy tales, 73–75, 91–95
   Dummling figure, 16, 195–96,
      211, 212–14
faith. *See* leap of faith
fantasies, 170, 171
Farrell, Suzanne, 29
Farrow, Mia, 29
Fassbinder, Rainer Werner, 29

Index

fear
  anxiety vs., 107
  facing, 95–96, 105–7
  as inner tyrant, 104–7
  of perfectionist, 193
Fellini, Federico, 29, 68, 87, 191
Field, Sally, 108
films
  Celebrant portrayals, 264–66
  critical love of, 240–46
  Critic portrayals, 224–26
  Dummling portrayals, 212
  muses, 28, 29
  Star portrayals, 172–77
  Stars vs. Artisans, 179–85
  Voyeur portrayals, 227–28
  See also specific actors, films, and
    filmmakers
Firebird legend, 13, 87, 90, 91–95,
  111
Fool. See Dummling
Forrest Gump (film), 212
Four Seasons, The (Vivaldi), 6
Frame, Janet, 211
Frankl, Viktor, 95–96
fraudulence, feelings of, 18–19, 192,
  194–97
Freud, Sigmund, 137, 215–16
Frog Prince, The (fairy tale), 74–75
From the Canyons to the Stars (Messiaen),
  31
Fugard, Athol, xv, 39–40, 43–44, 60,
  69–70

gardening, 41
Garland, Judy, 28
Gate of Hell, The (Rodin), 153, 156
Gauthier-Villars, Henri, 158,
  159–60

Giacometti, Alberto, 108
Gigi (Colette), 163–64
Goethe, Johann Wolfgang, 88, 209
Golden Fleece, 118
Goncharov, Ivan, 115–16
Gonne, Maud, 29
Good Earth, The (Buck), 6
Górecki, Henryk, xiv
Gorns, Marleen, 49
Gossipers, The (Claudel), 154
Goudeket, Maurice, 163
Graham, Martha, 6
Grateful Dead, 28
Greece, ancient, 4, 5–6, 24–26
Green Mansions (Hudson), 32–33, 98
Grimm brothers, 74, 211
Gropius, Walter, 30
group support, 103
guilt, 18, 105, 115, 126, 193
Gumilyov, Nikolay, 97

Haile Gebrselassie, 5
Hamilton, William, 172
Havel, Vaclav, 95–96
hedonism, 68, 124
Hepburn, Audrey, 163–64
Hesiod, 25–26
Hesse, Hermann, 140, 141, 211, 226
hibernation, 122–23
Hildegard von Bingen, 261
Hillesum, Etty, 81, 95–96
Hitler, Adolf, 84–85
Holiday, Billie, 28
Homer, 25, 88
Hopkins, Anthony, 108, 179
Hopper, Dennis, 179
Hour of the Star (film), 170
House of the Dead (Dostoyevsky), 90
Hudson, W. H., 32–33

Index

humility, 85
hypervigilance, 89

Icarus, 178–79
Ice Storm, The (film), 144
I Ching, 266
idealism, 60
Iliad (Homer), 25
imagination, 12, 30, 42, 86, 123
inertia, 116–17, 120
Inner Critic, 229–33
Inner Tyrant, 83–86, 89–91, 97
Inner Witness, 102–4
insecurity, 86
inspiration. *See* Muse of Nature
inspire, etymology of word, 30
Interrupted Life, An (Hillesum), 96
intimidation, 84
I-Thou relationships, 35, 245, 255
It Takes a Village (Clinton), 180
Ivanov (Chekhov), 116
Ivory, James, 142

Jackie and Hilary (film), 169
Jacob, Irène, 28
Jesus of Nazareth, 43
John of the Cross, Saint, 76–77
journal keeping, 102
Journal of a Solitude (Sarton), 257
Jouvenal, Henri de, 161, 162, 163
Juliet of the Spirits (film), 29
Jung, Carl Gustav, 4, 88, 135,
    137–38, 149, 171
    and Dummling, 211–12, 215–17,
    218
    school experience, 207–10

Kafka, Franz, 222–23
Kahlo, Frida, 108

Keaton, Diane, 29
Keitel, Harvey, 29, 179
Kennedy, Jacqueline, 118
Kennedy, John F., 29
Kierkegaard, Søren, 143
Kieslośki, Krzysztof, 28, 60, 180,
    181–85, 241–45, 264–67
King, Martin Luther, Jr., 29
King Lear (Shakespeare), 211
Klee, Paul, 88
Klimt, Gustav, 29–30
Kokoschka, Oskar, 30
Kollwitz, Käthe, 142
Kosinski, Jerzy, 114

Lange, Jessica, 179
Lascaux caves (France), 5
La Strada (film), 29, 87
laziness, 113
leap of faith, 69, 98, 115, 148
Leaving Las Vegas (film), 70
legends. *See* fairy tales; mythology
Léud, Jean-Pierre, 29
libido, 6, 88
Life Is Beautiful (film), 212
life's wonders, 257–60
listening, 51–55, 57, 108–11
literature, 6, 28, 30–33. *See also specific
    authors and works*
Lonely Crowd, The (Riesman), 142
Look Homeward Angel (Wolfe),
    128–29
Lorenzo's Oil (film), 28
Lover, 10, 17, 63, 220–46
Luxemburg, Rosa, 5, 95

Mahler, Alma, 29–30
Mahler, Gustav, 6, 30, 60
Mallarmé, Stéphane, 30, 31

Index

Mandela, Nelson, 95–96, 99
Mandelstam, Osip, 97, 99
Man's Search for Meaning (Frankl), 96
Mary, mother of Jesus, 17, 98
Masina, Giulietta, 29
Mastroianni, Marcello, 28
Matisse, Henri, 23, 34–35, 260
Maugham, Somerset, 255
Maxwell, Florida Scott, 112
McCullers, Carson, 226
McIntosh, Peggy, 197
Medea, 87, 118
Medea (film and opera), 87, 118
Melpomene, 26
Memories, Dreams, Reflections (Jung), 207
memory, goddess of, 24, 25, 26
Mephisto (film), 87
Messiaen, Olivier, 31
Metamorphoses (Ovid), 25
Michelangelo, 88
Mikhalkov, Nikita, 115
Miller, Alice, 90
Miller, Arthur, 30
Miller, Henry, 29, 256
Mitsou (Colette), 162
Mnemosyne, 24, 25, 26
Modigliani, Amedeo, 97
Monroe, Marilyn, 28, 30, 169
Montenegro, Fernanda, 69
Morrison, Toni, 28, 56, 139
Mother Nature, 98, 148
Mother Teresa, 105–6, 107
Mountain, The (Carr painting), 233, 234
Mr. and Mrs. Bridge (film), 142
Mrs. Dalloway (Woolf), 140–41
Muir, John, xiii, 59, 126

Munch, Edvard, 202
Muse of Nature, 10, 11–12, 13, 23–36, 249
  Cynic and, 62, 69–70, 71, 78, 98, 177
  Firebird as, 93
  Tyrant and, 83, 85
  as Witness, 96–102
Muses (mythology), 24–26, 261, 262
music, 6, 28, 29, 30–32. *See also specific composers and works*
mythology, 24–26, 44–47, 118, 178–79, 262–63

nature, xiii–xiv
  and call to create, 2–7, 59–60
  cyclical rhythms of, 7–10, 12, 38–39, 78
  as inspiration, 10, 11–12, 13, 23, 31–33, 98
  and seeds of creativity, 41–42
  wonder of, 257–60
  See also Muse of Nature
Nausea (Sartre), 226
Newman, Paul, 28, 179–80
Nietzsche, Friedrich, 29, 66, 229
Night (Wiesel), 48
Nights of Cabiria, The (film), 29
Nijinsky, Vaslav, 6, 30
Nin, Anaïs, 29
Nuit Blanche (Colette), 161

Oblomov (Goncharov), 115–16
Odyssey (Homer), 25
O"Faolain, Sean, xii
Oiseux exotiques (Messiaen), 31–33
O'Keeffe, Georgia, 6, 24, 31, 253, 258, 259–60

Index

Old Blind Singer, The (Claudel), 154
Oliver, Mary, 6
Onassis, Aristotle, 117–18
Ophuls, Max, 163
Ordinary People (film), 144
Orpheus and Eurydice, 161–62
overwork, 114, 115, 119, 123, 124, 135
Ovid, 25

Pacino, Al, 69
Pan, 52
Pasolini, Pier Paolo, 87, 118
passion, 83
passive-aggression, 84, 89
passivity, 114–15, 117
Pasternak, Boris, 99, 257, 260
Pastoral Symphony (Beethoven), 6
patient waiting, 12, 13, 51–57, 72, 187, 214
Pegasus, 25
Perfectionist, 10, 16, 18, 133, 192–218
    as Critic collaborator, 220
    Cynic's despair and, 69
    Dummling vs., 212–17
    feelings of fraudulence and, 194–97
Perkins, Maxwell, 128–29
Perrault, Charles, 74
Pesci, Joe, 29
Piaf, Edith, 28
Picasso, Pablo, 29, 203
Pindar, 25
Plague, The (Camus), 6
Plath, Sylvia, 114
Plato, 88
Plato's cave, 68
play, power of, 191, 215–18, 246

Pleasantville (film), 68, 142
pleasure, 68, 124
"Poem Without a Hero" (Akhmatova), 101
Poitier, Sidney, 28
Polyhymnia, 26
praise. *See* Celebrant
Prejean, Sister Helen, 108–10
Presley, Elvis, 28, 179
procrastination, 115, 136
Prokofiev, Sergey, 88
Psyche's tasks, 44–47, 51–52, 56, 75–76, 109, 115
    Artisan and, 187–888

Ravel, Maurice, 163
Razor's Edge, The (Maugham), 256
rebirth. *See* death and rebirth
Red (film), 28, 241–45
Red Shoes, The (film), 87
regressive patterns, 114–15
rejection, fear of, 193
"Requiem" (Akhmatova), 101
resentment, 156
Rhys, Jean, 200–201
Riesman, David, 142
Rilke, Rainer Maria, 18, 28, 29, 34, 42–43, 55–56, 88–89, 126, 128, 138, 189, 247, 258, 262, 267–68
Rite of Spring, The (Stravinsky), 202
Robbins, Jerome, 30–31
Rodin, Auguste, 24, 29, 87, 153–54, 155, 156
Roethke, Theodore, 78, 262
Rome, ancient, 5–6, 25, 26
Ross, Gary, 142
Rothko, Mark, 114
Russian revolution, 99, 100

Index

Salinger, J. D., 226
Salomé, Lou-Andreas, 29, 34
sand play therapy, 131–32, 199
Sarandon, Susan, 28, 108
Sarton, May, 31, 41, 126, 257, 258
Sartre, Jean-Paul, 171, 226
scapegoating, 84–85
Scent of a Woman (film), 69
Schumann, Clara, 29
Schumann, Robert, 29
Schygulla, Hanna, 29
Scorsese, Martin, 29
Scream, The (Munch), 202
Sea Around Us, The (Carson), 258
Second Sex, The (de Beauvoir), 142
security. *See* Conformist
"self-talk," defeatist, 64–66, 267
Sense of Wonder, The (Carson), 257
Sentinel, 10, 14, 113, 121, 129–38,
    246
    Conformist and, 148
    wake-up call of, 129–35
Sexton, Anne, 114
Shakespeare, William, 11, 211
shame, 19, 105, 115, 193, 195–96
Short Film About Love, A (film), 183
Shostakovich, Dmitri, 96
Sickness unto Death (Kierkegaard),
    143
Silent Spring, The (Carson), 257
Singleton, John, 226
sleep, 89, 118, 120
Sluggard, 14, 113–23
    positive aspect of, 122–23
    Star as, 170
    wake-up call to, 130–35
Solitary, 126–29
Solzhenitsyn, Alexander, 99
Song of the Earth, The (Mahler), 6

Sonnets to Orpheus, The (Rilke), 18, 43,
    267
soul, 46
    adventure of, 1–7
    creative challenge of, 68
    "dark night of the," 76–77, 100,
        262
    loss of, 220
soul-work, 71, 78, 82, 171
Sower, 10, 12, 17, 18, 37–57, 177
    as commitment, 48–51, 137
    patience and, 55–57
    seeds of, 43–44, 46, 47, 246,
        259–60
    Sluggard vs., 115
    See also Psyche's tasks
"Sower, The" (van Gogh), 50
Stalin, Joseph, 90, 96, 99, 101
Star, 10, 15, 169–77
    Artisan and, 177–88
    as Critic collaborator, 220–21
Steppenwolf (Hesse), 141, 226
stereotyping, 84–85
Stranger, The (Camus), 226
Stravinsky, Igor, 13, 24, 30, 202
Sukowa, Barbara, 29
Sunset Boulevard (film), 172–77
Swanson, Gloria, 173
Sydow, Max von, 29
Symposium (Plato), 88

Tarkovsky, Andrey, 108, 149–50,
    203, 253–54, 258
temptation, 13–14
Terpsichore, 26
Thalia, 26
thanksgiving, 256–57
Thelma and Louise (film), 28
Theogony (Hesiod), 25–26

Index

Thoreau, Henry David, 37, 59, 126
transformation
  challenges of, 67–68, 138
  disorientation prior to, xii
  leap of faith and, 69, 98
  Psyche's tasks as tasks of, 45–46
  of self, 17–18
  See also Muse of Nature
Tree Grows in Brookly, A (Smith), 5
Trial, The (Kafka), 223
Truffaut, Françoise, 29
Tsvetayeva, Marina, 97, 99
Tyrant, 10, 13, 14, 16, 27, 82–89,
    149
  Conformist and, 142, 144, 147
  coping with, 89–91, 100–104
  as Critic collaborator, 220
  Perfectionist as, 192, 201
  Star and, 177
  Witness and, 89–111

Ullmann, Liv, 29, 180, 224
unchartered territory. *See* wilderness
unconscious, 14, 42, 114, 143
  collective, 135–38, 215
Urania, 26

Vagabonde, La (Colette), 161
Valley Song (Fugard), 39–40, 43–44,
    69–70
Van Gogh, Vincent, 6, 24, 50, 202
Victim, 82, 86–89, 99, 104, 109
  Conformist as, 144, 145, 146,
    147
  Critic and, 223

Virgil, 25
Vivaldi, Antonio, 6
Voyeur, 226–30
vulnerability, 214

waiting. *See* patient waiting
Walker, Alice, 41
Weir, Peter, 226
Werfel, Franz, 30
Wiesel, Elie, 48
Wild Child, The (film), 29
Wilder, Billy, 172
wilderness, xii-xv, 4–5
  dark side of, 61
  solitude and, 127
  See also nature
Winfrey, Oprah, 29
Witness, 10, 13, 27, 82–111,
    246
  artist as, 150
  confronting Tyrant, 89–111
  Victim and, 86–89
Wolfe, Thomas, 127–29
Woodward, Joanne, 179
Woolf, Virginia, 140–41, 259
Wordsworth, William, 23
writer's block, 56, 61

Yeats, William Butler, 24, 29, 39,
    88
Yourcenar, Marguerite, 57

Zemlinsky, Alexander von, 30
Zeus, 24, 26

ABOUT THE AUTHOR

Linda Schierse Leonard, Ph.D., is a philosopher who trained as a Jungian analyst at the C. G. Jung Institute in Zurich. She is the author of many best-selling books, among them *The Wounded Woman* which has been translated into twelve languages, *Meeting the Madwoman,* and *On the Way to the Wedding.* She is an international lecturer and has held teaching positions in the California State Universities and the University of Colorado at Denver. She has been in private practice for nearly thirty years and currently practices in Aspen, Colorado.